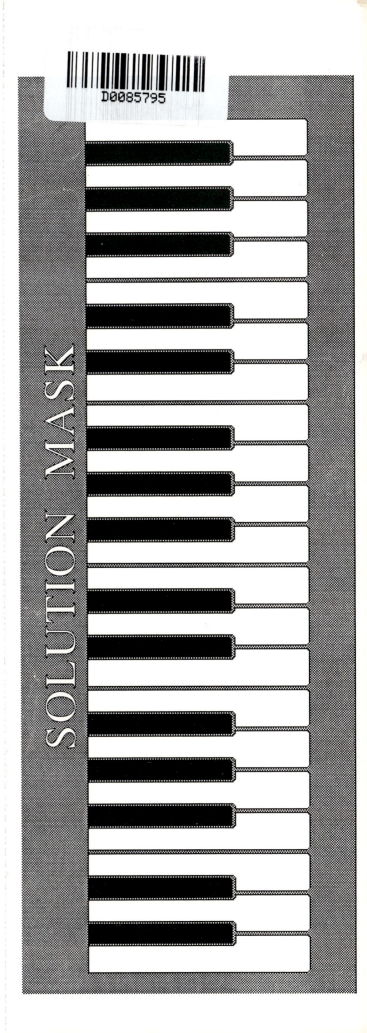

SOLUTION MASK

WRITING SATB SCORES

1. THE CLOSE SCORE

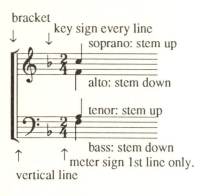

bracket
key sign every line
soprano: stem up
alto: stem down
tenor: stem up
bass: stem down
meter sign 1st line only.
vertical line

2. STAVES NOT CONNECTED BY BAR LINES.

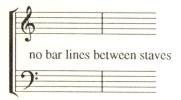

no bar lines between staves

3. THE PARTS OF A NOTE.

up stem on right → flag always on right

note head→

down stem on left

4. ALIGNMENT

Notes are placed horizantally to reflect their position in time.
Notes which occur at the same time are aligned vertically.

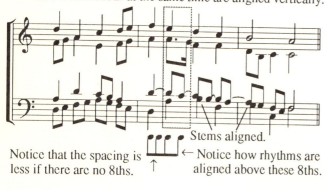

Stems aligned.

Notice that the spacing is
less if there are no 8ths.

← Notice how rhythms are
aligned above these 8ths.

Introduction to
MUSICAL DESIGN

Introduction to
MUSICAL DESIGN

volume 1

Kenneth R. Rumery
Northern Arizona University

WCB Wm. C. Brown Publishers

Book Team

Editor *Meredith M. Morgan*
Developmental Editor *Dean Robbins*
Production Editor *Suzanne Guinn*
Developmental Visuals/Design Consultant *Marilyn A. Phelps*

WCB

Wm. C. Brown Publishers

President *G. Franklin Lewis*
Vice President, Publisher *Thomas E. Doran*
Vice President, Operations and Production *Beverly Kolz*
National Sales Manager *Virginia S. Moffat*
Group Sales Manager *John Finn*
Executive Editor *Edgar J. Laube*
Senior Marketing Manager *Kathy Law Laube*
Marketing Manager *Kathleen Nietzke*
Managing Editor, Production *Colleen A. Yonda*
Manager of Visuals and Design *Faye M. Schilling*
Production Editorial Manager *Julie A. Kennedy*
Production Editorial Manager *Ann Fuerste*
Publishing Services Manager *Karen J. Slaught*

WCB Group

President and Chief Executive Officer *Mark C. Falb*
Chairman of the Board *Wm. C. Brown*

Consulting Editor
Frederick W. Westphal
California State University, Sacramento

Cover design by Jeff Storm

Cover illustrated by Melinda Fine, titled: Midnight Serenade

Printed in the United States of America by Wm. C. Brown Publishers,
2460 Kerper Boulevard, Dubuque, IA 52001

10 9 8 7 6 5 4 3 2 1

CONTENTS

Contents of Cassette (Selected Examples and Exercises)

Chapter 18

FOREWORD

The Philosophy of *Introduction to Musical Design*

Introduction to Musical Design is a theory book for music makers. It emphasizes practical skills and information relevant to performing and creating music. It is concerned with both the grammar of musical structure and the artistic mental processes which lie behind it. The book begins with the study of musical primitives, their characteristics, and how they are used to build longer, more complex patterns. These more complex patterns include melody, harmony, the interaction of melody and harmony, and, ultimately, the synthesis of all these patterns in musical texture.

The author has attempted to identify and describe some of the thought processes involved in music making. These concepts are presented to the students to explain how music works and to help them understand their own development as it relates to music processes. Students are continually asked to determine **why** a composer chose a particular effect, and to test their conclusions in actual performance.

Music making stems from mental processes associated with the perception of musical pattern, music cognition, and memory. The study of music perception and cognition is an emerging field. Although we live in a graphics intensive culture, studies on musical intelligence have begun to keep pace with studies on visual and lingual processes. Many of the ideas on musical thought included in this book were inferred from studies on visual and language perception and cognition.

The central aim of this book is to equip students with tools for understanding the musical literature they work with daily. A musician should be able to look at a passage, see the sense of it in musical terms, and form an opinion about it that can be expressed in musical action. The tools to accomplish these objectives are designed for the general musician—one who might become a composer, conductor, arranger, performer, teacher, scholar, critic, business person, jazz musician, or enthusiast (gifted amateur, audiophile). Students are guided through the process of opinion formation with sample descriptive analyses. These samples can be used by the students to develop approaches to a broad spectrum of musical styles and periods—including modern jazz and popular music.

Healthy discourse begins by sharing of different viewpoints about musical compositions. The music maker who participates in this discourse develops a musical intelligence and sensitivity that is reflected in his or her musical product. The student is urged to embrace this discourse and strive to preserve a connection between theory, performance, and interpretation. The whole point of a passage may be lost if separated too far from the act of performance. At the same time, all fine products in performance and original work stem directly from musical intelligence and thought. Theorists can no more detach themselves from processes of music making than music makers can detach themselves from the formation of musical intellect. One derives from the other.

PREFACE

About *Introduction to Musical Design*

This book is meant for students who have taken music fundamentals classes or possess the equivalent in experience (performance experience and ability to read in at least one clef, theory in private lessons). The material in the first part of this book is meant to provide a bridge between fundamentals and theory sequence courses. This is accomplished through a concentrated review of basics to solidify foundation knowledge and skills. During this review, students can work toward fluent, intuitive thinking and performance. Also, the review can be used by students to help remove any deficiencies in music literacy.

A wide range of student needs and interests are addressed in *Introduction to Musical Design*. An attempt was made to keep the book relevant to a variety of career futures such as teaching, performance, arranging, composition, jazz, studio music, music criticism, and scholarship.

Today's students have a unique challenge. Musicians of the past concentrated mainly on the music of their own times. Now, students must be trained to cope with a body of literature drawn from a broad spectrum of styles and historic periods. Today's concerts can include a mixture of literature from the Renaissance Period (16th century) to the present, a span of about 400 years. Musicians of today need the resources to "read between the lines," to "get behind the notes," to "get into the composer's head" while working with music written yesterday, 500 years ago, or tomorrow.

While preparing music for performance, musicians must work sensitively and insightfully with a wide variety of textures and period styles. Melody and rhythm are particularly important in day-by-day music-making. This book includes instruction in these areas and encourages the students to apply the knowledge immediately to their daily tasks. It also offers broad introductory experiences that lead the students toward advanced courses in theory, analysis, counterpoint, conducting, orchestration, arranging, and composition.

The book fosters the development of descriptive analysis skills. The student learns how to form considered opinions by thoughtfully studying examples of music. This opinion formation establishes a foundation for interpretation and musical criticism—all needed to develop well conceived acts of expressive performance, composition, arranging, conducting, and scholarship. This development of musical criticism forms a strong bridge between theory and performance that allows students to transfer experience and knowledge freely from area to area. An appreciation of the workings of a composition comes from an appreciation of the composer's thoughts and feelings that were built into the work. Writing experiences help to improve this appreciation.

The student is encouraged to develop writing skills. Numerous opportunities are provided for composing original melodies, chorales, and compositions. A long developmental process is built into the topic path strategy of the book. Instruction is designed to take the "mystique" out of the creative process so students realize that creative writing ability is developed through application rather than magic.

Progression of material is carefully stepped within a topic in topic "paths" (continued through several chapters), and within the exercises and applications. Checkpoints occur along each topic path. These include self-help components to give students a structured review of the material. Students can use the self-help frames to complete on-the-spot checks of their learning and to prepare themselves for the more complex applications that follow.

The union between theory and practice is encouraged in *Introduction to Musical Design* through efforts to blend practical musicianship with artistic musicality. Information on perception and memory is related to the improvement of reading, hearing, and learning techniques in ear-training/sight-singing classes and all performance activities. Music pattern recognition is particularly related to skills classes and everyday rehearsal tasks (reading, memorizing, phrasing, interpreting). Students are urged to graduate from note-by-note to pattern-reading skills as soon as possible.

The Chapters

Early chapters include a concentrated review of fundamentals. Instruction on *intervals, scales, and rhythm* is presented as topic "paths" that course through several chapters. These pathways merge into broader paths on *melody* and *harmony*, which also course through several chapters. All pathways merge in the final chapter on *texture*.

Students are required to analyze and write music in every chapter. A long developmental process leads the student to the writing of four-part texture in Chapter 14. This developmental process includes the writing of melody, the harmonization of melody, and two-part writing. The students gain a broad perspective on music writing and analysis. By the time they get to part writing, they have had a variety of writing and analysis experiences that can be applied to the specifics of part writing. This allows them to learn part writing quickly and enables them to produce work of high musicality.

Foundations of harmony are provided in the first six chapters. Chapters 7 through 10 contain preparatory experiences for later chapters.

Chapter 7 details the harmonic implications that can be discovered in skeletonized melody. This serves as a preparation for later chapters on the harmonization of melody. Chapter 8 is devoted exclusively to different aspects of triads. Concentration on harmony is continued in Chapter 9. Chapter 10 focuses on two-part texture and serves as a preparation for writing the two-voice outer framework needed in good four-part writing.

Chapters 11 and 13 are devoted exclusively to the harmonization of melody. A complete method is developed for the design of chord progressions. Chapters 14 through 17 are devoted exclusively to four-part writing and harmonization. Chapter 18 is a culminating chapter that shows how harmony, melody, and rhythm are integrated to create a real musical environment.

The Examples

The book is built around the examples. Thus, the careful study and performance of the examples is a most important activity. A tape of many of these examples is included as a study aid and to stress the importance of listening.

The Checkpoints

Some chapters contain more than one topic path. Checkpoints conclude each "leg" of a topic path to assist the student in review, reinforcement, and application of the topic. Most checkpoints include a list of terms and self-help exercises. Broader applications occur after some checkpoints, especially at the ends of chapters. Much of this material is included on the tapes so the student can form impressions of the problems as a listener.

Solutions and problems to the self-help framed exercises are included on the same page. The solution column should be covered while the student works on the problem. However, no harm will be done by looking at an answer if this will help the students to complete the next problem on their own. These framed exercises are intended to help students organize and structure their review of the material.

The exercises provide stepping stones to broader applications. Frequently, the framed exercises help students form questions about the material or its application. Perhaps the most difficult task for the student is to learn how to ask for help.

Acknowledgments

The organization and content of *Introduction to Musical Design* is influenced in part by those who participated in the Manhattanville Project (especially the "spiral" strategy) and the Contemporary Music Project (CMP). It also incorporates the influences of some of my own teachers, especially Robert Beadell, Jack Snider and Immanuel Wishnow of the University of Nebraska at Lincoln; and Cecil Effinger, William Kearns and Alan Luhring of the University of Colorado at Boulder. Perhaps these good influences will be passed on to those who would use this book.

This project has been personally supported over a period of years by my friend and colleague Thomas M. Kirshbaum. I gratefully acknowledge his gifts of unwavering encouragement and countless hours of review, criticism, class-testing, and dialogue.

I gratefully acknowledge the contributions made by the reviewers of this publication. Their careful consideration, candor, and numerous valued suggestions are greatly appreciated.

The Reviewers:

Daniel R. Bakos
West Georgia College

Kenton Bales
University of Nebraska–Omaha

George Beyer
Cypress College

Steven Block
Northeast Illinois University

Howard B. Brockington
Delaware State College

Gregory D. Carroll
UNC–Greensboro

Arthur S. Danner
West Los Angeles College

Lisa A. Derry
Western Michigan University

Paul J. Dickinson
(William Rainey) Harper College

Andrew Fowler
Cornell College
Mt. Vernon, IA

William G. Harbinson
Appalachian State University

Thomas M. Kirshbaum
Northern Arizona University

Alice Main Lanning
University of Oklahoma

Robert Nelson
University of Houston

Donald J. Para
California State University–Long Beach

Tressa Reisetter
No school affiliation

Carey M. Smith
Meridian Community College

Larry J. Solomon
Pima Community College

John Steffa
Murray State University

Stephen Yarbrough
University of South Dakota

I personally thank all the theory students at Northern Arizona University who used and freely commented on prototypes of this book. Their suggestions helped tailor this product for student use.

I invite all of these individuals to join me in dedicating *Introduction To Musical Design* to our students past, present, and future.

I am most grateful to the book team who patiently and skillfully led me through the complexities of textbook production. I especially appreciate the steady faith in the project shown by Meredith Morgan, Acquisitions Editor and the unerring suggestions and rigorous standards provided by Frederick Westphal, Consulting Editor. The expert and friendly guidance of Dean Robbins, Developmental Editor, and Suzanne Guinn, Production Editor, contributed greatly to the quality and timely completion of both volumes of this project.

I wish to express deep personal gratitude for the support given me by my spouse Leanne and son David throughout the whole development of this book.

Kenneth R. Rumery

CHAPTER

1 COMMUNICATION IN MUSIC, INTERVALS, DIATONIC SCALES

OVERVIEW   This is the first in a series of six chapters that lays a foundation for the study of melody, harmony, and texture. This chapter introduces the reader to modes of communication in music, an important basis of musical thought. Topic paths on *intervals* and *scales* are introduced here. These paths merge into *Melody, Harmony,* and *Texture* paths in later chapters. An overview of intervals serves as an introduction to detailed instruction on seconds, the basic building block of pitch patterns in Western music. A general introduction to diatonic scales is followed by detailed instruction on tetrachords and pentachords, important scale divisions.

COMMUNICATION IN MUSIC

Musical Message   The impact music has on us results from a message carried by a musical composition and the way it is performed. This message of music is evident whenever the listener experiences changing moods or becomes aware of the unfolding and changing patterns in the music. The composer and the performer communicate ideas, moods, and images through the vehicle of a musical composition.

Music communicates ideas and moods in a manner similar to the language process. For example, in an ordinary conversation, a speaker encodes a message in spoken words. The listener decodes the words and receives the message. The listener provides the speaker with feedback in the form of spoken reply, gestures, facial expressions, and posture.

In music, the process operates on a different channel and involves more steps. This channel of communication uses sounds other than words (although vocal music has a verbal dimension to it). In musical communication, a composer encodes a message using various kinds of musical patterns and effects, then translates this aural code into a graphic code (score and parts). The performer decodes the score, then decodes the aural message the score implies. The performer indicates understanding of the composer's message through interpretations of the original message.

The performer's response to the message is superimposed onto the composer's message through expressive performance practices. The performer is both part of the channel for the composer's message and the originator of an additional message. The listener decodes and receives the composer/performer message. The listener then provides feedback to the performer through mood changes, bodily movement, and attentiveness during a performance. The composer, if present at the performance, receives feedback from both the audience and the performer.

A jazz performer encodes a message in a pattern of various sounds, rhythms, and effects during an improvisation. Detailed parts and scores are seldom used. Fellow musicians decode the message and provide feedback in the way they respond and accompany the improvisor. The listener decodes the message delivered by the improvisor and accompanists and provides feedback through mood change, rhythmic movement, facial expressions, and voiced sounds, both verbal and nonverbal.

A conductor studies an orchestra score prior to a rehearsal. This helps the conductor imagine how the score will be decoded as musical sounds, to interpret the message carried by the sounding patterns and effects, and to plan a course of action intended to bring out the conductor's ideas about the composer's message. Later, during rehearsals, the conductor blends and balances parts, calls for specific expression techniques, and coordinates feedback from the musicians in the ensemble. The conductor uses spoken commentary, facial expressions, hand gestures, and bodily movement to communicate his ideas about the music to the musicians and to coordinate their efforts. The objective of these rehearsals is to bring out the composer's message as influenced by the conductor's and performers' interpretation.

Chamber music is a team effort because the musicians rehearse without a conductor to perfect the performance of a composition. Their main objective is to coordinate their personal interpretations of the composer's message to arrive at a mutually acceptable group interpretation. The interpretation shows how the musicians understand the composer's message as it is built into the various patterns and events in the composition.

When creating the message, the composer may attempt to imagine what effect his/her ideas will have on both the performers and the listeners. Some composers believe they can completely control the performers' responses by supplying detailed markings in the score. These composers expect the performers to perform their compositions exactly as originally conceived. Other composers believe the performers are part of the message-creating process and assume that interpretation will be involved. These composers do not expect their compositions to be performed exactly as originally conceived.

Vocal performers have the added task of decoding the verbal message and determining how the verbal and musical messages interrelate. Composers of vocal music often attempt to code their own response to the words in the musical patterns and effects they create. This response becomes part of the composer's message, an important consideration for the vocal performer or conductor.

Message and Sound Recording

An improvisor spontaneously creates and encodes a message in the patterns of the music and the style of performing it. The improvisor is both the originator and sender of a message. The improvisor might change messages from performance to performance, partly based on feedback received from fellow musicians and listeners in a live setting. A sound recording may capture the spontaneity of a single live performance on the surface of a record or a tape, and the listener can hear the identical message over and over again. In a general sense, a sound recording resembles the coding of musical ideas in graphics, perhaps more inflexibly and statically than any musical score.

The development of sound recording has simultaneously broadened the listening audience and detached it more from live performance. The same is true of the broadcast medium, including radio and television. This larger, more detached audience adds a new dimension to the transmission of musical message. Performers can be completely isolated from listener feedback. Sound recordings can be edited to nearly flawless states. Yet in all this fragmentation of communication lines, composers and performers still manage to imagine the effects of their work as though they were performing in a live setting. Throughout this book, we will consider music as a carrier of message transmitted in the context of **live performance.**

Message and Notation

Musical notation is used extensively to communicate ideas about musical message. This notation is not, of itself, the essence of the ideas. Notation is simply a means of representing ideas in a musical score so these ideas can be retrieved at a later time. The actual musical message is encoded in sounds that are represented by musical notation. In music, just as in language, a message can be delivered without notation or the written word. Writing is a way to represent spoken ideas in graphic form. Printing has become so much a part of our culture that there can now be a distinction between a spoken verbal channel and a printed verbal channel. There is a similar distinction in music. Music has a rich aural tradition, but the printed score has become an important way to store musical ideas.

In language, words may have to be written in order to preserve a large and complex structure like a play or long poem. The full impact of the message is not available until a reader imagines the lines as interpreted spoken words, hears them, or actually says the lines aloud. This is very similar to musical communication. Yet, because we will place so much emphasis on notation, we might falsely conclude that the notation itself is the message. Because the message is not always evident in the notation, one can study a score *but miss the message.* We do not receive the full impact of the music until we imagine how the score should sound.

A musical composition is an object of art that exists momentarily in the environment of sound. In the nature of all art objects, the musical object itself can be the message. In literature for example, the impact of poetry has as much to do with the sound and beauty of the words as with what the words say. Numerous essays and books have been written about meaning, idea, and beauty in music. A whole body of literature on this aspect of music exists within a field of inquiry called aesthetics.

Remember that musical performance is a live act of communicating a sounding message. Keep this in mind throughout your theory studies. The chief function of musical notation is to represent sounds graphically so that a large and complicated structure can be preserved for later use. For this reason, always perform the music examples when using this book. Make sure examples are performed with expression to avoid dry, uncommitted performance. In music, performance without message is deadly.

Message and Musical Pattern

Musical message is carried by musical patterns and effects. These sounding patterns and effects are the substance of a channel which links composer to performer to listener. In broad terms, these patterns are embodied in the elements of **MELODY, RHYTHM, HARMONY, TEXTURE, SOUND**, and **SHAPE.** How the music relates to another medium is also important as, for example, vocal music or dance music. Music has become an important integral part of film and television production. The combination of music with words, bodily movement, or animation can have a great effect on the composer's treatment of the elements of musical composition. This book is devoted to the study of these elements and how they are interrelated to create a musical composition as a whole. Certain aspects of the musical message might be carried by the melody or the harmony, or the message itself can result from the interplay between those elements active in a particular composition. A view of the whole composition (or improvisation) should be maintained even when one's attention is limited to the study of just a few of its aspects.

Elements of Musical Composition

The following elements are important carriers of musical message and are fundamentally important to composers, arrangers, performers, conductors, and teachers. Definitions of these elements are given, but these should be regarded as tentative at this stage of the course. A general idea about these elements will do for now. Definitions of these terms will develop as the book unfolds.

1. MELODY: (a) theme or tune, (b) melodic line, (c) string of contiguous notes.
2. RHYTHM: (a) pattern made up of durations, (b) process of organizing rhythm patterns in meter, (c) large scale timing of major events in a composition.
3. HARMONY: (a) chords that accompany a melody, (b) pitch structures underlying a melody and its setting, (c) large scale pitch architecture of a composition.
4. TEXTURE: (a) "fabric" of a composition, (b) pattern which results from different combinations and relationships of basic elements of melody, rhythm, and harmony, (c) categories of compositions based upon particular relationships of the basic elements.
5. SOUND: (a) timbre of the performance medium, (b) effects of various combinations of sound and silence, (c) combined effect of timbre, texture, and harmonic sounds.
6. SHAPE: (a) pattern of an element (melody, rhythm, harmony) or combination of elements, (b) pattern perceived to have closure, or boundaries and thus identity, (c) music form or structure.

An important aim of this book is to present these elements and show how they act together to contribute to the wholeness of a musical composition, its message, and the way it's performed.

INTERVALS

An Overview

An **interval** is a pattern made up of two pitches. It is **harmonic** if the two pitches sound at the same time. It is **melodic** if the two pitches sound one after the other.

Example 1. Harmonic and Melodic Intervals

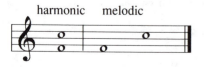

Interval size is determined by the number of contiguous notes spanned by the interval.

Example 2. Interval Sizing

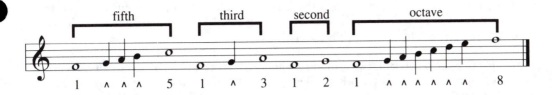

Simple Intervals

Simple intervals include the unison through the seventh. **Prime** has the same meaning as **unison.**

Example 3. Simple Intervals

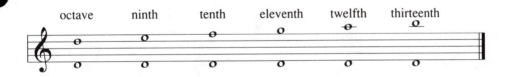

Compound Intervals

Compound intervals are an octave or larger. In a sense, a compound interval is a simple interval to which an octave is added. An octave can be seen as either the largest simple interval or the compound version of the unison.

Example 4. Compound Intervals

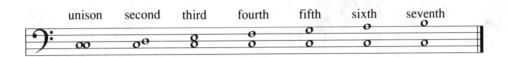

Intervals, Seconds

Seconds are spelled with adjacent letters in the musical alphabet and are written on adjacent positions in the staff (second = step).

Example 5. Seconds

Several terms can be used interchangeably when referring to seconds:

whole step = tone = major second = M2

half step = semitone = minor second = m2

5

A Building Block

The second is a **pitch primitive.** It is the building block of the entire pitch system in Western music, its scales, chords, and thematic ideas. Many traditional musical instruments are designed on the second. For example, the frets of a guitar divide the strings into half step increments. The piano keyboard is constructed in half steps as are many wind, brass, and mallet instruments.

On the piano keyboard, two pairs of white keys (E–F and B–C), are a **half step** apart. All other white keys are a **whole step** apart. In the following example, notice that B–C and E–F are adjacent white keys. Also, notice that there are black keys between the rest of the white keys making these a whole step apart (i.e., 1/2 + 1/2 = 1).

Example 6. White-Key Half Steps and Whole Steps

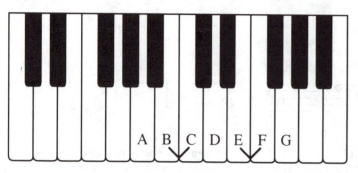

Accidentals

Accidentals can be used to change **minor seconds** to **major seconds** (or major seconds to minor seconds). A **sharp sign** raises a pitch one half step. A **flat sign** lowers a pitch one half step. A **natural sign** cancels any accidental. Notice how the accidentals can be used to change white-key minor seconds to major seconds—and white-key major seconds to minor seconds.

Example 7. Effect of Accidentals

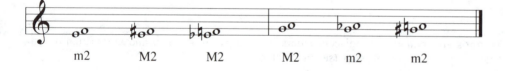

Diatonic versus Chromatic

A distinction must be made between a **diatonic half step** and a **chromatic half step.** The diatonic half step (mi2) is spelled with adjacent letters. The chromatic half step is spelled with different versions of the same letter.

Example 8. Diatonic and Chromatic Half Steps

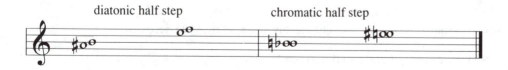

The **white-key half steps** are diatonic half steps if spelled with consecutive letters (i.e., E–F, B–C). They are chromatic half steps if both notes are spelled with the same letter (i.e., E–E sharp, B–B flat).

6

Transposition

Transposition is the shift of a pitch pattern to a different pitch level. A white-key half step or whole step can be transposed up or down a chromatic half step by sharping or flatting both notes in the interval. The transposition is diatonic if the letter spelling of the pitch pattern is changed.

Example 9. Transposition by Chromatic Half Steps

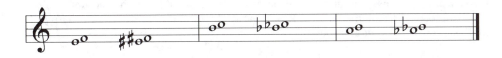

Double Sharps and Flats

A **double sharp** is used to raise a sharped note an additional half step. A **double flat** is used to lower a flatted note an additional half step. The next example shows how accidentals are used to change the size of major and minor seconds that already contain sharps or flats. These spellings are rare, so their appearance in a score may cause the unprepared reader to make an error. See if you can find an easier diatonic spelling for these intervals.

Example 10. Use of Double Sharps and Double Flats

Neighbor Tones

The following five-note pattern is based on a selected pitch and its upper and lower **neighbor tones** (notes a diatonic step above and below a given pitch). The upper and lower neighbors function as satellites around a central pitch. This pattern occurs regularly in melodies, etudes, and vocalises (vocal etudes).

Example 11. Five-Note Step Pattern

Neighbor Group

This five-note pattern is called a **neighbor group** because it includes a note and all of its diatonic neighboring notes (i.e., spelled with adjacent letters of the musical alphabet). Four diatonic versions of the neighbor group pattern can be made by changing the distance between the starting note and its neighbors. These patterns can be transposed to every step in the chromatic scale. **W** is used to represent the whole step. **H** is used to represent the half step. These patterns are best spelled diatonically.

Practice sing-spelling all transpositions of these four patterns (i.e., sing the letter names and accidentals of the notes).

Example 12. Four Diatonic Versions of Neighbor Groups

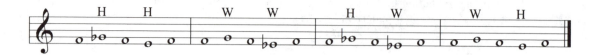

As you work with this pattern, you will occasionally use double sharps and double flats to preserve the diatonic pattern. Respell any pattern that requires you to sharp a double sharp (or flat a double flat).

CHECKPOINT I (Intervals)

1. Define and/or illustrate these terms:

elements of musical composition

interval	harmonic interval	interval size
melodic interval	prime	pitch primitive
unison	simple interval	neighbor tones
compound interval	white-key half steps	chromatic half step
second	major second	transposition
minor second	neighbor group	half step
accidental	sharp sign	natural sign
flat sign	double sharp	double flat
tone	semitone	
whole step	diatonic half step	

2. Self-help Problems. Problems are in the right column. Solutions are in the left column. Cover the answers while solving the problems. Some of the solutions depend on your interpretation of the pattern. Although these exercises are designed to have definite solutions, you may encounter differences between your solutions and those of others, including those given in this book. If your solution differs from the sample solution, raise a question about it in class. You may have a valid solution, or you may have made a mistake. Part of the learning process is sharing differing solutions, discussing the differences, and correcting mistakes.

Solution 1	Problem 1
harmonic simple compound melodic	An interval is _____ if both its notes sound at the same time. Intervals smaller than an octave are called _____intervals. Intervals larger than an octave are called _____ intervals. An interval is _____ if its notes sound one after the other.
Solution 2	**Problem 2**
diatonic (scale) five second diatonic chromatic	Interval size is calculated in_____ steps. This means that an interval of a fifth involves _____ contiguous letters of the musical alphabet. The interval of a _____ is spelled with adjacent letters of the alphabet. A _____ half step is spelled with adjacent letters of the musical alphabet. Notes in a _____ half step share the same letter name.
Solution 3	**Problem 3**
 E F B C two	Write the names of the notes included in the white-key half steps on the keyboard. There are _____ white-key half steps.

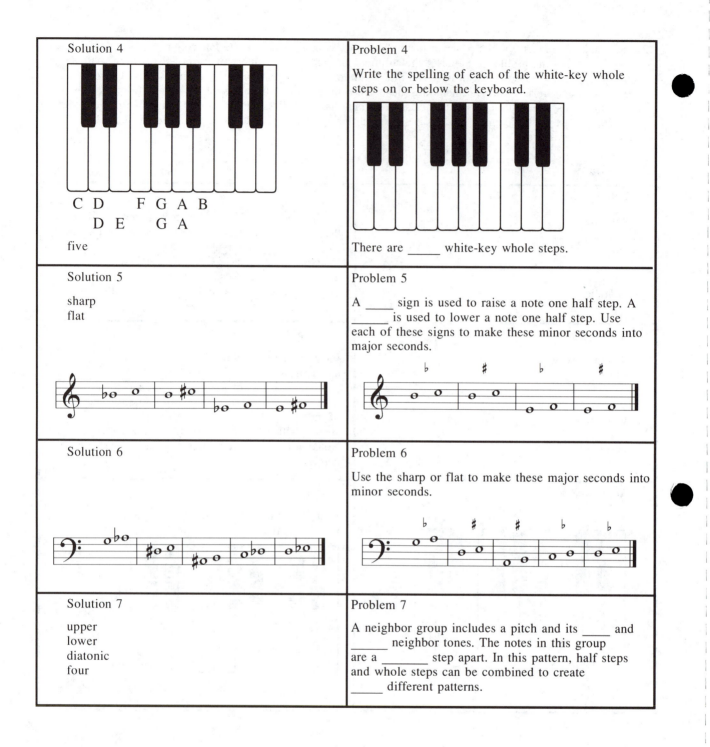

Solution 4

C D F G A B
D E G A

five

Problem 4

Write the spelling of each of the white-key whole steps on or below the keyboard.

There are _____ white-key whole steps.

Solution 5

sharp
flat

Problem 5

A _____ sign is used to raise a note one half step. A _____ is used to lower a note one half step. Use each of these signs to make these minor seconds into major seconds.

Solution 6

Problem 6

Use the sharp or flat to make these major seconds into minor seconds.

Solution 7

upper
lower
diatonic
four

Problem 7

A neighbor group includes a pitch and its _____ and _____ neighbor tones. The notes in this group are a _____ step apart. In this pattern, half steps and whole steps can be combined to create _____ different patterns.

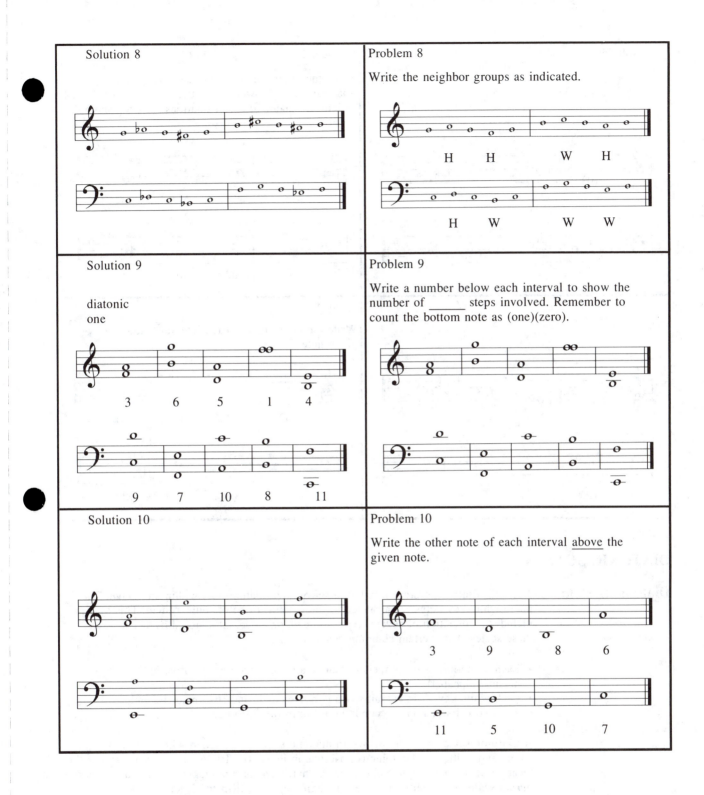

Solution 8

Problem 8

Write the neighbor groups as indicated.

H   H   W   H

H   W   W   W

Solution 9

diatonic
one

3   6   5   1   4

9   7   10   8   11

Problem 9

Write a number below each interval to show the number of _____ steps involved. Remember to count the bottom note as (one)(zero).

Solution 10

Problem 10

Write the other note of each interval above the given note.

3   9   8   6

11   5   10   7

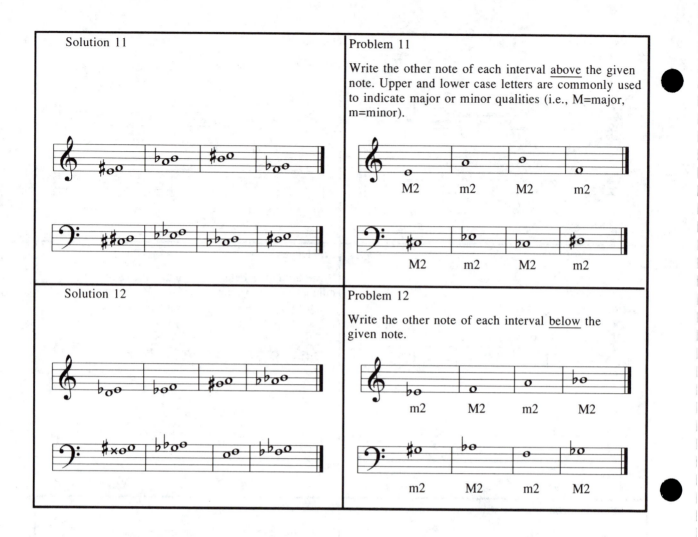

Solution 11

Problem 11

Write the other note of each interval <u>above</u> the given note. Upper and lower case letters are commonly used to indicate major or minor qualities (i.e., M=major, m=minor).

M2   m2   M2   m2

M2   m2   M2   m2

Solution 12

Problem 12

Write the other note of each interval <u>below</u> the given note.

m2   M2   m2   M2

m2   M2   m2   M2

DIATONIC SCALES

Diatonic System

The term **diatonic system** refers to a set of step relationships within an octave. The piano white-key notes are arranged in the pattern of the diatonic system. This system includes a collection of several types of scale or mode. Although different in sound, these scales share certain common characteristics.

- Each white-key scale is spelled diatonically (i.e., with consecutive letters of the musical alphabet).
- Each white-key scale contains two minor seconds and five major seconds.
- The two pairs of minor seconds lie a fourth (or fifth) apart.

A **diatonic scale** spans the octave in diatonic steps (i.e., spelled with contiguous letters and written on contiguous positions in the staff). The ^ shaped mark shows the location of the half steps. Notice that the half steps occupy degrees 3–4 and 7–8 in the **major scale.** The interval between the half steps is a **fifth.**

Example 13. The C Major Scale

The next example shows a different white-key diatonic scale (or **mode**), the A **minor scale.** Half steps now occupy degrees 2–3 and 5–6 of the scale. The interval between the half step pairs is a fourth (this shows the location of the half steps). This form of minor is also called **natural minor** (more on this later).

Example 14. The A Minor Scale

Relative and Parallel Modes

The C major and A minor scales are called **relative modes** because they use the same collection of diatonic pitches (the white keys in this case) but each starts on a different pitch in the collection.

Example 15. Relative Major and Minor

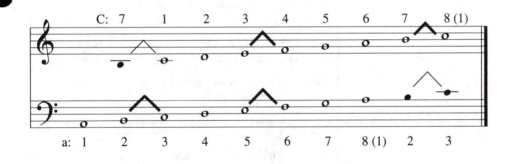

Parallel modes begin on the same pitch but are different types. Each parallel mode is based on a different collection of diatonic pitches to ensure the unique location of half steps of the mode. Three notes must be altered in order to convert C major to parallel minor.

Example 16. Parallel Major and Minor

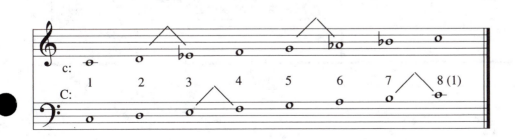

13

CHECKPOINT II (Diatonic Scales)

1. Define and/or illustrate these terms:

   diatonic scale   mode   diatonic system

   minor scale   fifth   natural minor

   major scale   parallel mode   relative mode

2. Self-help Problems.

Solution 1 diatonic consecutive two five fourth (or fifth)	**Problem 1** A **diatonic scale** spans the octave in _____ steps. Each white-key diatonic scale is spelled with _____ letters of the musical alphabet. Each white-key diatonic scale contains _____ minor seconds and _____ major seconds. The two pairs of minor seconds lie a _____ apart.
Solution 2 modes major minor	**Problem 2** The diatonic white-key scales include several types of scales called _____. The two modes currently under study are the _____ and _____ scales.
Solution 3 relative parallel half	**Problem 3** Modes (scales) that have the same key signature but start on different notes are called _____ modes. Modes which use different key signatures but start on the same notes are called _____ modes. Major and minor scales sound different because of the unique location of the _____ steps in each scale.
Solution 4 	**Problem 4** Use a ^ mark to show the location of half steps in each major scale.

Solution 5

natural minor

Problem 5

Use a ^ mark to show the location of half steps in each scale.

This is the pattern of the _____ _____ scale.

Solution 6

Problem 6

Use a ^ mark to show the location of half steps in each major scale. Add accidentals where needed to maintain the step pattern of major.

Solution 7

Problem 7

Use a ^ mark to show the location of half steps in each natural minor scale. Add accidentals where needed to maintain the step pattern of natural minor.

SCALE SUBSETS

Tetrachords and Pentachords

A **tetrachord** is a four-note segment of a scale (in the boxes). A **pentachord** is a five-note segment of a scale (in the oval).

Example 17. Tetrachord and Pentachord Segments

G major scale

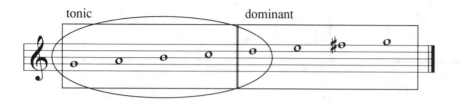

A white-key scale can be transposed to other pitch levels. When the collection of notes is transposed, one or more notes must be altered with flats or sharps to preserve certain relationships among the pitches. In the previous example, the white-key major scale was transposed to G. An F# was required to maintain a half step between the seventh and eighth scale degrees.

The starting pitch of a scale (i.e., the pitch name of the scale) is also called the **tonic** pitch. The fifth step of a scale is called the **dominant** pitch. The **tonic tetrachord** is a four-note scale segment starting on the tonic pitch. The **dominant tetrachord** starts on the dominant pitch. The next example shows a scale divided into tonic and dominant tetrachord segments.

Example 18. Tonic and Dominant Tetrachords

F major scale

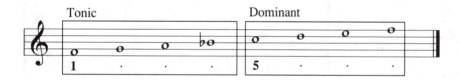

In the previous example, the white-key major scale was transposed to F. A B flat was required in order to maintain the half step between the third and fourth scale degrees.

The next example shows a scale divided into a tonic pentachord (in oval) and a dominant tetrachord (in box). This way of dividing up a scale is fairly common in simple melodies. Notice how the two segments overlap on the dominant pitch.

Example 19. Tonic Pentachord, Dominant Tetrachord

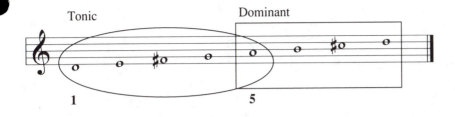

Tetrachords and pentachords are important subdivisions (**subsets**) of diatonic scales as can be seen in numerous melodies. There are several types of tetrachord and pentachord. Each type is named after the mode in which it appears as the tonic tetrachord or pentachord. Each has its own unique pattern of half and whole steps. For example, a **major tetrachord** is the first four steps of a major scale. A **minor pentachord** is the first five steps of a minor scale. The **Phrygian tetrachord** is the dominant tetrachord in natural minor and the tonic tetrachord in the Phrygian scale (to be discussed in later chapters). The step pattern of each type is illustrated in the next two examples. The letter **H** indicates a half step, **W** indicates a whole step.

Example 20. Tetrachord and Pentachord Types: Major, Minor

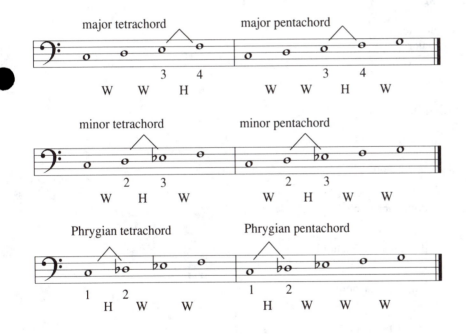

Major and minor scales have unique sounds because of the location of the half steps in each scale. Each scale also has an unique arrangement of tetrachords. Knowledge of tetrachord arrangements in different types of scales can be used to learn the scales in all keys more efficiently. This knowledge can also be used to develop pattern reading and memorization skills. All **major** scales consist of two major tetrachords. All natural minor scales consist of a minor tetrachord and a Phrygian tetrachord.

17

Example 21. Tetrachords in Major and Natural Minor Scales

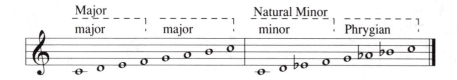

Harmonic Minor

The **harmonic minor** scale is a natural minor scale that contains a raised seventh scale degree. This alteration results from borrowing the leading tone from parallel major. The tonic tetrachord is unaffected by the alteration but the dominant tetrachord is changed to a **harmonic tetrachord.** The step pattern for this tetrachord is H –+2 –H. The harmonic tetrachord mixes features of the dominant tetrachords of parallel major and minor.

Example 22. Harmonic Minor and Harmonic Tetrachord

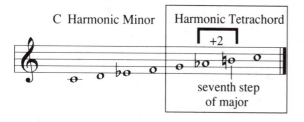

CHECKPOINT III (Scale Subsets)

1. Define and/or illustrate these terms:

tetrachord	pentachord
tonic pitch	dominant pitch
tonic pentachord	dominant pentachord
major tetrachord	major pentachord
minor pentachord	minor tetrachord
Phrygian tetrachord	harmonic tetrachord
scale subset	harmonic minor

2. Self-help Problems.

Solution 1 tetrachord pentachord tonic pentachord dominant tetrachord	**Problem 1** A four-note section of a scale is called a _____. A five-note section of a scale is called a _____. The five-note segment which begins on the first step of the scale is called the _____ _____. The four-note segment which begins on the fifth step of the scale is called the _____ _____.
Solution 2 major W, W, H (whole, whole, half) minor W, H, W (whole, half, whole)	**Problem 2** The first four steps of the major scale is a _____ tetrachord. The step pattern of this tetrachord is _____, _____, _____. The first four steps of the natural minor scale is a _____ tetrachord. The step pattern of this tetrachord is _____, _____, _____.
Solution 3	**Problem 3** Add accidentals as needed to make these tetrachords major.
Solution 4	**Problem 4** Add accidentals as needed to make these tetrachords minor.

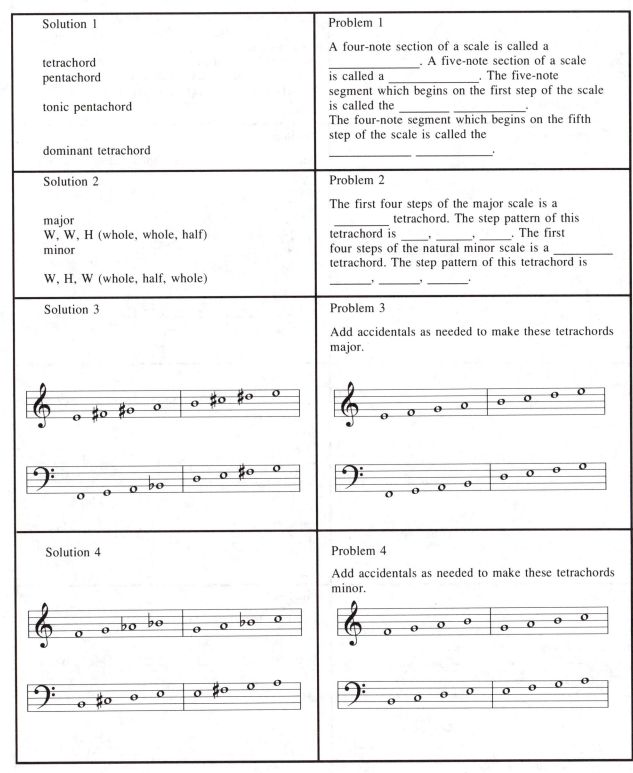

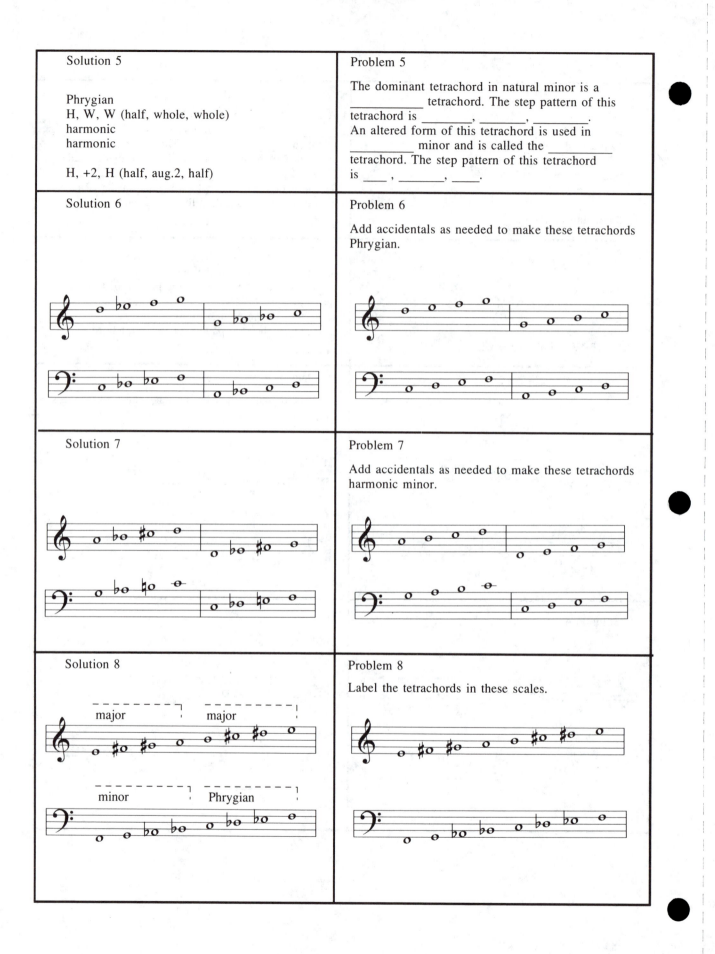

Solution 5

Phrygian
H, W, W (half, whole, whole)
harmonic
harmonic

H, +2, H (half, aug.2, half)

Problem 5

The dominant tetrachord in natural minor is a
_____ tetrachord. The step pattern of this
tetrachord is _____, _____, _____.
An altered form of this tetrachord is used in
_____ minor and is called the _____
tetrachord. The step pattern of this tetrachord
is ____ , _____, ____.

Solution 6

Problem 6

Add accidentals as needed to make these tetrachords
Phrygian.

Solution 7

Problem 7

Add accidentals as needed to make these tetrachords
harmonic minor.

Solution 8

major   major

minor   Phrygian

Problem 8

Label the tetrachords in these scales.

20

APPLICATIONS

1. Write and sing-spell major and minor pentachords, up and down, starting on each of these pitches: C, G, D, and A; C, F, B flat, and E flat. When transposing the patterns, be sure to keep the half and whole steps in their proper locations for each type of pentachord. Be able to write all these patterns quickly.

2. Find a melody based primarily on the notes of a tonic pentachord. Write the melody in the staff provided below. Perform it for others as a dictation exercise.

3. Find a melody that alternates between notes of the tonic pentachord and the dominant tetrachord. Write the melody in the staff below. Perform it for others as a dictation exercise.

4. Write and sing-spell the four different five-note neighbor group patterns with C as the starting note. Use a piano (or other instrument) to check your intonation. Next sing-spell the four neighbor groups on each of the remaining white-key notes. Then, sing them on B, E, and A flat. Finally, sing them on F and C-sharp. Be able to write all these patterns quickly.

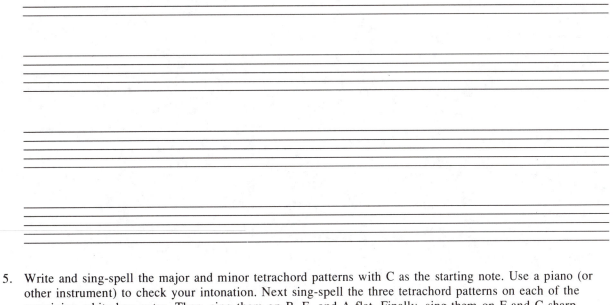

5. Write and sing-spell the major and minor tetrachord patterns with C as the starting note. Use a piano (or other instrument) to check your intonation. Next sing-spell the three tetrachord patterns on each of the remaining white-key notes. Then, sing them on B, E, and A flat. Finally, sing them on F and C sharp. Repeat this exercise using the Phrygian and harmonic tetrachords. Remember that the harmonic tetrachord contains <u>two</u> half steps and an augmented second. Be able to write these patterns quickly.

2 RHYTHM AND METER

OVERVIEW

The *Rhythm Path* begins in this chapter. This path includes foundation concepts on rhythm, pulse, and meter. Simple and compound meter, note beaming customs, rhythmic chanting and analysis, and rhythm reading skills are discussed in detail. This path merges with *Melody*, *Harmony*, and *Texture* paths in later chapters.

INTRODUCTION TO RHYTHM AND METER

The term **rhythm** has several meanings. Generally, rhythm is the timing, duration, or temporal organization of any element in a composition or an improvisation. It is the ''engine'' of music. More specifically, a rhythm is a short idea made of various durations. A rhythm can also be a recurring pattern of pulses caused by strong and weak beats.

Musical time is marked off in **beats,** also called **pulses.** These beats are organized by meter. **Meter** is the cycling of pulse patterns of equal or unequal length. In musical notation, meter is indicated by a meter sign.

The **meter sign** is a stack of numbers that follows the key signature on a line of music. The top number refers to the number of units in a recurring pattern of pulses. The term **unit** is used here because the top number does not always indicate the number of beats per measure. If the tempo is very fast, we feel only one beat every two or three units. If the tempo is very slow, we feel two or three beats per unit. The bottom number refers to the note value assigned to represent the unit.

For example:
- **2** - each measure contains two units
- **4** - each unit has the value of a quarter note

- **3** - each measure contains three units
- **2** - each unit has the value of a half note

- **7** - each measure contains seven units
- **16** - each unit has the value of a sixteenth note

Perception of Pulse

Tempo affects how we hear the pulse of the music. Thus, the indicated unit (the bottom number of the meter sign) is not always heard as the beat. In a slow tempo, for example, notes smaller than the unit will be heard as the beat. Under these circumstances, an indicated quarter note unit will be heard as a duration of two beats. The next smaller value (the eighth note) will be heard as a duration of one beat.

In a very fast tempo, the indicated unit will be heard as a fraction of the beat. Under these conditions, an indicated quarter note will be heard as half of one beat. Fast 3/4 meter is heard as one beat per measure. The dotted half note is felt as the beat and the indicated unit (the quarter note) as a third of the beat. Try saying "1-2-3" repeatedly aloud. Start slowly and gradually increase speed. Do you have a tendency to accent "1"? As you increase speed, does "1" seem to become the beginning of a triplet rather than the first count in a group of separate beats?

Simple Meter

Meters are classified according to the ratio between beats and **beat divisions. Simple meter** is any meter with a division-to-beat ratio of 2:1. This ratio is based on note values inherent in the meter. The moderate tempo 2/4 meter is classified as a simple meter because the indicated beat, the quarter note, divides into two eighth notes (duple division of the beat). The next example shows how indicated units are divided in simple meter.

Example 1. Simple Meters, 2:1 Rhythms

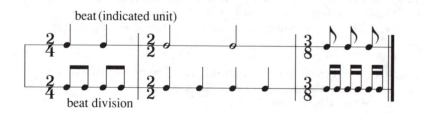

If composers use note and rest values no shorter than half of the indicated unit, they have only a few ways to write any beat-long rhythm pattern. Notice how note beams are used to show these one-beat groups.

Example 2. Possible Rhythms in One Quarter Note Beat

A close mental connection between the visual and aural image of a rhythm must be developed for efficient, error free reading skills. The following chart shows a kind of "family tree" of visual images of one-beat patterns (based on quarter note units). Each one-beat rhythm is enclosed in a circle. Imagine how each should sound. Look away from the book and see how many of these one-beat patterns you can visualize in your mind's eye and ear.

Example 3. One-beat Rhythms as Visual Images

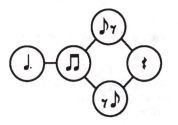

Compound Meter Perform a series of equal-length notes using a neutral syllable like "da." Do not accent any of the notes. Now, accent every other note. Next, accent every third note. Continue to perform these two patterns while attempting to visualize how each would be notated in eighth notes. Use beams to organize the notes into groups of two and three parts. Now, look at the next example. Each measure contains the same number of eighth notes, but each is organized and beamed differently. After completing this exercise, can you put the difference between simple and compound meters into words?

Example 4. Eighth Notes in Simple and Compound Meters

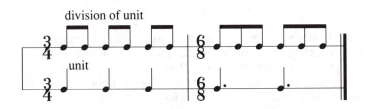

In **compound meter,** the indicated unit is combined into three-unit groupings. For example, 6/8 meter consists of two 3/8 groups. At moderate or fast tempos, these groups are felt as a beat with three parts. At a slow tempo, each unit is felt as the beat and can be divided by two. In this sense, slow 6/8 operates as simple meter.

Example 5. Slow 6/8 Meter as Simple Meter

In a fast tempo, the three-unit group (3/8 or dotted quarter) is heard as the beat and the indicated unit is now one-third of the beat (a **3:1 rhythm**).

Example 6. Fast 6/8 Meter

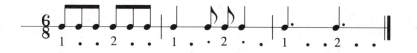

How do examples 5 and 6 relate to the exercise you performed in **Perception of Pulse** above (counting 1-2-3 at various speeds)?

If one uses note and rest values no smaller than the indicated unit (a third of a beat), any beat-long rhythm pattern in compound meter can be written only a few ways. In the next example, notice how note beams are used to show these one-beat groups (each beat contains three units).

Example 7. Possible Rhythms in a Dotted Quarter Beat

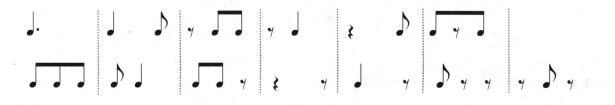

The following chart shows a "family tree" of one-beat patterns possible in compound meter. Each one-beat rhythm is enclosed in a circle and has the net value of a dotted quarter note, the perceived beat in fast compound meter. Notice how the beams show the triplet organization of each beat. Imagine how each should sound. Look away from the book and see how many you can visualize in your mind's eye and ear.

Example 8. One-beat Rhythms in Compound Meter as Visual Images

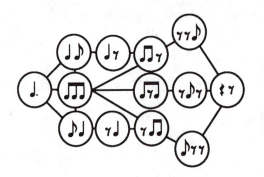

Note Beaming Customs

Beams connect the stems of eighth notes and smaller values, reflecting the internal organization of the beat. Recall that the units in 2/4 meter are arranged in eighth note pairs by beams. The units in 6/8 meter are arranged in eighth note triplets.

Example 9. Beams in Simple and Compound Meter

In simple meters, beats and whole measures can be grouped under a common beam. Such groups begin on an important accent in the measure. In 4/4 meter, notes can be beamed together in two two-unit groups. This beaming shows graphically that 4/4 meter is made up of two measures of 2/4 meter.

Example 10. Beats Grouped by Beams

Beams visually support the beat, accent, and beat-group organization of a meter. A few incorrect ways to beam notes are shown in the next example. Can you explain what is wrong with each sample error?

Example 11. Incorrect Beaming

Later, you will see that some of these incorrect beaming patterns are used by modern composers to indicate special rhythm patterns. Generally, the errors above were the result of

- Inconsistent beaming within the measure; for example, uniting some units with beams but not others, or not using beams in <u>all</u> one-unit groups
- Note groupings inconsistent with the standard strong-weak patterns of a particular meter; for example, connecting beats 2–3 of 4/4 meter with a beam (instead of beats 1–2 or 3–4), or not starting beams at the beginning of a beat
- Inconsistent illustration of 2:1 or 3:1 beat organization

29

Beaming in Vocal Music

These beaming customs also apply to vocal music when there is more than one note per syllable.

Example 12. Refrain from "Angels We Have Heard On High"

Glo - ri - a

Rhythmic notation in vocal music is **syllabic.** This means values less than a quarter note are written as flagged notes unless there is more than one note per syllable.

Example 13. Syllabic Rhythmic Notation

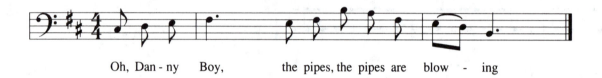

Oh, Dan - ny Boy, the pipes, the pipes are blow - ing

Rhythmic Chanting

Rhythmic chanting is the performance of rhythms with syllables that indicate the rhythmic organization. The use of rhythmic chanting can aid learning rhythmic reading, diagnosing reading problems, and communicating ideas about rhythms.

Several approaches to chanting are generally used. A few of these will be introduced to provide an overview of rhythmic chanting vocabularies and approaches.

Kodaly used the syllable "ta" for durations a beat or more in length. The syllable "ti," pronounced "tee," was used for durations less than a beat in length.

Example 14. Elementary Rhythmic Chanting

Ta Ta ti ti ti ti Ta ti ti Ta Ta

Another approach uses "one—and" or "one—trip—let" syllables for simple or compound meter. An alternate form of compound meter chanting is "one-la-li-two-la-li," etc. ("li" is pronounced "lee").

Example 15. Chanting in Simple and Compound Meters

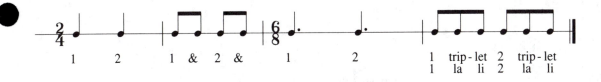

The organization of the divided simple meter beat can be described in several ways. Notes on the beginning of a beat are considered to be stronger than notes on other parts of a beat. **Down** and **up** refer to the finger or foot tapping motions ordinarily associated with counting rhythm.

Example 16. Description of Beat Divisions (simple meter)

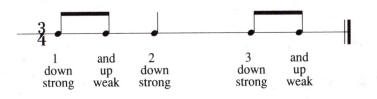

Apply these chants to the rhythm exercises at the end of the chapter. You should be familiar with all of these approaches to teach someone else how to read rhythms or to communicate ideas about rhythms quickly to other musicians. It is helpful to think about rhythms as **multilayer** patterns, shown in the next example.

Example 17. Multilayer Rhythmic Thinking

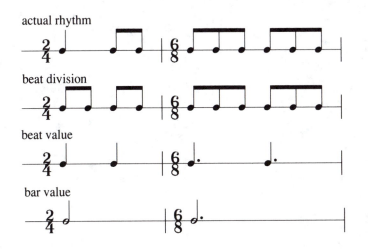

CHECKPOINT

1. Define these terms:

   rhythm   beat

   pulse   indicated unit

   simple meter   2:1 rhythm

   beat division   syllabic notation

   multilayer   meter sign

   meter   tempo

   compound meter   3:1 rhythm

   beaming customs   rhythmic chant

2. Briefly explain the following:

   a. value of rhythmic chants

   b. effect of tempo on the perception (hearing, feeling) of beat

   c. organization of beats

3. Self-help Problems.

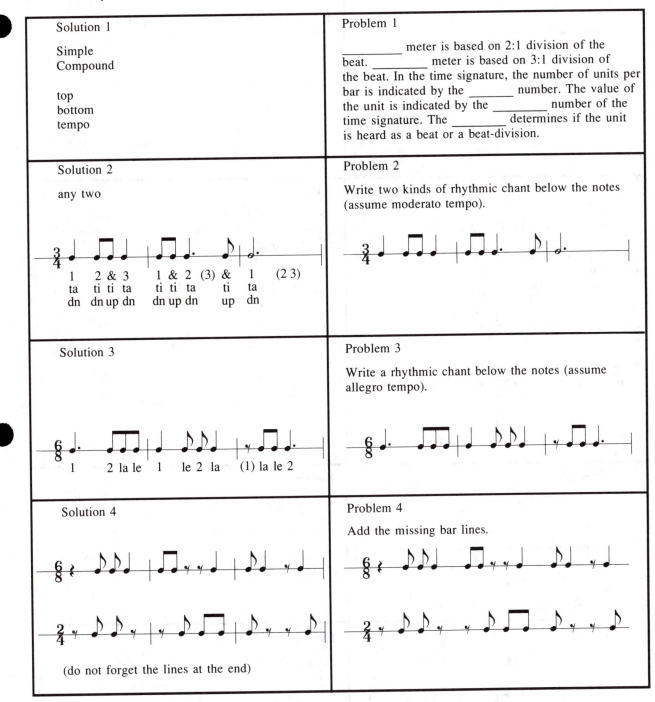

Solution 1

Simple
Compound

top
bottom
tempo

Problem 1

_____ meter is based on 2:1 division of the beat. _____ meter is based on 3:1 division of the beat. In the time signature, the number of units per bar is indicated by the _____ number. The value of the unit is indicated by the _____ number of the time signature. The _____ determines if the unit is heard as a beat or a beat-division.

Solution 2

any two

3/4 1   2 & 3   1 & 2 (3) &   1   (2 3)
     ta ti ti ta ti ti ta ti ta
     dn dn up dn dn up dn   up dn

Problem 2

Write two kinds of rhythmic chant below the notes (assume moderato tempo).

Solution 3

6/8 1   2 la le   1 le 2 la (1) la le 2

Problem 3

Write a rhythmic chant below the notes (assume allegro tempo).

Solution 4

6/8

2/4

(do not forget the lines at the end)

Problem 4

Add the missing bar lines.

6/8

2/4

33

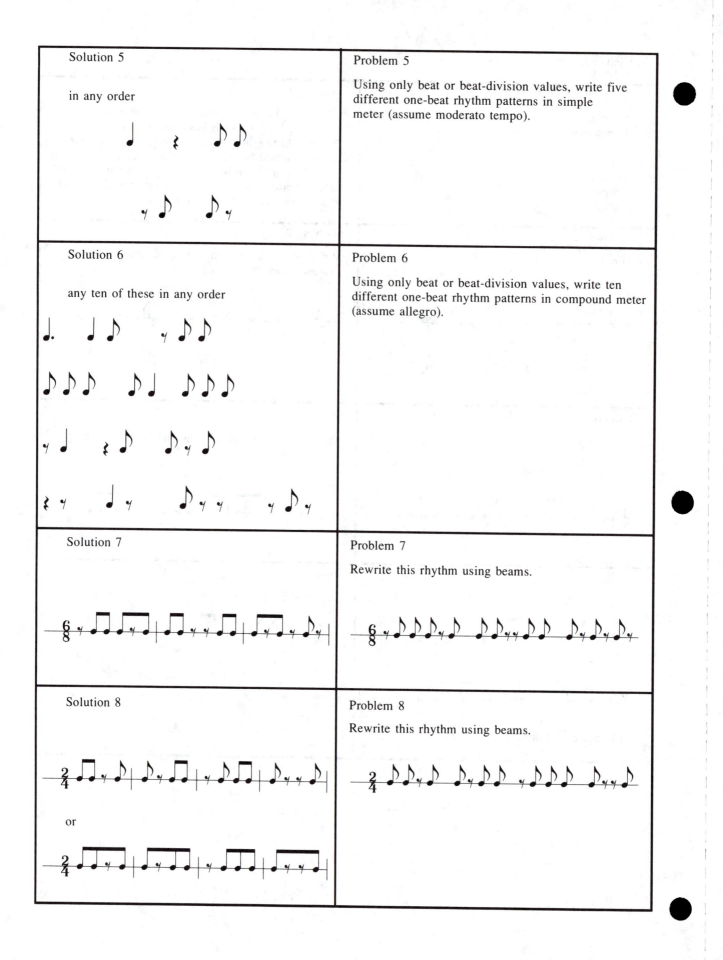

Solution 5

in any order

Problem 5

Using only beat or beat-division values, write five different one-beat rhythm patterns in simple meter (assume moderato tempo).

Solution 6

any ten of these in any order

Problem 6

Using only beat or beat-division values, write ten different one-beat rhythm patterns in compound meter (assume allegro).

Solution 7

Problem 7

Rewrite this rhythm using beams.

Solution 8

or

Problem 8

Rewrite this rhythm using beams.

34

APPLICATIONS

1. The following patterns are in two-pulse meter. To the viewer, the two-pulse conducting pattern looks something like this:

Use this conducting pattern when performing the rhythms below. Begin with a preparatory beat (i.e., the beat that precedes the first beat in the music). Use these exercises as an opportunity to apply the rhythm syllables included in this chapter. Also use neutral syllables, especially when working for speed.

2. The following rhythms are in three-pulse meter. To the viewer the three-pulse conducting pattern looks something like this:

Practice chanting and conducting when performing the rhythms. At first, practice the exercise one line at a time. Later, perform the whole exercise non-stop at a medium or fast tempo.

3. Two-Part Ensembles (simple meter)

Perform these patterns alone, with a study partner, or with a study group. For variation, use contrasting sounds for each part (i.e., contrasting syllables, hand claps, taps, clicks, nonsense mouth sounds, etc.). Try conducting and chanting when performing. Switch parts.

4. The following rhythms are in four-pulse meter. To the viewer, the four-pulse conducting pattern looks something like this:

Practice chanting and conducting when performing these rhythms.

5. Two-Part Ensembles (simple meter)

Perform these patterns alone, with a study partner, or with a study group. For variation, try conducting, chanting, and performing each part with a contrasting sound.

6. The following rhythms are in two-pulse and three-pulse compound meters. Try using two-pulse and three-pulse conducting patterns when performing the rhythms. Try rhythmic chanting, too.

38

7. Two-Part Ensembles (compound meter)

3 THIRDS, DOTS AND TIES, MAJOR SCALES

OVERVIEW *Interval*, *Rhythm*, and *Scale* paths continue in this chapter. The *Interval Path* includes details on thirds and enharmonic notation. The *Rhythm Path* includes instruction on dots and ties, rhythm chanting, analysis, reading, scanning, and performance. The *Scale Path* includes instruction on the circle of fifths in major, major key signatures, relative and parallel modes, and enharmonic and chromatic pairs of major scales.

Thirds A **third** spans three diatonic notes (or three positions of the musical alphabet). This span includes both notes in the interval. As shown in the example, a third is spelled with every other letter of the musical alphabet (i.e., C–E, F–A, etc.). The notes of a third span three positions in the staff.

Example 1. Thirds

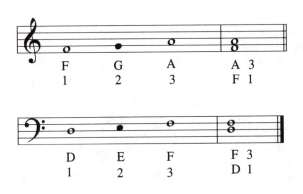

On the keyboard, the **white-key major thirds** are C–E, F–A, and G–B. The major third is one half step larger than the minor third. Notice that a white-key half step is never included in any white-key major third.

Example 2. White-Key Major Thirds

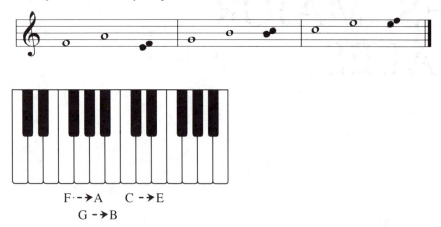

F ··➤ A   C ➤ E
G ➤ B

The **white-key minor thirds** are A–C, B–D, D–F, and E–G. Notice that one white-key half step pair is always included in each minor third. Also, the white-key minor thirds are arranged in two pairs of thirds a step apart.

Example 3. White-Key Minor Thirds

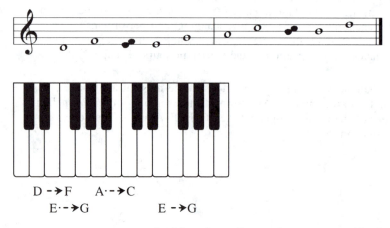

D ➤ F   A ··➤ C
E ··➤ G   E ➤ G

Accidentals can be used to convert white-key major thirds to minor thirds.

Example 4. Changing Major Thirds to Minor Thirds

M3   m3   m3   M3   m3   m3

Accidentals also convert white-key minor thirds to major thirds.

Example 5. Changing Minor Thirds to Major Thirds

Augmented and Diminished Intervals

Augmented intervals are a chromatic half step larger than major intervals. **Diminished intervals** are a chromatic half step smaller than minor intervals. Both notes of a chromatic half step are spelled with the same letter name.

Example 6. Changing Major Thirds to Augmented Thirds

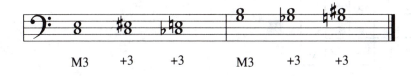

Example 7. Changing Minor Thirds to Diminished Thirds

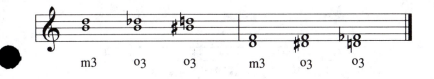

Example 8. Changing Major Seconds to Augmented Seconds

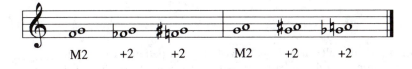

Example 9. Changing Minor Seconds to Diminished Seconds

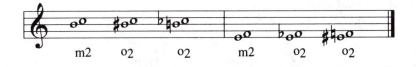

Enharmonic Notation

Enharmonic notation provides alternate ways to write a pitch. The next two examples show how enharmonic notation relates to the piano keyboard and to treble clef. Notice each white key can be spelled three ways, all practical spellings. The sharp and flat signs on the black keys indicate that each black key has two practical spellings. If sharp, the black key takes the letter name of the white key below it. If flat, the black key takes the letter name of the white key above it.

Example 10. Enharmonic Spellings on the Piano Keyboard

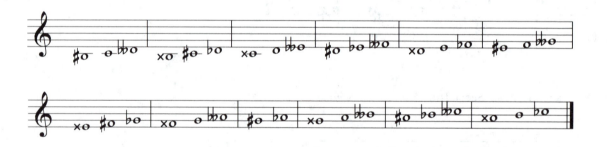

Compare the next example to this keyboard.

Example 11. Enharmonic Spellings in Treble Clef

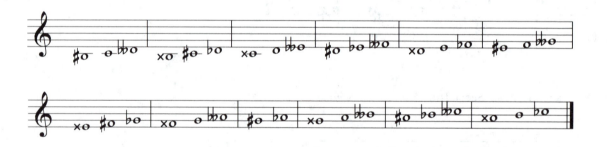

Enharmonic notation provides alternate ways to write a pitch pattern of the same sound. For example, a minor third is a half step larger than a major second. If the second is augmented, it sounds like a minor third. Conversely, if the third is diminished, it sounds like a major second (the equals sign indicates that two intervals share the same sound).

Example 12. Enharmonic Notation of Intervals ("Sound alikes")

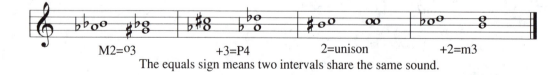

M2=º3   +3=P4   2=unison   +2=m3

The equals sign means two intervals share the same sound.

CHECKPOINT I (Intervals)

1. Define these terms:

   third   augmented interval

   white-key minor thirds   diminished interval

   white-key major thirds   enharmonic notation

2. Self-help Problems. Problems are in the right column. Solutions are in the left column. Cover the answers while solving the problems.

Solution 1	Problem 1
three F–A G–B a–c, b–d, d–f, e–g	A third spans _____ letter names. The spelling of white-key major thirds is C–E, ___-___, and ___-___. The spelling of white-key minor thirds is ___-___, ___-___, ___ – ___, and ___-___.
Solution 2 accidentals smaller lowering (flatting) raising (sharping)	Problem 2 One type of third can be converted to another type through _____. The minor third is a half step _____ than a major third. The major third can be converted to a minor third by _____ the top note or _____ the bottom note .
Solution 3 larger raising (sharping) lowering (flatting)	Problem 3 The augmented third is a half step _____ than a major third. The major third can be converted to an augmented third by _____ the top note or _____ the bottom note.
Solution 4 smaller lowering (flatting) raising (sharping)	Problem 4 The diminished third is a half step _____ than the minor third. The minor third can be converted to a diminished third by _____ the top note or _____ the bottom note.

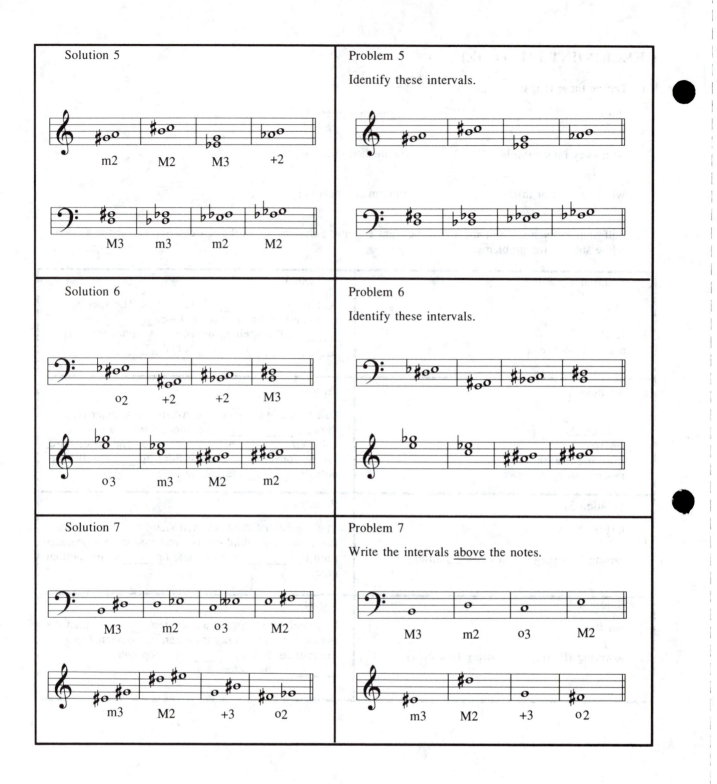

Solution 5

m2   M2   M3   +2

M3   m3   m2   M2

Problem 5

Identify these intervals.

Solution 6

o2   +2   +2   M3

o3   m3   M2   m2

Problem 6

Identify these intervals.

Solution 7

M3   m2   o3   M2

m3   M2   +3   o2

Problem 7

Write the intervals above the notes.

M3   m2   o3   M2

m3   M2   +3   o2

46

47

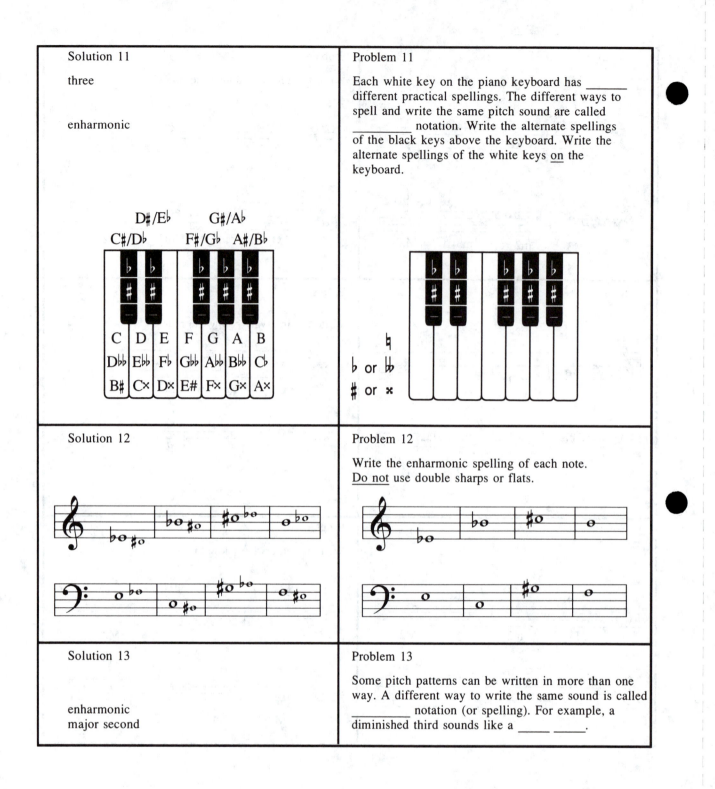

Solution 11

three

enharmonic

Problem 11

Each white key on the piano keyboard has _____ different practical spellings. The different ways to spell and write the same pitch sound are called _____ notation. Write the alternate spellings of the black keys above the keyboard. Write the alternate spellings of the white keys on the keyboard.

Solution 12

Problem 12

Write the enharmonic spelling of each note.
Do not use double sharps or flats.

Solution 13

enharmonic
major second

Problem 13

Some pitch patterns can be written in more than one way. A different way to write the same sound is called _____ notation (or spelling). For example, a diminished third sounds like a _____ _____.

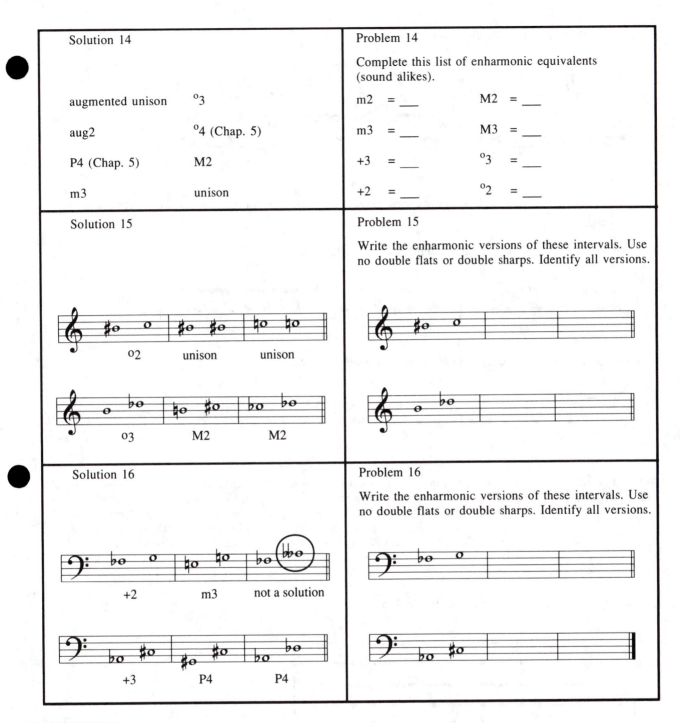

Solution 14

augmented unison	°3
aug2	°4 (Chap. 5)
P4 (Chap. 5)	M2
m3	unison

Problem 14

Complete this list of enharmonic equivalents (sound alikes).

m2 = ___		M2 = ___
m3 = ___		M3 = ___
+3 = ___		°3 = ___
+2 = ___		°2 = ___

Solution 15

°2   unison   unison

°3   M2   M2

Problem 15

Write the enharmonic versions of these intervals. Use no double flats or double sharps. Identify all versions.

Solution 16

+2   m3   not a solution

+3   P4   P4

Problem 16

Write the enharmonic versions of these intervals. Use no double flats or double sharps. Identify all versions.

RHYTHM

Dots and Ties   Dots and ties lengthen the value of a note. A dot is worth half of whatever it follows. If it follows a whole note, the dot is worth a half note. If a dot follows another dot, it is half as long as the first dot. Dots and ties can sometimes be used interchangeably. The next example shows dotted rhythms and their tied rhythm equivalents.

Example 13. Dots and Their Tie Equivalents

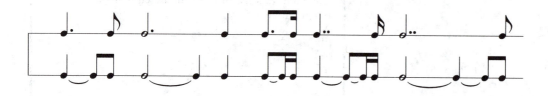

Sometimes, ties are used to extend a value past a bar line or across a break in beams.

Example 14. Ties Across Measure and Beam Breaks; Simple Meter

Example 15. Ties Across Measure and Beam Breaks; Compound Meter

Accuracy in Performance

Dots and ties can cause errors in reading and in performance accuracy. These signs make music notation more elaborate, more complex. Also, it is easy to ignore the rhythmic significance of these signs and to guess when reading and performing dotted or tied rhythms. For the sake of accuracy, one should make time to take a closer look at rhythm details. A break down of this rhythm into chants and **rhythmic layers** will help.

Example 16. Rhythmic Break Down (analysis); Simple Meter

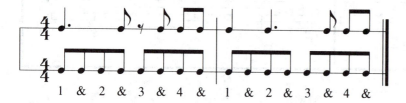

Example 17.

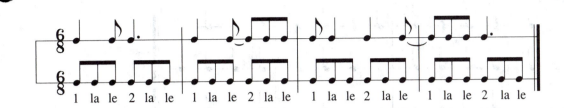

Mental and Physical Coordination

Music performance is a complex activity that requires considerable physical and mental coordination. Consider all the things a musician must do and think about when performing (fingerings, enunciation, intonation, tone quality, rhythm, interpretation, ensemble, and more). This coordination would be impossible unless we had a way of putting some thoughts on "automatic." While reading music, a particular part of thinking or doing is switched to "manual" control if a problem occurs. If the performer fails to respond to this signal, one or more mental or physical processes might be called too late to manage the problem. Concentration might break, causing the performance to falter or fail.

Fortunately, there are ways to refine and strengthen this automatic control and its occasional switches to manual. One way is to rehearse patterns to set them solidly in one's memory. Drill and practice, as old as this technique may be, still works best for this purpose. Sometimes a trouble signal is set off by an unfamiliar pattern. When this happens, look at the pattern (or the particular sequence of patterns) that caused the problem. Attempt to identify the specific cause of the problem (an awkward interval, rhythm, or fingering). Drill the problem area at a slow tempo. Concentrate on the cause. Think in terms of pattern, not separate notes. Gradually, work back up to speed.

Scanning

One technique that improves reading is **scanning.** To develop good scanning techniques, always keep your eyes moving and ahead of the real-time performance point. Do not stop for a mistake. Do not look back. If necessary, "fake it" in order to avoid a failure in performance. This technique will increase your capacity to recall longer and longer patterns, to scan further and further ahead, and generally to read and perform with fewer errors and greater confidence. When working at scanning, do not allow yourself to get in a tempo "rut." Change tempo. Push yourself at times but not to the point which absolutely guarantees failure.

Scanning can be improved by developing the ability to think in simultaneous rhythmic layers. Try to break down rhythms into layers for rehearsal purposes. This helps program your **internal "clock,"** part of the process of developing dependable automatic response. As suggested in the next example, body "intelligence" and "memory" are part of this development process.

Example 18. Rhythm Layer Breakdown

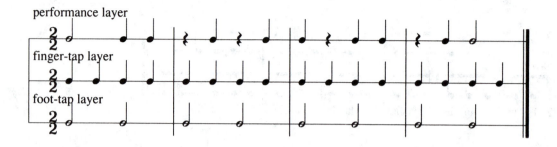

CHECKPOINT II (Rhythm)

1. Define these terms:

    internal clock   tie

    dot   rhythmic layers

    scanning

2. Briefly comment on the following:

    a. advantages of scanning

    b. advantages of analyzing, breaking down, and chanting rhythms

    c. advantages of drill and practice

3. Self-help Problems. Problems are in the right column. Solutions are in the left column. Cover the answers while solving the problems.

Solution 1	Problem 1
increased half half tie measures beamed	The value (and duration) of a note can be _____ by using a dot or a tie. A dot adds _____ the value of the preceding rhythm. A second dot adds _____ the value of the first dot. A _____ can be used to join the values of notes in adjacent _____ or groups of _____ notes.

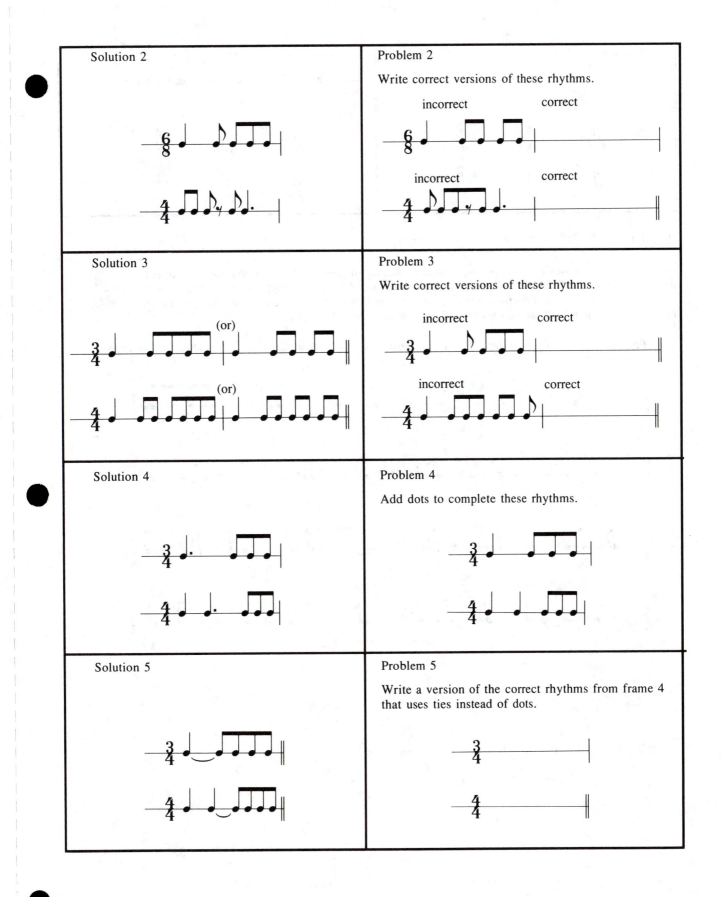

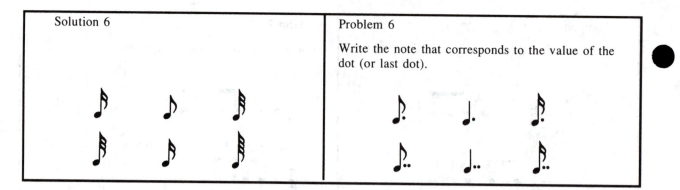

APPLICATIONS

In the rhythm exercises that follow, work on scanning techniques, mental and physical coordination development, and multilayer rhythmic thinking and action. Accompany rhythmic performance with bodily movement or gestures (conducting, tapping, etc.). At first, practice the exercise line by line. Later, strive for non-stop performance of the entire exercise at a medium or fast tempo.

1. Perform the following rhythms. Strive for nonstop accuracy. For variation, try conducting and chanting.

54

2. Two-Part Ensembles (Simple Meter)

Perform these patterns alone, with a study partner, or with a study group. For variation, try conducting, chanting, or performing each part with a contrasting sound.

3. Perform the following rhythms. Strive for nonstop accuracy. For variation, try conducting and chanting.

4. Two-Part Ensembles (Compound Meter)

SCALES
The Major Circle of Fifths

The white-key C scale is major and has the following characteristics:

a. It is made of two major tetrachords. Both the tonic and dominant tetrachord have the step pattern, W-W-H. The tonic pentachord is major, W-W-H-W.
b. Its half steps are located at steps 3–4 and 7–8.
c. It can be transposed to other pitch levels by relocating its tonic pitch and adding the flats or sharps needed to preserve all the characteristics of the scale at the new level.

The white-key F scale (Lydian mode) has a raised fourth step in comparison to major. This step must be lowered a half step to convert the scale to major.

Example 19. C and F Major Scales

The white-key G scale (Mixolydian mode) has a lowered seventh step compared to major. This step must be raised a half step to convert the scale to major.

Example 20. C and G Major Scales

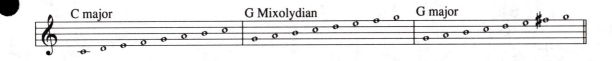

The major scales with one sharp or one flat lie a fifth above or below C, respectively. A **circle of fifths** can be constructed by continuing this pattern upward or downward in fifths and adding one accidental each time.

The circle of fifths has these characteristics:

a. Each time a major scale is transposed up or down a fifth, one accidental must be changed to preserve the characteristics of major.
b. If the major scale is transposed up a fifth, a sharp must be added (or a flat removed). If it is transposed down a fifth, a flat must be added (or a sharp removed).
c. This process of transposing the scale a fifth and adding an accidental can be continued systematically until all seven sharps or flats are accumulated in the key signature.
d. Sharps are added to the key signature in the order **F C G D A E B**. Flats are added to the key signature in the order **B E A D G C F**.

Key signatures containing seven accidentals are written as follows:

Example 21. Key Signature Notation Format

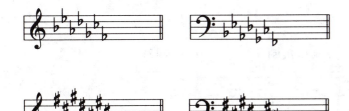

The flats follow a zig-zag pattern, up four, down five. Sharp key signatures zig-zag down four and up five. Notice the break in pattern after the fourth sharp. Key signatures always follow these formats in bass and treble clefs throughout the entire range of accidentals.

A diagram of the complete major circle of fifths follows.

Example 22. The Major Circle of Fifths

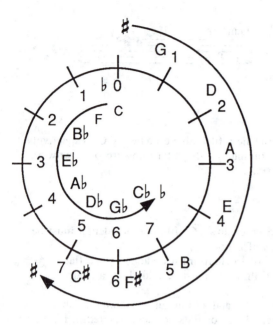

Enharmonic Scales in Major

Keys of five or more sharps or flats were arranged in pairs in the circle-of-fifths example (see the bottom of the example). These pairings follow. Notice that the number of accidentals in the key signatures of each pair add up to twelve.

enharmonic pairs   C sharp ma: (7 sharps) → D flat ma: (5 flats)   (7 + 5 = 12)

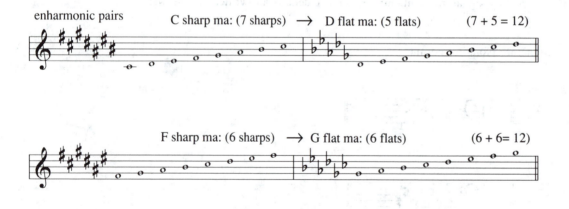

F sharp ma: (6 sharps) → G flat ma: (6 flats)   (6 + 6 = 12)

B ma: (5 sharps) → C flat ma: (7 flats)   (5 + 7 = 12)

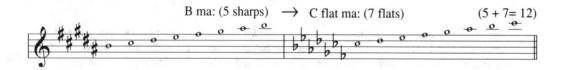

Chromatic Transposition Pairs

Scales a chromatic half step apart (e. g., C, C sharp or C flat major) form a special relationship similar to comparing a black and white photograph to its negative. What is white in the print is black in the negative. For example, the D and D flat major scales are chromatic transpositions of each other. The notes sharped in D major are natural in D flat major. Conversely, the notes that are natural in D major are flatted in D flat major.

The idea of comparing a scale to its chromatic transposition can be used to learn or to recall scales and key signatures. For example, if you cannot remember the key signature for G flat major, try the following connection:

IF *G* has one sharp (and six naturals)
    THEN *G flat* has one natural (and six flats)

OR

IF *B flat* has two flats (and five naturals)
    THEN *B* has two naturals (and five sharps)

If one knows the order of sharps or flats of key signatures, and knows how many accidentals there are in a particular key signature, the key signature for the unknown key can be determined and constructed quickly through the method of comparing chromatic pairs of scales. The chromatic transposition pairs in major are:

chromatic pairs   D ma: (F and C sharp) → D flat ma: (F and C natural)

E flat ma: (B, E, A flat) → E ma: (B, E, A natural)

F ma: (B flat) → F sharp ma: (B natural)

G ma: (F sharp) → G flat ma: (F natural)

B flat ma: (B and E flat) → B ma: (B and E natural)

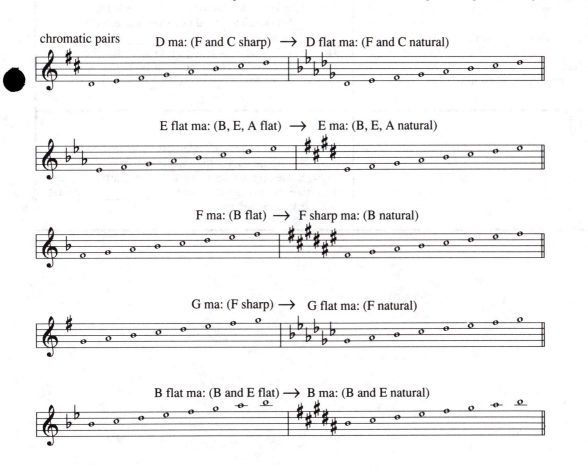

59

Summary This section of the chapter illustrated some relationships among scales within the greater system of scales. Remembering these relationships will help you work with scales in a broader framework.

CHECKPOINT III (Major Circle of Fifths)

1. Discuss, explain, or define these terms:

   characteristics of the major scale

   circle of fifths

   order of sharps   order of flats

   enharmonic scales   chromatically paired scales

2. Self-help Problems. Problems are in the right column. Solutions are in the left column. Cover the answers while solving the problems.

Solution 1	Problem 1
Lydian lowering (flatting) fourth Mixolydian raising (sharping) seventh	The white-key scale starting on F is called the _____ mode. This mode can be converted to parallel major by _____ its _____ step. The white-key scale starting on G is called the _____ mode. This mode can be converted to parallel major by _____ its _____ step.
Solution 2 fifth one	Problem 2 The C, F, and G major scales can be arranged so their starting notes are the interval of a _____ apart. Scales (of the same mode) with starting notes a fifth apart have a difference of _____ accidental in their key signatures.

Solution 3 B E A D G C F F C G D A E B	**Problem 3** Flats are added to the key signature in this order: ___ ___ ___ ___ ___ ___ ___. Sharps are added to the key signature in this order: ___ ___ ___ ___ ___ ___ ___.
Solution 4 mode (type) fifth one seven	**Problem 4** A circle of fifths occurs if scales of one _____ are arranged so: • their starting notes are a _____ apart; • their key signatures increment by _____ accidental; • all practical keys are present (key signatures through _____ sharps and flats).

Solution 5
 	
  1   2   3   4   5   6   7
  G D A E B F$^\sharp$ C$^\sharp$
  F B$^\flat$ E$^\flat$ A$^\flat$ D$^\flat$ G$^\flat$ C$^\flat$
	Problem 5
	
	Write the names of the major keys that match the key signatures below.
	
	  1 2 3 4 5 6 7
	___ ___ ___ ___ ___ ___ ___ sharps
	
	___ ___ ___ ___ ___ ___ ___ flats

Solution 6
 	
	Problem 6
	
	Write the key signatures of these major keys in the proper format.
	
	    C flat major C sharp major
	
	    D flat major B major

Solution 7

Problem 7

Write the key signatures of these major keys in the proper format.

G flat major E major

F sharp major A flat major

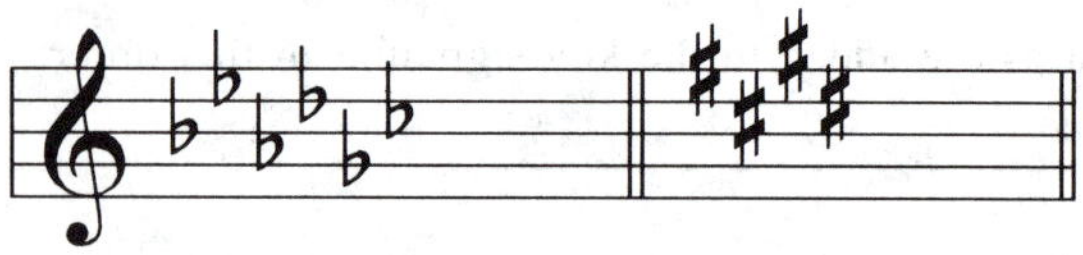

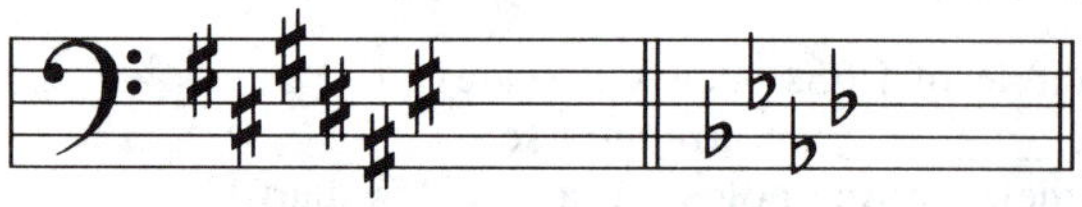

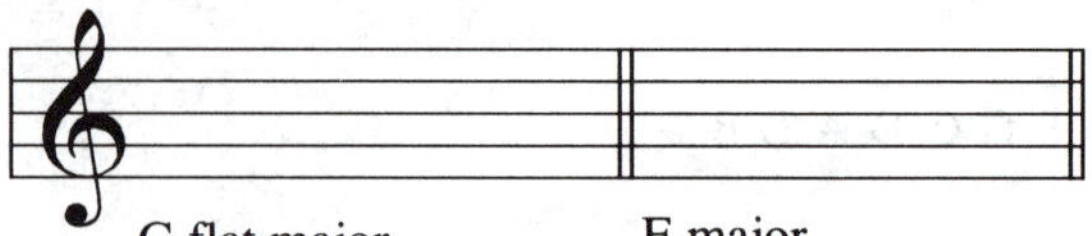

3. Compare Lydian and Mixolydian to their parallel major scale in regard to:

   a. tetrachord makeup

   b. difference in key signature

   c. location of half steps

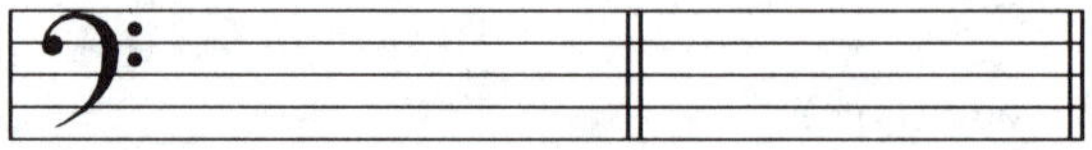

4. Briefly comment on the following:

   a. advantage of knowing about enharmonic scale pairing

   b. advantage of knowing about chromatic scale pairing

5. Complete the diagram of the major circle of fifths.

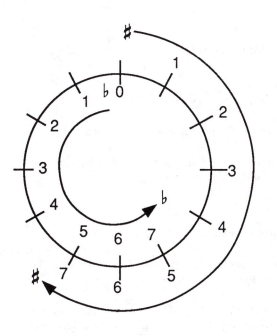

APPLICATIONS

1. Starting from each pitch in the chromatic scale, write and sing-spell the following:

   a. ma 3 above

   b. ma 3 below

   c. mi 3 above

   d. mi 3 below

2. Modify the neighbor group patterns by replacing seconds with thirds above and below the central pitch. Practice sing-spelling the following patterns on selected starting pitches. In the patterns, "s" represents the starting note.

   a. s ma 3 s ma 3 s

   b. s mi 3(up) s mi 3(dn) s

   c. s mi 3 s ma 3 s

   d. s ma 3 s mi 3 s

3. Sing the major thirds in any major scale, 1–3, 4–6, and 5–7. Now, select a few major scales and sing-spell the following patterns:

   a. 1–3 4–6 5–7 8

   b. 3–1 6–4 7–5 8

4. Sing-spell the scales in the order they occur in the major circle of fifths, up and down. Then, sing-spell the major thirds of each scale as shown in exercise 3.

5. Sing-spell all the major scales in chromatic pairs.

6. Sing all the thirds in a major scale up and down using this pattern:

| starting up from the tonic pitch |

"major-3rd minor-3rd minor-3rd major-3rd major-3rd minor-3rd minor-3rd T"

| starting down from the tonic pitch |

"minor-3rd major-3rd major-3rd minor-3rd minor-3rd minor-3rd major-3rd T"

Note: "T" refers to the keynote. Sing the letter name of the keynote instead of the letter "T."

7. Write all the scales in the major circle of fifths in five minutes or less. Write them in either bass or treble clef. For practice, use the clef in which you are *least* fluent. Follow this pattern:

a. Start with C flat major (seven flats). Write the scale.

b. Find the next keynote in the circle a fifth above the current keynote (in this case, G flat).

c. Carry over the accidentals of the previous scale. Write the new scale, but raise its seventh step. The new scale will have one less flat or one more sharp than the previous scale.

Continue this pattern until you have removed all seven flats and added all seven sharps. C major (no flats) is an important check point on the way to C sharp major (seven sharps). Notice that flats are deleted in the order of sharps in key signature.

8. *Try this* to improve your fluency with key signatures. On one side of a 3 × 5 card, place a key signature from the range of seven sharps to seven flats. Write the name of the major keynote on the other side of the card. Practice naming the keynote given the key signature and naming the accidentals in the key signature given the keynote. This works well with a study partner. [Practice naming the parallel Lydian and Mixolydian keynotes, too. Remember that Lydian has one more sharp than parallel major and Mixolydian has one more flat than parallel major.]

4 PERFECT AND INVERTED INTERVALS, SYNCOPATION

OVERVIEW

Interval and *Rhythm* paths continue in this chapter. Instruction on perfect intervals and interval inversion is included. The rhythm section contains information on syncopation and how principles of syncopation can be used to create various kinds of rhythmic contexts. Continued emphasis is placed on the analysis and performance of rhythm.

INTERVALS

Perfect Intervals

Intervals can be placed in one of two principal groups. Intervals such as seconds and thirds belong in the **major/minor** group. The **perfect** group includes unison (prime), octave, fourth, and fifth.

Perfect Fourth

A **perfect fourth** spans four diatonic notes. With one exception, all white-key fourths are perfect. This exception is the augmented fourth, F–B. An **augmented interval** is a half step larger than a perfect interval.

Example 1. White-key Fourths

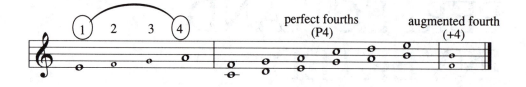

Notice that only one white-key fourth is not perfect in the previous example. This interval is built on the fourth step of the C major scale. This feature remains true of all major scales within the circle of fifths: all fourths are perfect except those built on the fourth degree of major.

Example 2. Augmented Fourth in Major Scales

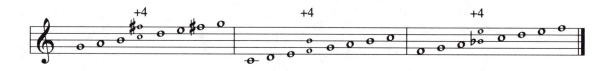

A perfect fourth can be augmented by raising its top note or lowering its bottom note a chromatic half step.

Example 3. Altering Perfect Fourths

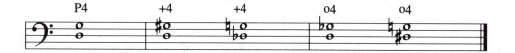

An augmented fourth can be made perfect by raising its bottom note or lowering its top note a chromatic half step.

Example 4. Altering Augmented Fourths

The diminished fourth has the same sound as the major third. The augmented third has the same sound as the perfect fourth.

66

Example 5. Enharmonic Equivalents

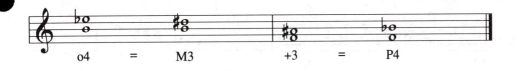

o4 = M3 +3 = P4

Interval Inversion

Interval inversion involves the octave transposition of one note of the interval in the direction of the other note (the change of vertical position between the two notes of an interval). As shown in the next example, an interval becomes inverted if its bottom note is moved above its top note or vice versa. Notice that an interval and its inversion equal an octave (interval + inversion – common tone = eight). Thus, an interval and its inversion are **octave complements.**

Example 6. Interval Inversion

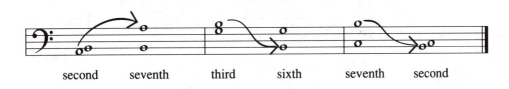

second seventh third sixth seventh second

Perfect intervals remain perfect when inverted, but major intervals change to minor when inverted. The inversion of a minor interval is major.

Example 7. Inversion Properties

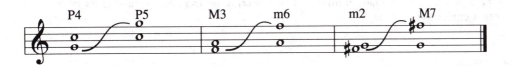

P4 P5 M3 m6 m2 M7

Perfect Fifth

The **perfect fifth** spans five diatonic notes and is the inversion of the perfect fourth. All white-key fifths are perfect except the fifth built on B. The B–F fifth is diminished and is the inversion of the F–B fourth, an augmented fourth. A **diminished interval** is a chromatic half step smaller than a perfect interval.

Example 8. White-key Fifths

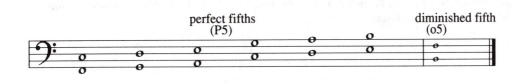

perfect fifths
(P5)   diminished fifth
(o5)

Notice that the diminished fifth occurs on the seventh step of the white-key major scale. This is true for all major scales in the circle of fifths.

67

Example 9. Diminished Fifth in Major Scales

The diminished fifth and the augmented fourth are identical in sound and are **enharmonic equivalents** of each other. Their sound is called the **tritone**. The tritone divides the octave into two segments of six half steps each. **Tritone** means "three tones" (three whole steps counting the bottom note as "zero").

Example 10. Tritone

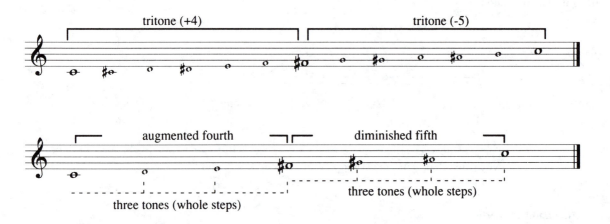

A perfect fifth can be made diminished by lowering its top note or raising its bottom note a chromatic half step.

Example 11. Altering Perfect Fifths

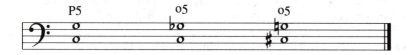

A diminished fifth can be made perfect by lowering its bottom note or raising its top note a chromatic half step.

Example 12. Altering Diminished Fifths

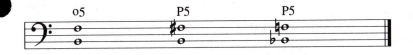

White-key fourths and fifths can be transposed chromatically by sharping or flatting <u>both</u> notes in the intervals.

Example 13. White-key Intervals, Chromatic Transposition

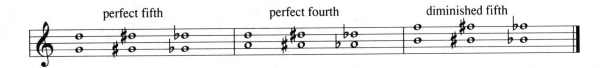

One note of the white-key diminished fifth and the augmented fourth must be altered to convert them to perfect intervals. Unlike white-key perfect intervals, the two notes in a tritone do not carry identical accidentals. This remains true if the intervals are transposed chromatically.

Example 14. Altered Intervals, Chromatic Transposition

CHECKPOINT I (Intervals, Inversion)

1. Explain these terms:

   major/minor intervals   perfect intervals

   perfect fourth   white-key perfect fourths

   white-key augmented fourth   augmented fourth

   white-key diminished fifth   diminished fifth

   diminished fourth   augmented third

   perfect fifth   tritone

   white-key perfect fifths   enharmonic equivalents

   octave complement   diminished interval

2. Self-help Problems.

Solution 1 octave inverted	**Problem 1** Notes of an interval exchange vertical position if one note is transposed an _____ in the direction of the other note. If the notes in an interval change vertical position, the interval is _____.
Solution 2 complements octave	**Problem 2** An interval and its inversion are called octave _____ of each other because the interval plus its inversion (minus the common tone) add up to an _____.
Solution 3 fifth sixth seventh minor diminished major perfect	**Problem 3** The inversion of a fourth is a _____. The inversion of a third is a _____. The inversion of a second is a _____. The inversion of a major interval is _____. The inversion of an augmented interval is _____. The inversion of a minor interval is _____. The inversion of a perfect interval is _____.

Solution 4		Problem 4

Problem 4

Complete this table of interval inversions.

	Inversion		Inversion
M3 → m6		P5 → P4	
m3 → m6		M2 → m7	
°5 → +4		+4 → °5	
P4 → P5		m2 → M7	

(Problem 4 side)

	Inversion		Inversion
M3 →		P5 →	
m3 →		M2 →	
°5 →		+4 →	
P4 →		m2 →	

Solution 5

major/minor
perfect
perfect

Problem 5

All intervals are members of one of two groups. These groups are named _____/_____ and _____. The intervals of a fourth and fifth are members of the _____ group.

Solution 6

augmented
diminished
alike (the same)
enharmonic

tritone

Problem 6

The fourth above F (f–b) is _____.
The fifth above B (b–f) is _____.
Both intervals contain the same pitches and sound _____. These intervals are _____ spellings of each other. Both intervals can be identified by the same name, the _____.

Solution 7

lowering (flatting)
raising (sharping)
raising (sharping)
lowering (flatting)

Problem 7

A P5 can be changed to a °5 by _____ its top note or by _____ its bottom note. A P4 can be converted to a +4 by _____ its top note or by _____ its bottom note.

Solution 8

P5   +4   o5   P4

P5   o5   P4   +4

Problem 8

Write these intervals above the given notes.

P5   +4   o5   P4

P5   o5   P4   +4

Solution 13

Problem 13

Write these intervals below the given notes.

o4   +3   P4   P5

o5   +4   o4   +3

Solution 14

Problem 14

Write enharmonic versions of each interval.
Identify all versions.

+3   P4   P4

o4   M3   M3

Solution 15

Problem 15

Write enharmonic versions of each interval.
Identify all versions.

o4   M3   M3

o5   +4   +4

73

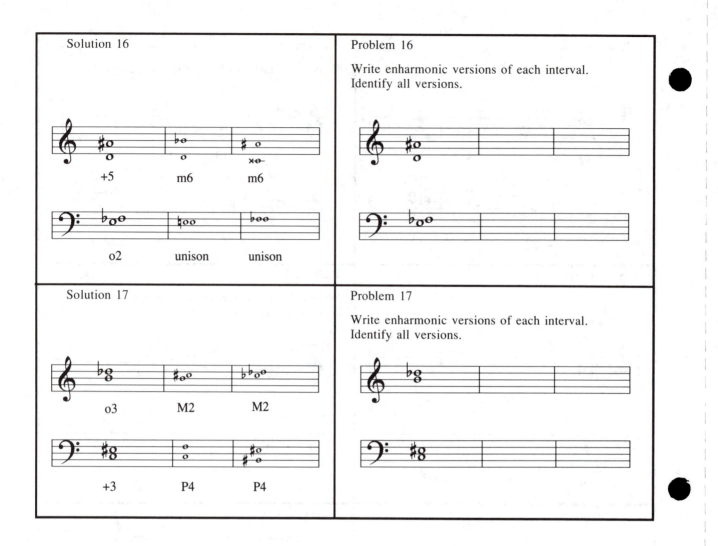

APPLICATIONS

1. Starting from each pitch in the chromatic scale, practice writing and sing-spelling the following:

   a. P4 above   b. P4 below

   c. P5 above   d. P5 below

   e. dim5 above   f. dim5 below

   g. aug4 above   h. aug4 below

   This is a good activity for group study.

2. Try the following patterns on selected pitches. "S" represents the starting pitch.

   a. S P5(up) S P4(dn) S   b. S P4(up) S P5(dn) S

   c. S P5(up) S P5(dn) S   d. S P4(up) S P4(dn) S

   This is a good activity for group study.

3. Try this interval pattern in several major and minor keys. The third step is lowered in minor.

   a. 1-2-1-3-1-4-1-5::5-4-5-3-5-2-5-1

   b. Use the pattern and sing the interval sizes (i.e., "major-second, major-third," and so on).

   c. Sing-spell the pitches of the pattern.

RHYTHM

Accent and Rhythmic Ground

Meter provides a ground for rhythmic figure. Recurring accent is one of the most important features of **rhythmic ground.** Accents are **periodic** and usually mark off equal units of time. Periodic and/or meter accents are customarily emphasized in performance. Accents are listed below in order of declining strength (accent customs).

- accent the first beat in the measure
- accent the beginning of any division of the measure
- accent the beginning of each beat

Look for these three levels of accent in the next example. Perform the example giving appropriate weight to each accent.

Example 15. Accenting Customs in Meter

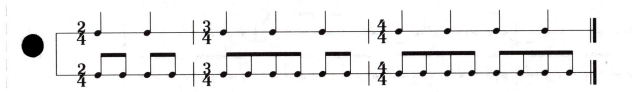

Meter accent can be reinforced by placing relatively long notes at accent points. Groups of notes that begin at these points have a similar reinforcing effect. The next example shows how the placement of duration accents and note groups can agree with accenting customs.

Example 16. Figure Reinforcing Ground

Figure accents can be made to disagree with accenting customs by putting long notes or note groups on unaccented beats. This causes an interesting interplay between figure and meter accents. The context formed by figure accents will sometimes become dominant, obscuring the accent pattern in the established meter.

Example 17. Figure in Disagreement With Meter

Syncopation,
Displaced Accent

Syncopation is the displacement or offsetting of conventional meter accents. The displacement is created by making a comparatively longer note bridge across a normal accent point. As shown below, the syncopation is ordinarily one value larger than surrounding notes.

Example 18. Displaced Accent

A series of accents can be offset (displaced).

Example 19. Displaced Accents in Series

Syncopation in Notes of Equal Value

Syncopation can be created through slurs or articulation marks in a series of notes of equal duration. In the following example, the articulation pattern places the notes into groups of three eighth notes, implying a series of dotted quarter note accents.

Example 20. Syncopation by Slurs and Articulations

Syncopation can be created by accent markings in a series of notes of equal duration. As before, the accents place the notes into groups of three eighth notes.

Example 21. Syncopation by Accent Marks

Syncopation can be created through beaming. Sometimes, unconventional beaming patterns are used to indicate syncopated note groupings. In example 22, the special beaming places the notes in groups of three eighth notes.

Example 22. Syncopation by Beaming

Perceived versus Indicated Meter

Displaced accents can be patterned to make the listener think that the music he/she hears is in a meter other than that indicated by the time signature. The next example has an indicated meter of 4/4. What is the **perceived meter**? How do you account for the difference between indicated and perceived meter in this example?

Example 23. Implied Meter

Cross Rhythm

Cross rhythm refers to any pattern that disagrees with the accenting customs for a given indicated meter. Special cases of cross rhythm include certain syncopation and implied meter patterns. A cross rhythm can also be established by writing patterns that are not intrinsic (built in) to a particular meter. One-beat triplets or quintuplets in simple meter are examples of this kind of cross rhythm.

Hemiola

The **hemiola** is a traditional cross rhythm based on a 3:2 rhythmic proportion. Any ''three-against-two'' rhythm can be called a hemiola.

Example 24. Hemiola, Two-beat Triplet

The next example illustrates the classic Flamenco hemiola. This pattern occurs frequently in Hispanic music and was used by Bernstein and Sondheim in the song ''America'' from *West Side Story* to underscore its cross-cultural message.

Example 25. ''America.'' Copyright © 1957 (Renewed) Leonard Bernstein Jalni Publications, Inc., U.S. and Canada. G. Schirmer, Inc. worldwide print rights and publisher rest of the world. International Copyright Secured. All Rights Reserved. Used by Permission.

CHECKPOINT II (Syncopation, Cross Rhythm)

1. Explain these terms:

   rhythmic ground   periodic accent

   accent customs   syncopation

   figure accent   hemiola

   displaced accent   cross rhythm

   perceived meter

2. Self-help Problems.

Solution 1	Problem 1
layers beats beat (-groups) measures, (measure-) groups	Performance customs call for accents at several _____ in a meter. Accents are located at the beginnings of _____, _____-groups, _____, and measure-_____.
Solution 2	Problem 2
ground figure disagree (be at odds)	Performance customs help provide a _____ for rhythmic figure. Rhythmic _____ can reinforce or _____ with the ground provided by meter.
Solution 3	Problem 3
offset displaced (do not)	Syncopation is cause by _____ or _____ accent. Points of syncopation (do) (do not) coincide with customary accent points in a meter.
Solution 4	Problem 4
displaced (offset) series imply (suggest, sound, etc)	A syncopated rhythm can result from a single, isolated _____ accent. It can also be part of a _____ of syncopations. If used systematically, syncopation can _____ a meter other than indicated by the time signature.

Solution 5 cross hemiola two 3:2 (three-to-two)	**Problem 5** Any rhythm figure that disagrees with meter accents is a _____ rhythm. One example of this is the _____ figure, sometimes associated with Flamenco or Hispanic music. The ___-beat triplet is the classic example of this figure. This pattern is a _____ mathematical ratio.
Solution 6 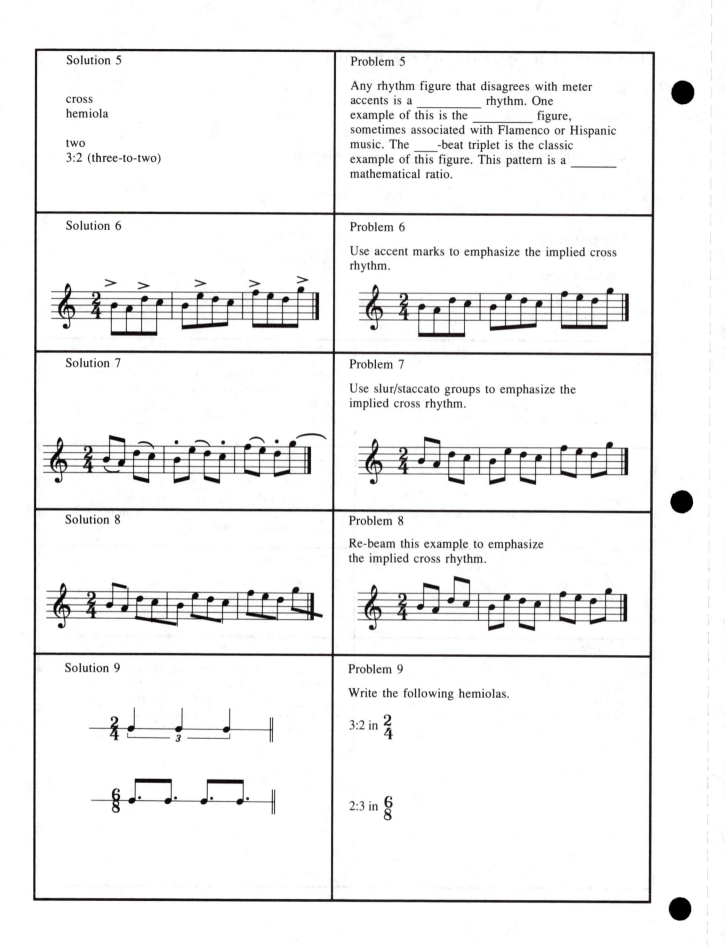	**Problem 6** Use accent marks to emphasize the implied cross rhythm.
Solution 7	**Problem 7** Use slur/staccato groups to emphasize the implied cross rhythm.
Solution 8	**Problem 8** Re-beam this example to emphasize the implied cross rhythm.
Solution 9	**Problem 9** Write the following hemiolas. 3:2 in $\frac{2}{4}$ 2:3 in $\frac{6}{8}$

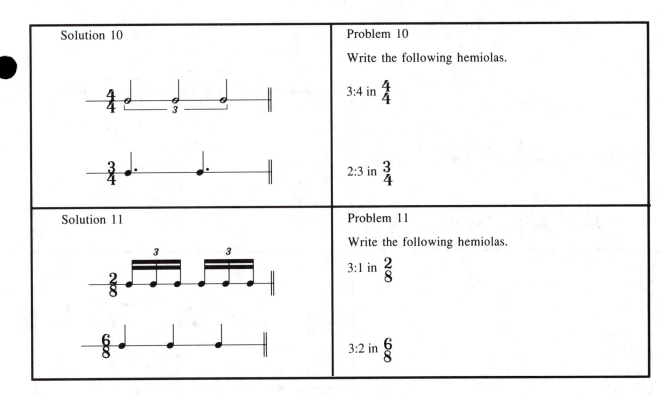

Solution 10	Problem 10
	Write the following hemiolas.
	3:4 in $\frac{4}{4}$
	2:3 in $\frac{3}{4}$

Solution 11	Problem 11
	Write the following hemiolas.
	3:1 in $\frac{2}{8}$
	3:2 in $\frac{6}{8}$

Find the cross rhythm patterns in the next three frames. Rewrite these patterns so that the implied meter is shown as a change of meter, as in the sample problem below.

original

sample

rewrite

sample

Solution 12	Problem 12
rewrite	original
	rewrite
or	$\frac{3}{4}$

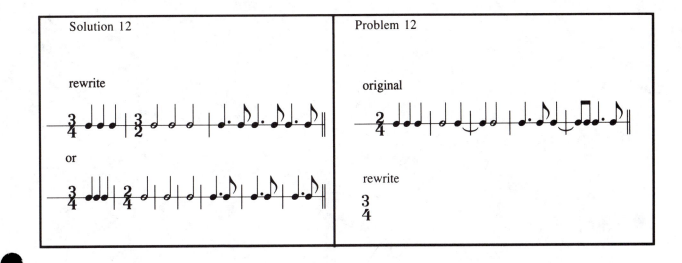

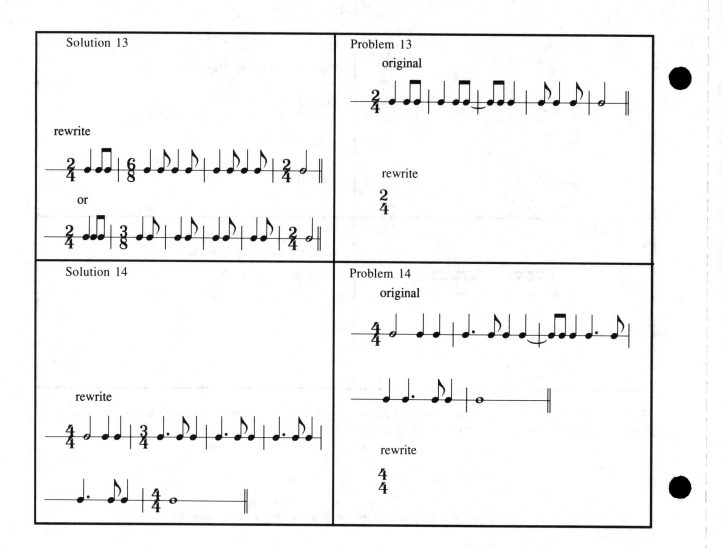

APPLICATIONS

1. Find the cross rhythms in this melody. Mark them in the music and describe them in detail. Does knowledge of this cross rhythm influence your interpretation and performance of the melody?

Third Symphony, Op. 97, First Movement   R. Schumann

2. Find the cross rhythms in this melody. Mark them in the music and describe them in detail. How do these patterns influence the way you perform this melody?

Symphony No. 40, Third Movement   Mozart

In the rhythm exercises that follow, work on scanning techniques, mental and physical coordination development, and multi-layer rhythmic thinking and action. For variation, try chanting, conducting, or performing the rhythms while tapping both the beat and the beat division.

3. Perform these rhythms. Strive for nonstop accuracy. Be aware of the relationship between the rhythm and the beat division.

4. Rhythmic Etude (the eighth note is common throughout)

5. Rhythmic Etude (the eighth note is common throughout)

6. Two-Part Ensembles. For variation, perform each part with a contrasting sound, like voice sounds against clapping sounds.

5 INTERVALS, MINOR SCALES

OVERVIEW

The *Interval Path* continues with information on sixths and sevenths. The *Scale Path* includes the circle of fifths in minor, minor key signatures, relative and parallel modes, mixed modes (harmonic and melodic minor), and enharmonic and chromatic pairs of minor scales.

INTERVALS

Sixths and Sevenths

Sixths and sevenths belong to the major/minor group of intervals. Both are inversions of smaller major/minor intervals. The **inversion properties** of these intervals are

a. Major inverts to minor, minor inverts to major
b. Augmented inverts to diminished, diminished inverts to augmented
c. An interval and its inversions are octave complements of each other (the interval plus its inversion span an octave)
d. The sixth is the inversion of a third (6 + 3 – common tone = 8)
e. The seventh is the inversion of a second (7 + 2 – common tone = 8)

These properties are shown in the next example.

Example 1. Sixths and Sevenths, Properties

M3 → m6   M2 → m7   m3 → M6   m2 → M7

The three **white-key minor sixths** are the inversions of the three white-key major thirds (C–E, F–A, and G–B). The three minor sixths appear in every major scale at the third, sixth, and seventh scale degrees.

Example 2. Minor Sixths

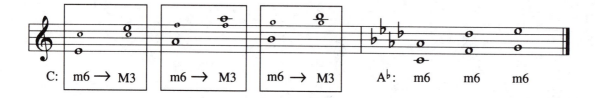

C: m6 → M3   m6 → M3   m6 → M3   A♭: m6   m6   m6

Major sixths are inversions of minor thirds. The four **white-key** major sixths (inversions of the white-key minor thirds) are c–a, d–b, f–d, and g–e. The four major sixths are located on the first, second, fourth, and fifth scale degrees of every major scale.

Example 3. Major Sixths

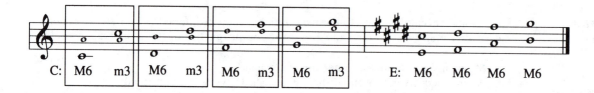

C: M6 m3 M6 m3 M6 m3 M6 m3   E: M6 M6 M6 M6

Major sevenths are inversions of minor seconds. The two **white-key major sevenths** (inversions of the white-key minor seconds) are c–b and f–e. The two major sevenths are located on the first and fourth scale degrees of every major scale.

Example 4. Major Sevenths

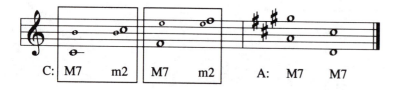

C: M7 m2 M7 m2   A: M7 M7

Minor sevenths are inversions of major seconds. The five **white-key minor sevenths** (inversions of the white-key major seconds) are b–a, d–c, e–d, g–f, and a–g. The five minor sevenths fall on all BUT the first and fourth scale degrees of any major scale.

Example 5. Minor Sevenths

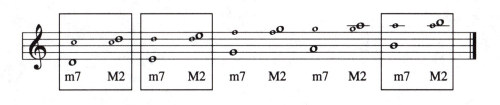

| m7 | M2 | m7 | M2 | m7 | M2 | m7 | M2 | m7 | M2 |

> **RULE:** Intervals <u>above</u> the tonic pitch of a major scale are either <u>major</u> or perfect. Conversely, intervals <u>below</u> the tonic pitch of a major scale are either <u>minor</u> or perfect.

This rule is illustrated in the next example and is a very useful guide for identifying and writing intervals. For example, the accidental for the top note of a major sixth can be determined by considering the bottom note of the interval, the tonic pitch of a major scale. In a major interval, the top note will bear whatever accidental is dictated by the key signature of that scale. If the bottom note is D flat, the top note must be B ♭ because this pitch is included in the D flat key signature. When figuring minor intervals, consider the <u>top</u> note of the interval tonic.

Example 6. Intervals Above and Below the Tonic Pitch in Major

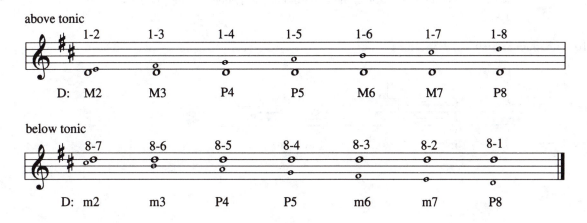

above tonic

| 1-2 | 1-3 | 1-4 | 1-5 | 1-6 | 1-7 | 1-8 |

D: M2 M3 P4 P5 M6 M7 P8

below tonic

| 8-7 | 8-6 | 8-5 | 8-4 | 8-3 | 8-2 | 8-1 |

D: m2 m3 P4 P5 m6 m7 P8

Major sixths can be made minor by lowering their top note or raising their bottom note a half step.

Example 7. Changing Major Sixths to Minor

M6 m6 m6

89

Minor sixths can be made major by raising their top note or lowering their bottom note a half step.

Example 8. Changing Minor Sixths to Major

When augmented sixths, diminished sevenths, and their inversions occur, they are usually parts of particular kinds of chords. These chords will be studied later. An **augmented sixth** is a half step larger than a major sixth. A **diminished seventh** is a half step smaller than a minor seventh.

Example 9. Augmented Sixths, Diminished Sevenths

The **augmented sixth** is the enharmonic equivalent of the minor seventh.
The **diminished seventh** is the enharmonic equivalent of the major sixth.

Example 10. Enharmonic Sixths and Sevenths

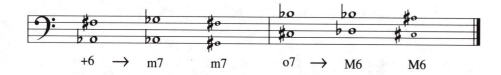

CHECK POINT I (Sixths and Sevenths)

1. Explain these terms:

   inversion properties

   white-key major sixths   white-key minor sixths

   white-key major sevenths   white-key minor sevenths

   augmented sixths   diminished sevenths

2. Explain how these ideas can be used in learning, writing, identifying, reading, and performing the intervals.

   a. white-key sixths and sevenths

   b. connection between sixths and their inversions, sevenths and their inversions

   c. intervals above and below tonic in major scales

3. Self-help Problems.

Solution 1	Problem 1
major/minor third second major	Sixths and sevenths are members of the _____ /_____ group of intervals. The inversion of a sixth is a ____. The inversion of a seventh is a ___. The inversion of minor is _____.
Solution 2 common position one eight (octave) complements	Problem 2 An interval and its inversion share a _____ tone. An inversion occurs when notes of the interval change _____ in relation to the common tone. An interval plus its inversion minus ____ (for the common tone) adds to _____. Thus, an interval and its inversion are said to be octave _____.

Solution 3	Problem 3
chromatic (i.e., same letter name)	Interval quality (major, minor, etc) can be changed by adding or subtracting _____ half steps. Any major interval can be made a half step larger by _____ its top note or _____ its bottom note chromatically. This alteration of notes changes major to _____. Any minor interval can be made a half step smaller by _____ its top note or _____ its bottom note chromatically. This alteration of notes changes minor to _____. The inversion of major is _____. The inversion of augmented is _____.
raising lowering	
augmented	
lowering	
raising	
diminished	
minor	
diminished	

Solution 4	Problem 4
augmented	The interval a chromatic half step larger than major is _____. The interval a chromatic half step smaller than major is _____. The interval a chromatic half step smaller than minor is _____. The interval a chromatic half step larger than minor is _____.
minor	
diminished	
major	

Solution 5	Problem 5
major (or) perfect	In a major scale, all intervals that have the tonic as the bottom note are _____ or _____. In a major scale, all intervals that have the tonic as the top note are _____ or _____.
minor (or) perfect	

Solution 6	Problem 6
	Write the specified intervals _above_ the given notes.

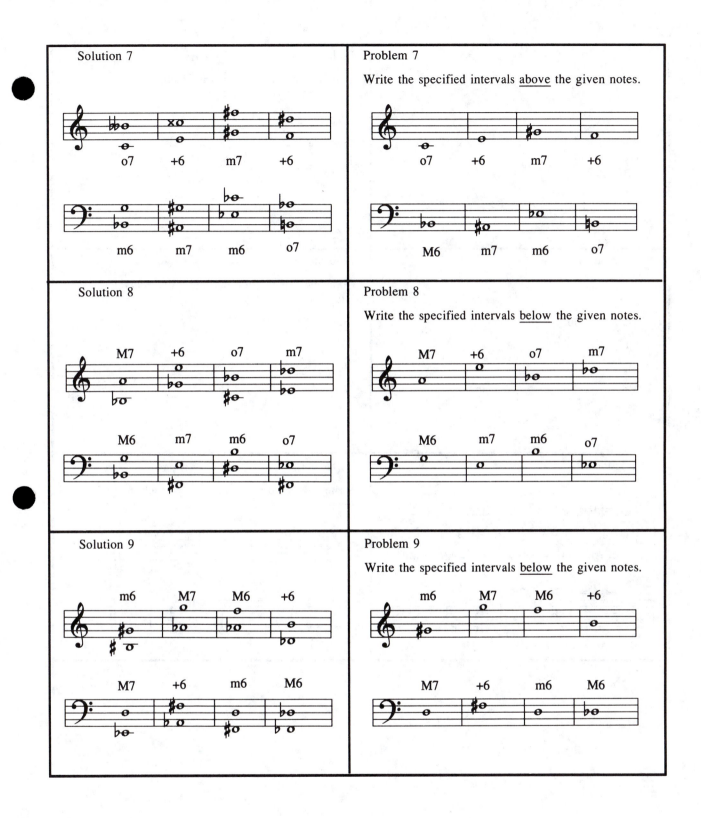

Solution 7

Problem 7

Write the specified intervals above the given notes.

o7   +6   m7   +6

M6   m7   m6   o7

Solution 8

Problem 8

Write the specified intervals below the given notes.

M7   +6   o7   m7

M6   m7   m6   o7

Solution 9

Problem 9

Write the specified intervals below the given notes.

m6   M7   M6   +6

M7   +6   m6   M6

Solution 10	Problem 10
m7　　　M6	Complete this list of enharmonically equivalent intervals.
m6　　　unison	+6 = _____　　　°7 = _____
P8　　　P5	+5 = _____　　　°2 = _____
	+7 = _____　　　°6 = _____

Solution 11	Problem 11
	Complete this list of enharmonically equivalent intervals.
M2　　　m3	°3 = _____　　　+2 = _____
P4　　　+4	+3 = _____　　　°5 = _____
M3　　　M7	°4 = _____　　　o8 = _____
M6　　　m7	°7 = _____　　　+6 = _____

Solution 12	Problem 12
	Write two enharmonic versions of each interval. Identify all intervals.

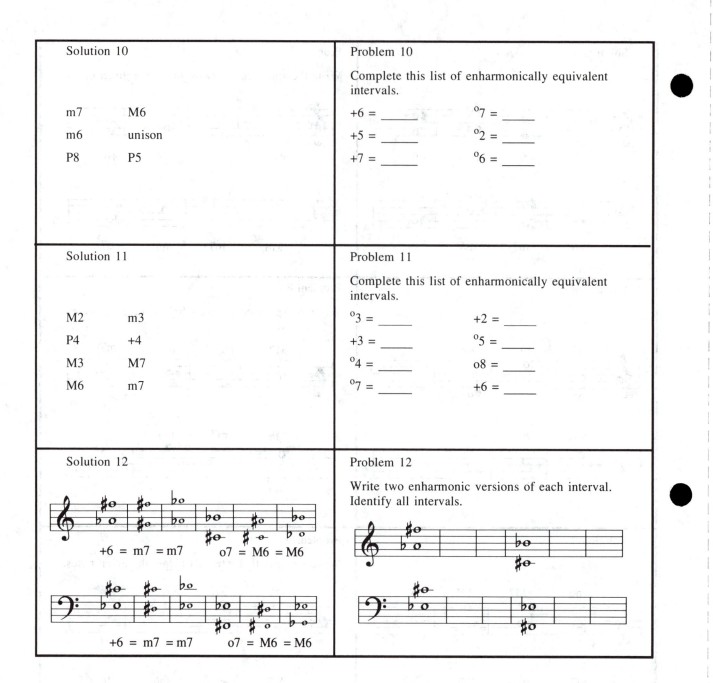

+6 = m7 = m7　　　o7 = M6 = M6

+6 = m7 = m7　　　o7 = M6 = M6

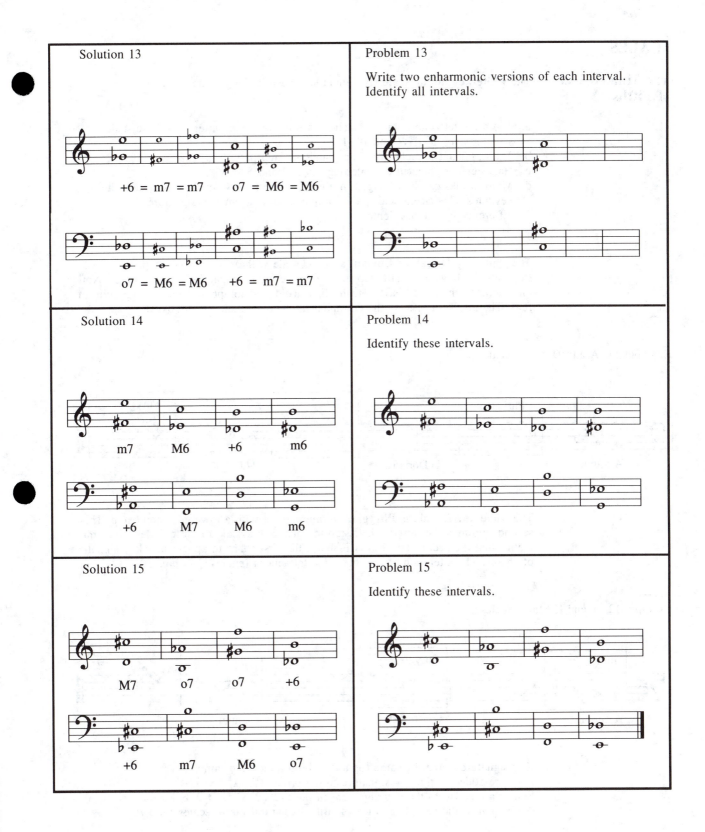

Solution 13

+6 = m7 = m7   o7 = M6 = M6

o7 = M6 = M6   +6 = m7 = m7

Problem 13

Write two enharmonic versions of each interval.
Identify all intervals.

Solution 14

m7   M6   +6   m6

+6   M7   M6   m6

Problem 14

Identify these intervals.

Solution 15

M7   o7   o7   +6

+6   m7   M6   o7

Problem 15

Identify these intervals.

SCALES

The Minor Circle of Fifths

The **white-key minor scale** (A minor) has the following characteristics:

    a. The tonic tetrachord and pentachord are minor. Step patterns in these scale segments are W-H-W and W-H-W-W.

    b. The dominant tetrachord is Phrygian. The step pattern is H-W-W.

    c. Half steps are located at scale degrees 2–3 and 5–6.

    d. Minor scales can be arranged in a circle of fifths system. In this system the keynotes of adjacent scales are P5 apart and adjacent key signatures have a difference of one accidental.

The white-key D scale is **Dorian**, a minor scale with a raised sixth step. This sixth step must be lowered a half step to change the mode to parallel natural minor. Notice that the accidental used is B flat, the first accidental to appear in a key signature of flats. The alteration affects the dominant tetrachord (enclosed in boxes).

Example 11. A and D Minor Scales

The white-key E scale is **Phrygian**, a minor scale with a lowered second step. This second step must be raised a half step to change this scale to the parallel minor mode. Notice that the accidental used is F sharp, the first sharp to appear in a key signature of sharps. The alteration affects the tonic tetrachord (enclosed in boxes).

Example 12. A and E Minor Scales

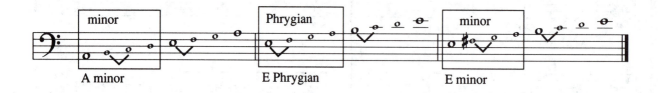

Key signatures have the same **format** in both major and minor keys.
Flats are added to the key signature in the order **B E A D G C F.**
Sharps are added to the key signature in the order **F C G D A E B.**
A diagram of the complete circle of fifths of natural minor scales follows.

Notice that adjacent keynotes are P5 apart and adjacent key signatures change by one accidental.

Example 13. The Minor Circle of Fifths

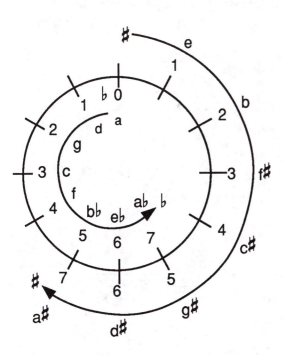

Scales in Enharmonic Pairs

In the previous example, scales of five or more sharps or flats were arranged in **enharmonic pairs.** Notice that the accidentals of paired key signatures equal twelve. These pairings are as follows:

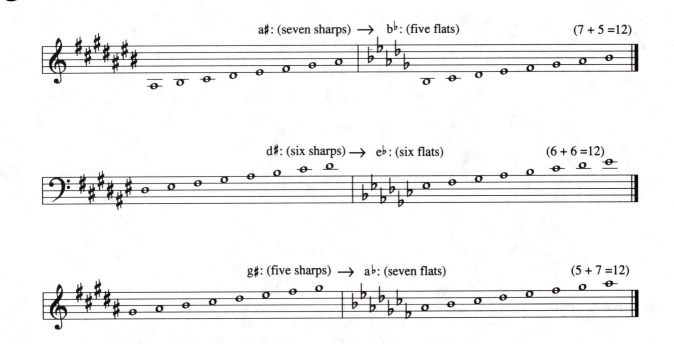

a#: (seven sharps) → b♭: (five flats)   (7 + 5 =12)

d#: (six sharps) → e♭: (six flats)   (6 + 6 =12)

g#: (five sharps) → a♭: (seven flats)   (5 + 7 =12)

Scales in Chromatic Pairs

As in major, minor scales can be transposed a chromatic half step to produce positive/negative pairing. The **chromatic transposition pairings** in minor are:

(F and C natural)

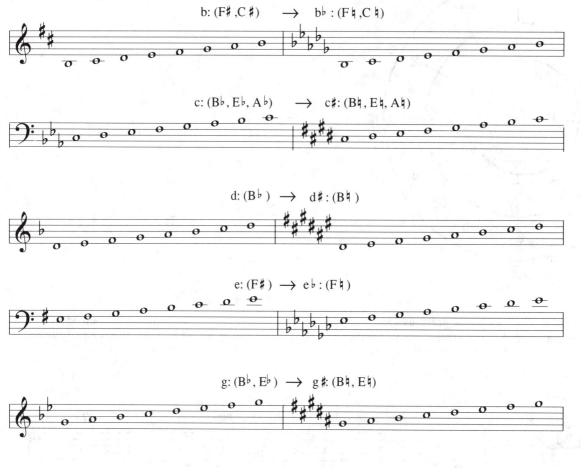

The concept of chromatic pairing of minor scales can be used as follows:

IF *A minor* has no sharps or flats

> **THEN** *A sharp minor* has seven sharps
> **AND** *A flat minor* has seven flats

OR

IF *D minor* has one flat (and six naturals)
> **THEN** *D sharp minor* has one natural (and six sharps)

Relative Modes

Relative modes share the same key signature but have different tonic pitches. A relative mode can be one of several diatonic modes contained within the same collection of pitches (as defined by a key signature). The tonic pitches of **relative major** and **minor** are a diatonic third apart (both keys share the same key signature). This relationship holds true throughout the entire circle of fifths. Knowledge of this relationship can be used as follows:

IF five sharps major is *B*

    THEN five sharps minor is *G sharp* (because the minor tonic is a third below the major tonic in any collection of pitches)

OR

IF three flats minor is *C*

    THEN three flats major is *E flat* (because the major tonic is a third above the minor tonic in any collection of pitches)

Parallel Modes

A **parallel mode** is any mode that starts on the same pitch as another mode but uses a different collection of pitches. Parallel modes share the same tonic but have different key signatures. Compared to **parallel major,** minor has a lowered third, sixth, and seventh step. Compared to **parallel minor,** major has a raised third, sixth, and seventh step. Thus, parallel minor has three more flats (or three fewer sharps) than its parallel major. Conversely, major has three fewer flats (or three more sharps) than its parallel minor. These parallels are consistent throughout the circle of fifths. This knowledge can be applied as follows:

IF *C major* has no sharps or flats

    THEN *C minor* has three flats (because minor has three more flats than its parallel major)

OR

IF *E major* has four sharps

    THEN *E minor* has one sharp (because minor has three fewer sharps than its parallel major)

OR

IF *B minor* has two sharps

    THEN *B major* has five sharps (because major has three more sharps than its parallel minor)

OR

IF *F minor* has four flats

    THEN *F major* has one flat (because major has three fewer flats than its parallel minor)

> **RULE:** The third, sixth and seventh <u>above</u> the tonic pitch of a natural minor scale are minor. Conversely, the sixth, third, and second <u>below</u> the tonic pitch in any natural minor scale are major.

Notice that the intervals in the second measure of the next example are inversions of those in the first measure.

Example 14. Thirds and Sixths Involving Tonic in Minor

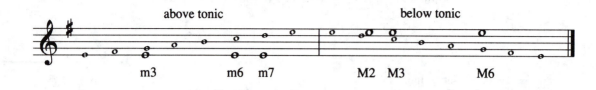

above tonic   below tonic

m3   m6 m7   M2 M3   M6

Tetrachords and Pentachords

Each diatonic mode contains an unique mixture of tetrachords and pentachords. This is very useful knowledge when applied to writing, playing, or memorizing scales. The pentachord and tetrachord makeup in the relative minor modes is shown in the next example. Notice the location of the half step in each type of tetrachord (i.e., minor = WHW, Phrygian = HWW).

Example 15. Tetrachords and Pentachords in Minor

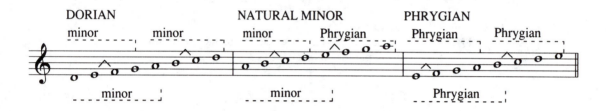

DORIAN   NATURAL MINOR   PHRYGIAN

minor   minor   minor   Phrygian   Phrygian   Phrygian

minor   minor   Phrygian

Mixed Modes

A **mixed mode** is a scale that combines features of two parallel modes. **Harmonic and melodic minor** are mixed modes because they combine the features of parallel major and minor. Harmonic and melodic minor are created by "borrowing" steps from parallel major. Mixed modes are hybrid scales rather than purely diatonic.

Harmonic Minor

If the seventh scale degree is a whole step below tonic, it is called the **subtonic**. If the seventh scale degree is a half step below tonic, it is called the **leading tone**. In **harmonic minor,** the leading tone is borrowed from parallel major. This alteration affects the dominant tetratchord (enclosed in boxes). The borrowed tone appears as an accidental in the music rather than a change to the key signature.

Example 16. Parallel Modes and Harmonic Minor

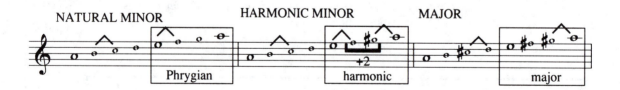

NATURAL MINOR   HARMONIC MINOR   MAJOR

Phrygian   harmonic   major

+2

As indicated by its extensive use during the past four centuries, harmonic minor has been favored by composers because *the borrowed leading tone improves focus on tonic*. Certain chords in traditional harmonizations almost always contain the raised seventh step. Harmonic minor is so named because of its strong tie to this traditional harmonic practice.

Melodic Minor   The interval between the minor sixth and the raised seventh step is an augmented second. This interval can present difficulties in performance. The augmented second may sound out of place in passages of whole and half steps. To avoid this, the sixth step is also raised when next to the raised seventh step. The scale is called **melodic minor** when both the sixth and seventh steps are raised. These alterations affect the dominant tetrachord. Notice that the dominant tetrachords of major and parallel melodic minor are identical.

Example 17. Parallel Modes and Melodic Minor

A composition in a minor key can change freely from one type of minor to another as the composition unfolds. The key signature of natural minor is used in all cases. Raised sixth and seventh steps are indicated as temporary changes through use of accidentals in the body of the music.

Adjacent raised sixth and seventh steps are not uncommon in descending lines in literature. Be careful not to assume that the classic melodic minor scale exercise (i.e., uses melodic minor while ascending and natural minor while descending) is the true model for melodic minor. In the next example, note the type of minor in each bracket. Notice the descending melodic minor pattern in measure 1 of the bass and the ascending natural minor pattern in measure 3 of the bass.

Example 18. From 371 Four-Part Chorales   J. S. Bach

Jesu, der du meine Seele

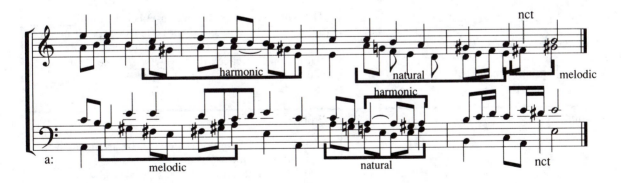

CHECKPOINT II (Minor Circle of Fifths)

1. Define these terms:

characteristics of the natural	minor scale
minor circle of fifths	order of flats, minor
key signature format, minor	order of sharps, minor
enharmonic pairs, minor	chromatic pairs of minor scales
relative mode	parallel mode
relative minor	relative major
parallel major	parallel minor
mixed modes	subtonic
leading tone	borrowed tone
melodic minor	Dorian
Phrygian tetrachord	harmonic tetrachord

2. Self-help Problems.

Solution 1	Problem 1
Dorian lowering (flatting) sixth (B♭) Phrygian raising (sharping) second (F♯)	The white-key scale starting on D is called the _____ mode. This mode can be converted to parallel minor by _____ its _____ step. The white-key scale starting on E is called the _____ mode. This mode can be converted to parallel minor by _____ its ____ step.
Solution 2 fifth one	**Problem 2** The E, A, and D minor scales can be arranged so that their starting notes are the interval of a _____ apart. When so arranged, these scales have a difference of _____ accidental in their key signatures.

Solution 3	Problem 3
parallel relative	Modes that start on the same pitch but have different key signatures are called _____ modes. Modes that start on different pitches but have the same key signatures are called _____ modes.

Solution 4	Problem 4
minor W H W (whole, half, whole) Phrygian H W W (half, whole, whole)	The tonic tetrachord in natural minor is a _____ tetrachord. Its step pattern is ____, ___, ____. The dominant tetrachord of natural minor is a _____ tetrachord. Its step pattern is ___, ___, ____.

Solution 5	Problem 5
	Add accidentals to make these tetrachords minor.

Solution 6	Problem 6
	Add accidentals to make these tetrachords Phrygian.

Solution 7	Problem 7
	Add accidentals to make these tetrachords minor.

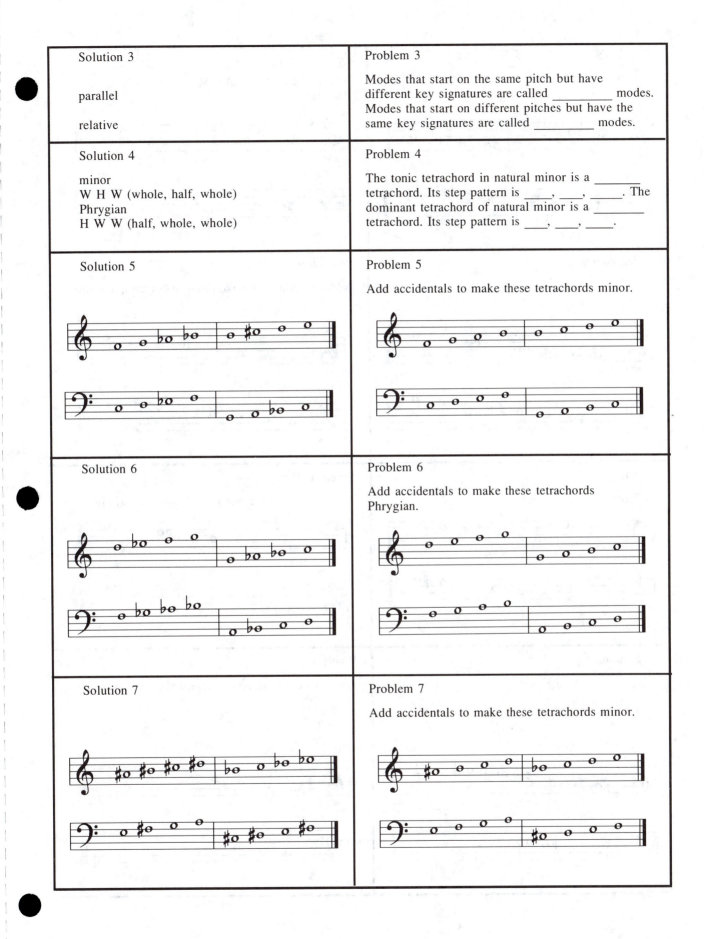

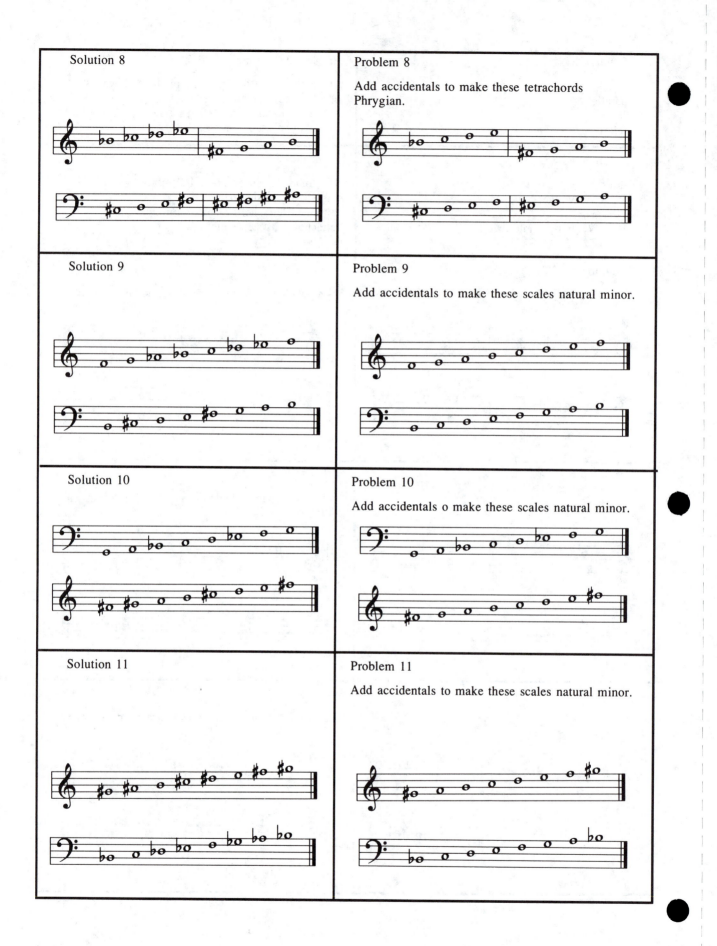

Solution 8

Problem 8

Add accidentals to make these tetrachords Phrygian.

Solution 9

Problem 9

Add accidentals to make these scales natural minor.

Solution 10

Problem 10

Add accidentals o make these scales natural minor.

Solution 11

Problem 11

Add accidentals to make these scales natural minor.

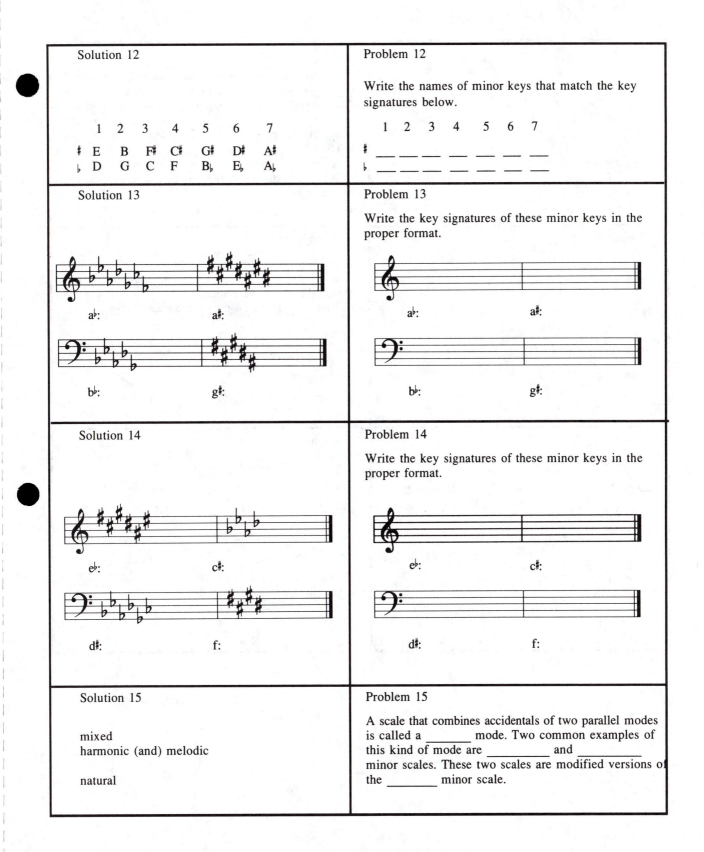

Solution 12

	1	2	3	4	5	6	7
♯	E	B	F♯	C♯	G♯	D♯	A♯
♭	D	G	C	F	B♭	E♭	A♭

Problem 12

Write the names of minor keys that match the key signatures below.

	1	2	3	4	5	6	7
♯	__	__	__	__	__	__	__
♭	__	__	__	__	__	__	__

Solution 13

a♭:   a♯:

b♭:   g♯:

Problem 13

Write the key signatures of these minor keys in the proper format.

a♭:   a♯:

b♭:   g♯:

Solution 14

e♭:   c♯:

d♯:   f:

Problem 14

Write the key signatures of these minor keys in the proper format.

e♭:   c♯:

d♯:   f:

Solution 15

mixed
harmonic (and) melodic

natural

Problem 15

A scale that combines accidentals of two parallel modes is called a _____ mode. Two common examples of this kind of mode are _____ and _____ minor scales. These two scales are modified versions of the _____ minor scale.

Solution 16	Problem 16
lowering raising natural harmonic melodic	Any major scale can be converted to parallel minor by _____ its third, sixth, and seventh steps chromatically. Conversely, any natural minor scale can be converted to parallel major by _____ its third, sixth, and seventh steps. The harmonic minor and melodic minor scales are modified forms of parallel _____ minor. If the seventh step is raised, the form of minor is _____. If both the sixth and seventh steps are raised, the form of minor is _____.
Solution 17	Problem 17
dominant Phrygian natural H W W harmonic H W+ H melodic W W H major	In all three forms of parallel minor, the mixed mode changes are made in the _____ tetrachord. In natural minor, the dominant tetrachord is _____. Complete this table of dominant tetrachord step patterns. natural minor: ____ ____ ____ harmonic minor: ____ ____ ____ melodic minor: ____ ____ ____ In melodic minor, the dominant tetrachord is _____.
Solution 18	Problem 18

Solution 18:

Scale	Tonic	Dominant
natural minor		Phrygian
harmonic minor	harmonic	harmonic
melodic	minor	major
same natural		

Problem 18:

Complete this table of tetrachords.

Scale	Tonic	Dominant
natural minor	minor	_____
minor	_____	_____
melodic minor	_____	_____

These three parallel forms of minor use the _____ key signature, _____ minor.

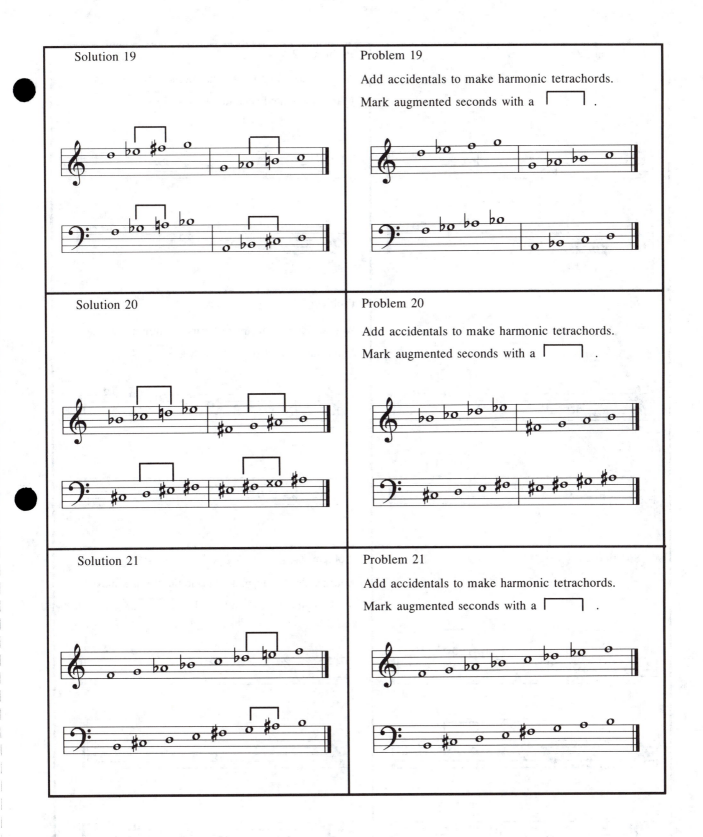

Solution 19

Problem 19

Add accidentals to make harmonic tetrachords.

Mark augmented seconds with a ⌐‾‾⌐ .

Solution 20

Problem 20

Add accidentals to make harmonic tetrachords.

Mark augmented seconds with a ⌐‾‾⌐ .

Solution 21

Problem 21

Add accidentals to make harmonic tetrachords.

Mark augmented seconds with a ⌐‾‾⌐ .

Solution 22

Problem 22

Add accidentals to make harmonic minor scales.

Mark augmented seconds with a ⌐‾‾⌐ .

Solution 23

Problem 23

Add accidentals to make harmonic minor scales.

Mark augmented seconds with a ⌐‾‾⌐ .

Solution 24

Problem 24

Add accidentals to make harmonic minor scales.

Mark augmented seconds with a ⌐‾‾⌐ .

3. Compare major and natural minor regarding:

    a. tetrachord makeup

    b. difference in key signatures (in both parallel and relative keys)

    c. location of half steps

4. Comment on the following:

    a. how to use knowledge of enharmonic pairings

    b. how to use knowledge of chromatic pairings

5. Complete the diagram of the minor circle of fifths.

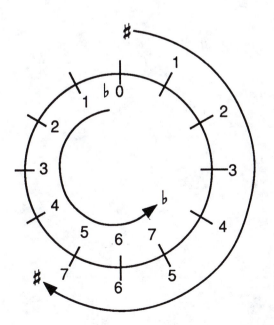

109

APPLICATIONS

1. Write all the scales in the minor circle of fifths in five minutes or less. Be able to write them in either bass or treble clef. For practice, use the clef in which you are least fluent. Use the procedure that follows.

    a. Start with A flat minor (seven flats). Write the letter names and needed accidentals of the scale.

    b. Count up five steps to find the keynote of the next scale in the circle (in this case, E flat).

    c. Carry over the accidentals from the previous scale, and raise the second step of the new scale. The new scale should have one less flat or one more sharp than the previous scale.

Continue this pattern until all seven flats are removed and all seven sharps are added. Important check points along the way are A minor (no flats) and A sharp minor (seven sharps). Notice that flats are deleted and sharps are added in the same order they appear in the sharp key signature format.

2. Sing-spell every scale in the minor circle of fifths. Follow the same pattern as in exercise 1. Instrumentalists should apply this to scale practice and memorization.

3. Practice exercises 1 and 2 in harmonic minor (raised seventh). Instrumentalists should apply this to scale practice and memorization.

4. Practice exercises 1 and 2 in melodic minor (raised sixth and seventh ascending, natural minor descending). Instrumentalists should apply this to scale practice and memorization.

5. Make key signature flash cards to improve your fluency with minor key signatures. Place one of the fifteen key signatures on one side of a card. Write the keynote of the corresponding minor scale on the other side. Practice naming the keynote given the key signature and naming the accidentals in the key signature given the keynote.

6 PERCEPTION AND MEMORY, MELODIC CONTOUR

OVERVIEW   This chapter presents material on musical thought processes that are based on the perception and memory of sound. Information about soundscapes, figure and ground, and masking and interference is included. The *Interval* and *Rhythm* paths merge into the beginning of the *Melody Path*. Ideas about melodic contour and continuity are presented. These ideas are applied to the interpretation and expressive performance of melody.

AURAL PERCEPTION

Senses and Memory   We sense the world through a mechanism called **perception**. Our world is understood when perceptions can be related to past experiences. Data obtained through our senses is sorted, indexed, and interpreted. As impressions are received, they are compared to the sense experiences, impressions, and knowledge we have accumulated over a life time. Notable impressions are stored in **short-term memory** (temporary), and some of these eventually find their way into **long-term memory** (permanent).

Soundscapes, Figure, and Ground   Sound is an important aspect of our environment. Sonic scenes or soundscapes continually shift and change. We have the ability to select meaningful patterns out of a seemingly chaotic soundscape. We can concentrate on a particular source and assign the rest of the sounds to the background. Our attention focuses on **foreground** patterns. Images that capture our attention are called **figure**. Material that does not receive our primary attention is called **ground**. In music, a melody is figure and its accompaniment is ground.

Silence

John Cage's composition, "Four Minutes and Thirty-Three Seconds," consists entirely of silence. During its performance (the performers make no sound) some listeners become very aware of **ambient** (residual) sounds in the concert hall. The composition illustrates our tendency to ignore the ambient sounds in a concert hall, to wear sonic blinders to mask out distracting background sounds so we can focus on the music and the musicians.

Interference and Masking

Interference is an intruding image that distracts one's attention from figure. Interfering patterns are disruptive because they are as strong and vivid as the figure. Imagine trying to understand what someone is saying to you on the telephone while another person in the room is vigorously telling you what to say to the caller. **Masking** occurs if another source of sound has qualities very similar to the figure. Imagine trying to single out the sound of one soprano in a large chorus, or the second chair clarinet player in a section. Interference and masking are both forms of sonic camouflage that routinely confront musicians during rehearsals. Musicians work to remove these problems so that the intended figure can be delivered clearly to the audience.

Aural Skills and the Musician

Musicians develop specialized aural skills, including image recognition, image interpretation, and sonic memory (searching, sorting, and recall). These skills are very important to hearing, remembering, performing, creating, reading and writing musical notation, rehearsing, directing, arranging, composing, and music research and scholarship. The study of musical perception, cognition, and memory is a growing field. Researchers are now focusing on the areas of aural perception, image recognition, memory development, aural learning, and musical communication. An awareness of these mental processes can improve both your musicianship and musicality. Your recognition of these factors will give you more insight into your own patterns of thought and learning.

Aural Image Processing

Musicians develop large indexed memory stores of aural images. Musical primitives are so indexed (like intervals, chords, and archetypical melodic fragments). These images have been fixed in long-term memory because they have repeatedly been heard or rehearsed.

Interpretation

Significance and meaning are assigned to the patterns we hear by **interpretation**. For example, listen to a rhythmic passage. This passage is made of a string of short-duration patterns. Are you aware of these separate patterns? Do you think of these patterns as they fit into the overall stream of patterns? Do you relate these patterns to a meter? Were accents performed to your satisfaction? As soon as you think about the rhythms as they relate to larger patterns, you are engaged in the process of interpreting.

Selection and Indexing

In a normal day, sensory information comes to us at random and without structure. Without a filtering mechanism, there is simply too much information to deal with. To solve this problem, we perceive information selectively, automatically designating some information to the background. Patterns we choose to perceive are selected and processed by our indexed memory. **Selection** and **indexing** is the first step of organizing and structuring the information we receive through our senses. Information is further organized by processes called **enlarging, simplifying, and closing**.

Enlarging

Enlarging is how we relate parts to the whole. Think of the patterns we perceive as pieces of a large puzzle. We select the pieces we want to work with and think how they fit into the imagined assembled puzzle. Individual pieces do not make much sense unless we can find a larger frame of reference in which to place them.

Simplifying

While imagining this larger framework for the pieces, we look for ways to generalize, to simplify complex and confusing features to more understandable essentials. We attempt to put the information in outline form with a process called **simplifying**.

Closure

We tend to think in terms of wholes. For example, we might regard two lines joined at one end as part of a triangle, square, or rectangle rather than as something complete in itself, and will imagine the line(s) needed to complete the shape. A pattern that we regard as a whole has **closure**, (it has boundaries and definition). Imagine someone playing a major scale up through the seventh step. Do you want to finish the scale by supplying the missing keynote? In order to be regarded as a whole, any pattern you hear has to satisfy your criteria for closure. If it does not, you will mentally supply the missing elements to create a whole in your own imagination.

More on Interpretation

As far as we know, all these processes of perceiving a pattern and making sense of it through selection, indexing, enlarging, simplifying, and closing take place simultaneously, instantly, and continuously. This happens whether the subject is chaotic and random or organized and structured. We tend to ignore chaos and pay attention to things that ''make sense.'' We relate the processed sensory input to our memories and past experience and assign meaning to it accordingly. This process is another aspect of **interpretation**.

Soundscapes

Sensory information in a musical composition is neither random nor unstructured. Most music we hear and work with is deliberately organized. Composers, improvisors, and arrangers intuitively know about aural perception and memory process, and create musical **soundscapes** (like artists' landscapes) according to its rules. We interpret a musical composition as a soundscape according to our past experience.

Musical pattern exploits figure and ground. During all musical activity composers, performers, and listeners engage in selecting and indexing figure, enlarging, simplifying, closing, and interpreting. *This is the foundation of musical thought and should be taken into account when considering all aspects of music making.* For example, this awareness will help explain how and why a composer organizes musical ideas in a particular way within a composition.

CHECKPOINT I (Perception)

1. Define these terms in reference to aural perception:

   perception   soundscape

   foreground   masking

   ground   interference

   figure   short-term memory

   image indexing   long-term memory

   pattern interpretation   ambient (residual) sound

2. How is drill-and-practice linked to memory?

3. In a rehearsal or practice session, observe how figure and ground are made to operate in music. How can an awareness of this be used in the rehearsal? Summarize your findings below.

4. Observe how interference and masking are dealt with in a routine rehearsal. Balance is a key word. Summarize your observations below.

5. What is the advantage of knowing about aural perception and memory processes?

MELODY

Contour

Contour is the general rise and fall of pitch in a melody. Contour carries part of the expressive message in a melody, somewhat like spoken inflection in language. The pattern produced by the general rise and fall of pitch also provides a general carrier for thematic patterns. With this in mind, try this exercise in musical perception, thought, and interpretation. Sing the melody in the following example. While doing so, think about the patterns you perceive, how you interpret these as they relate to the general flow of the melody, and how you feel in response to the melody. The graph below the example illustrates the general contour features of the melody. How does your perception of the melody relate to this graph?

Example 1. Agnus Dei   Gregorian Chant

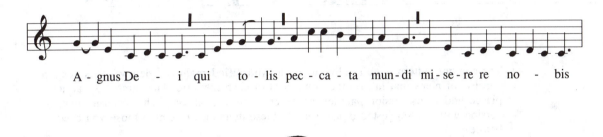

Did the way you expressively performed the melody have anything to do with its contour pattern? The rise and fall of pitch? Now, think about the words. They mean, "Lamb of God, that takes away the sins of the world, have mercy on us." Does the sense of these words change your interpretation of the melody?

Several factors contribute to the formation of a contour pattern. Differences between one melody and another can be explained according to how their contour factors are balanced, changed, and the changes timed as the melodies unfold. The uniqueness of a given melody may be caused by a unique contour pattern. A list of contour ingredients follows.

Contour Factors

Contour Factors:

a. **shape**: the overall pattern of the contour, any breakdown of this pattern into shorter, interrelated units
b. **direction change**: changes in general upward or downward movement, how often changes of direction occur, and the timing of these changes
c. **range**: distance between the highest and lowest points, rate of pitch change, any variation in this rate of change, distribution of low, middle, and high notes

Contourtabs factors in the next melody are
a. shape: an arch (up and down)
b. direction change: one major change at the top of the arch, the high point is reached before the midpoint of the melody
c. range: a ninth traversed within the first three measures, most of the notes fall within the E–B fifth (the tonic pentachord)

Perform the melody expressively. Is there a relationship between the contour factors and your use of dynamics and accents?

Example 2. Theme from the Moldau   Smetena

The contour pattern is quite obvious in the **simplified melody** (below). This version consists of notes that fall on the down beat of each measure. The sample dynamics placed under this version parallel the general rise and fall of pitch. Perform this version with the suggested dynamics. Do these dynamics resemble those you used before?

Example 3. The Moldau Theme Simplified

Notice how the melody is made almost entirely of seconds (stepwise motion). How does this compare to the melody in example 1 (Agnus Dei)?

The contour factors in the next melody are
a. shape: wave motion (up-down-up) with a separate upward moving segment added at the end
b. direction change: changes at high and low points of the wave, abrupt change at the beginning of the last segment
c. range: covers an eleventh, rapid upward movement, slower downward movement, contrast between upward "surge" and downward "meandering" patterns

Sample dynamics are included below this melody. Perform the melody, try the sample dynamics, then experiment with a dynamic scheme of your own.

116

Example 4. Theme from Second Piano Concerto   Rachmaninoff
From Piano Concertos Nos. 1, 2 and 3 in Full Score, Serge Rachmaninoff, Dover Publications 1990. Originally published by State Publications, Moscow 1965.

Continuity

Continuity is the general flow of effects caused by melodic intervals, rhythm values, articulation, and the duration and connection of ideas (figures). Differences between one melody and another depend on what continuity factors in each are developed as the melodies unfold.

Continuity Features

Continuity Features:
a. **intervals**: relative size
b. **activity**: relative slowness or quickness of rhythms
c. **articulation**: the mixture of sounds and silences; the degree to which sounds and figures are separated by silences
d. **duration**: the relative length of ideas, how these lengths are sequenced

The significant continuity features in the next melody are
a. intervals: all seconds (stepwise motion)
b. activity: slow-fast contrasts
c. articulation: contrasts between detached and connected sounds
d. duration: two ideas four beats in length and one idea eight beats in length, a balance between two ''shorts'' and one ''long''

The contour of this melody is a series of expanding waves, each returning to the starting pitch level. A change in rhythmic pace is associated with each wave. A sample dynamic scheme is placed below a composite graph of the contour and continuity features of the melody. Do you agree or disagree with this scheme? [Some ideas about continuity effects have been superimposed on this contour chart. The contrast between staccato and legato is charted as interrupted versus continuous line.]

contour/continuity graph of melody from Hàry Jànos

Compare the continuity features of examples 4 and 5. Do you note a difference in the treatment of intervals, range, articulation, and durations when comparing the two melodies?

The next melody is accompanied by a graph of its contour and continuity features, and by a simplified version of the melody. A sample dynamic scheme is included under the melody. Perform the melody with these dynamics and compare the three parts of the example. Be sure to perform the simplified version of the melody.

118

Example 6. *Un Bel Di* from Madame Butterfly   Puccini

Afterthoughts on *Un Bel Di*

Some important features of this melody are
  a. shape: inverted arch (down-up), low point near end of melody, contour breaks into four inverted arches of equal length, the melody is in a sense made of smaller versions of itself
  b. direction change: one fundamental change in the overall pattern at the melody's low point, many surface changes in each segment
  c. range: an eleventh covered gradually as the melody moves through its contour
  d. intervals: a balance of steps and small skips, skips are larger toward end of melody
  e. activity: recurring pattern with minor variations
  f. articulation: short span patterns are separated by rests (except midway in melody), otherwise continuous sound
  g. duration: length of short span patterns is uniform

The simplified version of the melody unfolds in equal-note rhythms. The first half of this version moves in steps. In contrast, the second half contains more skips. The effect of this change is to impart a greater sense of motion.

In the sample interpretation, each **segment** of the contour was treated as a melody within a melody. Each received a dynamic swell under the control of an overall crescendo and diminuendo. The lowest note in the melody was the goal of the crescendo. Dynamic change was small and gradual to complement what was seen as the calm and perhaps sad mood of the melody. The gradual descent, recurring equal-length patterns, and continuation of a rhythmic and interval norm seemed to create a mood of calm resignation.

119

The next melody differs in mood and effect from the previous melody. Comparing the contour/continuity features of the two melodies can help show the causes of this contrast. Features of the next melody are

a. contour: upward movement through two short inverted arches followed by a long descent, movement is temporarily "stalled" in bars 5–8
b. direction change: four major changes in quick succession
c. range: an eleventh is covered in the first five measures, creating rapid up and down movement in the first half of the melody, a contrasting slow descent follows in the second half
d. intervals: more skips in the first half, more steps in the second half
e. activity: long accented notes in first, third, and fifth measure, rhythm more active after fifth measure
f. articulation: continuous sound, no separation by rests
g. duration: two short segments (bars 1–4) and one long segment (bars 5–11)

Example 7. from Marriage of Figaro Mozart

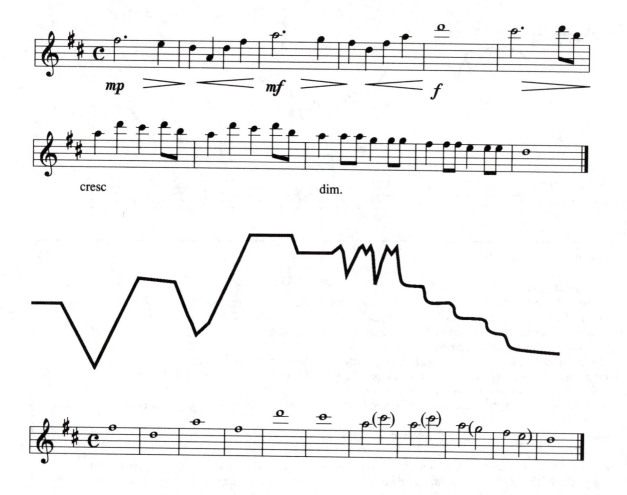

The notes enclosed in parentheses are included in the simplification to indicate an increase in background rhythmic pace. These are the only notes in the simplification that do not fall on the downbeat of a measure.

The agitated nature of the melody is underscored by rapid changes in loudness. These changes are under an overall crescendo in the first four bars. The suspense of the delayed motion in bars 6, 7, and 8 is heightened by a sudden reduction of loudness followed by a crescendo.

Compound Contour

The next melody illustrates a **compound contour**. Notice how the bracketed parts of this example seem to stand apart from the body of the melody, as though the example were made of two separate voices. This separation can also be seen in the contour/continuity graph. A contour with such separable elements is called a compound contour.

Example 8. from Capriccio for Recorder and Continuo   Teleman

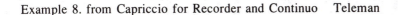

The compound elements of this melody can be seen as a conversation-like pattern, a dialogue. Notice that the contours of the two elements are in opposite directions. The bracketed notes can be intensified slightly to bring out the dialogue pattern in this melody.

PERSON TO PERSON: One objective of this book is to encourage you to think critically about music, and to convert this thinking into musical action such as singing, playing, conducting, writing, and responding to or talking about music intelligently. "Critical" should not be interpreted as "negative" or "faulty." Critical thinking means bringing all your knowledge and resources to consider a selection of music. These resources include your intelligence, feelings, aural memory, intuition, music skills, and "body" intelligence. As you might now suspect, you are the subject matter as much as the music is. You can understand music better if you know more about how you use it to communicate, how you perceive it, and how your aural memory stores your musical experiences. This self-knowledge is bound to help you as you continue to develop your own musical intelligence.

CHECKPOINT II (Melodic Contour and Continuity)

1. Define these terms:

   contour   shape

   direction change   range

   simplified melody   continuity

   interval continuity   rhythm continuity

   articulation continuity   duration continuity

   segment   relative activity

2. What is the value of awareness of contour and continuity features in a melody?

3. Explain how contour and continuity features could be related to simplifying, perceiving in wholes, and hearing closure.

APPLICATIONS

Regard musical thinking as something that can be disciplined like any other mental process. Try the following plan for investigating an example of music:
   a. develop a working hypothesis about the example based on your initial experience with it (apply some selected ideas about the nature of music to a specific example); then
   b. test and illustrate this hypothesis through performance.

The exercises on the following pages are intended to assist you in developing this investigation method. The instructions with each sample of music include directed questions that are designed to "step" you through the process.

1. Apply ideas about contour and continuity to this melody. Discuss how these ideas influence your response to the melody and how you perform it expressively. A cross rhythm occurs in the last four measures. Isolate and describe it. What affect does this rhythm have on the way you perform the melody? On staff paper, write a simplified version of this melody (restricted to primary accents). Allow no more than two pitches per measure. Some measures can be simplified to one note.

Brandenburg Concerto No. 1, Third Movement   J. S. Bach

2. Discuss your response to the contour and continuity features of this melody. Notice that part of this melody has a compound contour. What affect does this have on your interpretation of the melody?

from Wachet auf, Chorale Prelude   J. S. Bach

3. Describe the contour and continuity features of this melody. A compound contour occurs in the last four measures. Isolate and describe it. What affect does this have on your interpretation of the melody?

Bouree from Suite No. 3 for cello (unaccompanied)   J. S. Bach

4. Chart the contour and continuity features in this melody. Relate this to the cross rhythm patterns. Be able to explain your findings and describe how this knowledge influences your performance of the melody.

Symphony No. 40, Third Movement   Mozart

5. Chart the contour and continuity features of this melody. A shift in accent occurs in the second half of the melody. Isolate and describe it. How does this affect the rhythmic flow of the melody? On staff paper, write a simplified version of this melody that has no more than two pitches per measure. Some measures can be simplified to one note.

Concerto for Piano and Orchestra   Robert Schumann

allegro affettuoso (mm = 138)

6. Chart the contour and continuity features in this melody. Relate this to the cross rhythm patterns. Be able to explain your findings and describe how this knowledge influences your performance of the melody.

Third Symphony, Op. 97, First Movement   R. Schumann

7 MELODIC SKELETON

OVERVIEW

The *Melody Path* continues with instruction on the harmonic/rhythmic skeleton of melody. A method is presented for reducing a melody to its structural skeleton. This method is based on ideas about patterns of musical thinking presented in the previous chapter, and relates to the perception and recall of recurring pitch, pattern extremes, interval root, and rhythmic emphasis. The interplay between focal and satellite pitches is discussed. The way the structural skeleton reveals harmonic/rhythmic underpinnings of a melody is also illustrated. These concepts prepare students for the merging of *Melody* and *Harmony* paths in later chapters.

MELODIC SKELETON

Focal versus Satellite Notes

Listeners usually pay special attention to and remember particular notes in a stream of notes. Some notes seem more noticeable and more easily remembered than others. These notes are called **focal pitches** because they have qualities that cause us to focus our attention on them. Other notes in the stream seem dependent on these focal pitches and gravitate towards them. These dependent pitches are called **satellites**.

Melodic Skeleton   Every melody contains a series of focal pitches and their attending satellites. These focal pitches form a background or **skeleton melody** described as *simplified melody* in previous units. Satellites are "connector" notes that add detail, character, and individuality to a skeleton. Notes in a melody take on meaning based on their role and position in the skeleton/satellite structure. *The melodic skeleton carries important information about the harmonic content and architecture of the melody.*

Skeleton Notes   Factors that cause us to focus our attention on certain notes include **pitch recurrence, interval root, pattern extreme,** and **accent.** For now, the effect of rhythmic accent will be ignored. The next examples are written in equal note values to minimize the influence of accent and rhythm.

Perform this simple phrase.

Pitch Recurrence   One's attention tends to focus on pitches that reappear in a melody. Each recurrence of a note underscores its relative importance. A note can gain enough impact through repetition to dominate a whole passage. In the next example, the recurring pitches are indicated by bigger notes, and are tied together. Perform the first line of the example in equal note values. Then, omit the notes that are not tied together during your next performance. Finally, perform the second line of the example. Notice that A seems attached as a satellite to G. How do you think this relationship grew as the melody developed?

Example 1. Focus Through Repetition

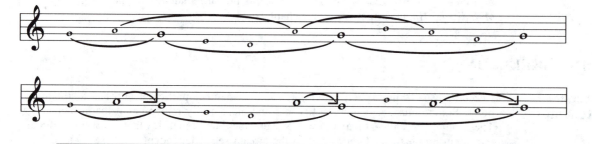

PERSON TO PERSON: Your observance of repeated tones can be helpful when sight singing or taking dictation. Recurring pitches form a background "drone" in your memory that can be used as aural references to help keep you "on track."

Interval Root   Sometimes, one pitch of an interval seems to "close" the interval more convincingly than the other. This note is the **root** of the interval, the dominating note of the interval. One's attention is attracted to interval roots in a melody. Listen for this phenomenon while performing the melodic intervals in the next example. Ask yourself which of the two notes seems to be the best ending note. The strength of the root varies from interval to interval. Some intervals have very obvious roots, others do not. Which note in each of the following intervals is the root—the top, bottom, or neither?

132

Example 2. Intervals to Perform

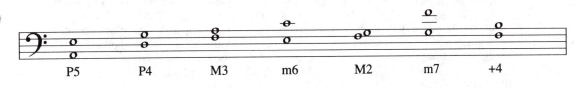

P5   P4   M3   m6   M2   m7   +4

Roots are very detectable in the major third, perfect fifth, and their inversions (the minor sixth and perfect fourth). In the next example, the bigger notes indicate the theoretical roots of each interval. Can you hear these notes as root tones? Additional information on interval root theory is included later with material on the harmonic series.

Example 3. Interval Roots

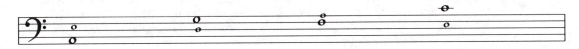

PERSON TO PERSON: If you have ever mistaken an interval for its inversion, an awareness of interval roots may hold a solution for you. Consider the perfect fifth, for example. Its root is the bottom note of the interval. The root is the top note of its inversion, the perfect fourth. You can train yourself to hear the position of interval roots as a way to tell an interval from its inversion. Interval roots provide important aural references in melodies and your awareness of them can help keep you "on track."

Pattern Extremes   **Pattern extremes** are the *first, last, highest,* and *lowest pitches* of a pattern. Like the frame of a picture, they limit the dimensions of a passage (they limit flow of pitch through time instead of physical space). Attention is attracted by pattern extreme notes because they are on the "edges" of a melody. Pattern extremes are circled in the following example. Notice how these pattern extreme notes are also part of strong root producing intervals, a fairly typical pattern in melody. Interval roots occur at the vertical leg of each bracket.

Example 4. Pattern Extremes

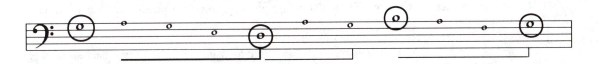

133

Rhythm Accent

Accent is any special stress or emphasis given to a note. In this general sense, any focal pitch is an accented note because it attracts special attention by its position and role in a pattern. In performance, a note can be accented by making it louder than nearby notes (**dynamic accent**) or by delaying (or anticipating) its attack slightly (**agogic accent**). Elongating or "stretching" the value of a note is another form of agogic accent. Special instructions to the performer can be written on the music in the form of accent or tenuto marks, or through style terms like *marcato* or *marziale*. *Performers must be able to detect focal pitches in order to give them appropriate emphasis.*

Rhythm accents are those notes that attract special attention by their position, value, or role in a rhythm pattern. A rhythm accent can be caused by the position of a note in a meter, the relative duration of the note, or the position of the note in a pattern of sounds and silences.

Accents in Meter

Usually, meter is set at the beginning of a composition and recycles continually unless a new time signature appears. For example, a 3/4 meter sign means that the meter unit is set to a length of three beats (assuming moderate tempo). The beats will recycle in three-beat groups until a new meter sign appears to reset the meter unit to a new value. The first beat of each group of beats is customarily accented to signify the beginning of a new cycle.

Example 5. Meter Accents

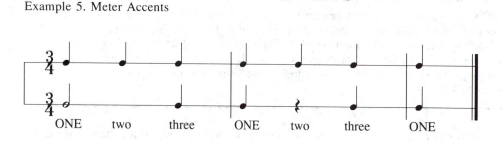

ONE two three ONE two three ONE

Parceling Incoming Data

We tend to organize incoming streams of information into small manageable packets to help our short-term memory handle input. This is called **parceling** (or "chunking") and is used to facilitate the learning of long strings of data, like numbers. A long number can be retained better by breaking it down and rehearsing it in two- and three-part subsets. Telephone and social security numbers are organized in subsets.

Parceling and Meter

Meter is the organization of temporal data into small rhythmic parcels. For example, if we hear a stream of equal-length unaccented notes, we tend to parcel these notes into two- and three-note subsets. Parceling underlies metered (measured) organization in music.

The number of beats in any measure can be divided into two- and three-beat subsets. The first beat of each subset is ordinarily accented. Accents vary in strength according to the performer's interpretation of the meter patterns and the style of the composition. The first beat of a meter is ordinarily stronger than subset accents.

Example 6. Meter and Subset Accents

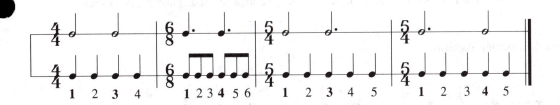

Duration Accent

Longer notes attract more attention than other nearby notes. A performer can stress this focus with dynamic or agogic accents (delayed or premature attacks, prolonged notes). The next example includes accents caused by the relative duration of notes. The bold numbers indicate that a note is accented. Notice that alternative interpretations are given for some of the rhythm patterns. Accent caused by the relative length of a note is a special case of agogic accent. As an experiment, single out a particular accent and delay its attack slightly when performing the phrase.

Example 7. Duration Accents

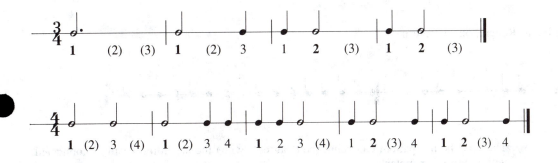

Accent and Serial Position

Recurring patterns (a recycling arrangement of notes and rests) attract attention to certain notes. A performer can emphasize these notes with dynamic or agogic accents. A few possibilities follow. Perform these unmetered examples. Are any recurring patterns present? How many ways can the flow of accents be interpreted?

Example 8. Recurring Patterns

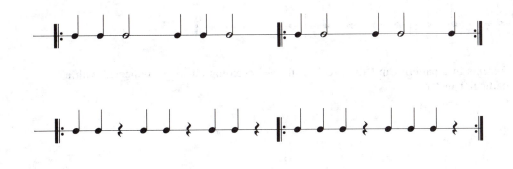

Consider the same patterns in metered contexts. How many ways can these patterns be interpreted when they are set into a meter? Does the context of the meters influence how the patterns are accented? How does the idea of recurrence apply to meter?

Example 9. Metered Recurring Patterns

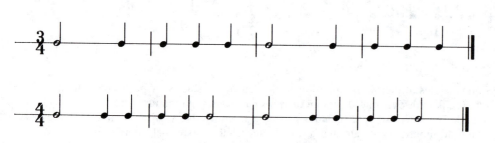

A rhythmic stream that contains little reiteration may not have a metered "feel" to it (a string of unaccented equal values, for instance). Unlike patterns that suggest particular meters, non-iterating patterns can be interpreted in several ways. Experiment with the rhythms in the next example. Envision them in different meters and accent them accordingly. How would these rhythms be written in these meters? Consider the possibility of changing meters.

Example 10. Minimum Reiteration of Pattern

The accents in a pattern can reinforce ("agree" with) the accenting customs connected with a particular meter.

Example 11. Rhythmic Focus Synchronized With Meter Accents

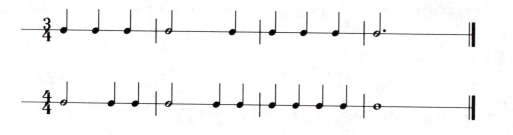

Accents in a pattern can "disagree" with the accenting customs connected with a particular meter.

136

Example 12. Rhythmic Focus Not Synchronized With Meter Accents

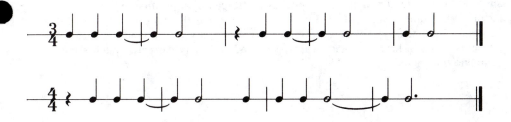

Accents can be patterned so there is a difference between how meter sounds and how it looks. Do the following patterns sound like they are in the indicated meter? If not, is a different meter implied?

Example 13. Differences Between Indicated and Perceived Meter

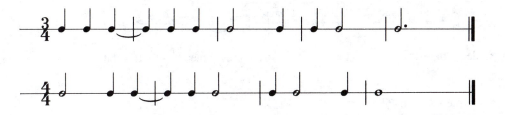

While performing the previous examples, did you notice a tendency to close a rhythmic stream just as you would a spoken phrase? The musical term for this "closing off" is **phrasing**, a way to give dimension and boundaries to rhythmic ideas. In fact, the term **cadence** once meant the same as "rhythmic phrase" (Arbot, *Orchesography*). Closure seems necessary to our memory processes and helps us make sense of a string of rhythmic ideas. Process is parcelling on a somewhat larger scale.

We tend to organize a composition into phrases when listening or performing. Phrasing is built into most of the music we encounter. There seems to be a connection between phrasing in music and in spoken language. If musical phrasing is indefinite or non-existent, we may want to supply our own closures to help the passage make more sense.

Our sense of phrases can be improved by a change of rhythm pattern near the end of each idea.

Example 14. Rhythm Phrases

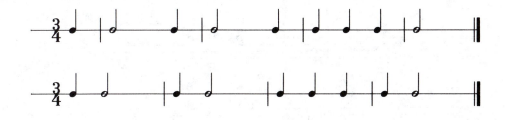

Interaction of Focus Factors

Perform the next few examples. Look for focal pitches caused by recurring pitch, interval root, and pattern extremes. Decide which notes are focal pitches and which are satellites. Were any of the focal pitches reinforced by more than one focusing factor? Which notes were attended by satellites? What is the pattern of the satellites? Can you visualize a simplified version of the melody (a skeleton made of focal pitches)? Can you hear a pattern in this skeleton? Does any particular pitch seem to dominate this melody?

Example 15. Aeterna Christi

A sample solution follows.

a. The focal pitches are the notes in the G major triad.
b. All other notes are satellites.
c. G is the low pattern extreme and D is the high pattern extreme. The higher note E always embellishes D, usually in a returning note pattern (neighbor tone). B is the most repeated mid-range note. G is the root of both the G–B and the G–D interval.
d. The notes A and C were part of note groups centered on B. These notes decorate and connect the notes of the G major triad.

Refer to the outline below while studying the analyzed version of "Aeterna Christi."

• Focal pitches are indicated by whole notes.
• Pattern extreme notes are marked by * in each phrase.
• Satellites are shown as black notes.

Perform example 16 in equal note values. Notice how your impression of the roles and functions of some of the notes grows and changes as the melody unfolds.

Example 16. Aeterna Christi Analyzed

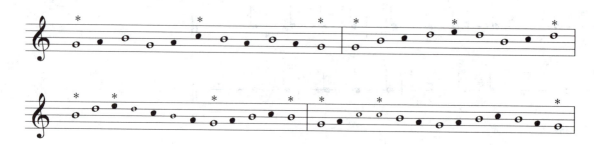

138

PERSON TO PERSON: You are regularly asked to perform the examples in this book while evaluating them. This union of thought and performance improves your ability to think critically about music. You should always test your ideas about music in terms of sound. Always think about the music as it is heard, performed, and expressed. Try different interpretations. Be curious about how another person might treat the same example. This will help you develop your own musical thinking, better understand your own responses to music, and appreciate the thinking of other musicians. Do not be surprised if your evaluations sometimes lead you to solutions that are different from others' solutions, or vary from the sample analyses given in this book.

Compare the two halves of the next example. Notice how the addition of a single pitch can change your whole perspective of this short tune (see second half of example). Can you explain how the addition of one note can change focal pitch, patterns formed by focal pitches, or focusing factors?

Example 17. A Tune Revisited

In the next melody, essential movement is on the weak beats. B♭, the fifth step of the E♭ major scale, is emphasized in the first four measures. The remainder of the melody outlines the notes of the tonic pentachord. This pattern can be seen in the skeleton version of this melody. The focus on the tonic pitch through interval roots and pattern goals seems obvious. Does this strong background pattern influence your interpretation of this melody? Perform both the original and skeletonized melodies with expression. Can you see the melody as a general movement from the dominant to the tonic pitch? What qualities does the rhythm add to the overall pattern?

Example 18. Waltz in E flat, Op. 18   Chopin

The next melody also features basic movement from the dominant to the tonic pitch. This movement has strong harmonic implications. Focus rests on the dominant pitch for the first two bars. Bars 3–4 contain a series of fifths leading to tonic. Bars 5–6 contain a neighbor group around tonic. This pattern is shown in the skeletonized version of the melody. Perform both the original and skeleton versions with expression. How does the background pattern influence your interpretation in this example? This melody could be reduced to the pattern of a melodic fifth (the first and last notes). Each note of this interval is decorated by its satellites (*A* by *B*, *D* by *E* and *C#*). How can this viewpoint be used to learn and memorize this melody more rapidly? Can you see "skeletonizing" as a kind of musical generalizing, outlining, or summarizing?

Example 19. Concerto in D for Piano and Orchestra, First Movement   Haydn

Sensitivity to Roots and Closure

A root may dominate an interval or a cluster of intervals. Hearing the root of an isolated interval is not as difficult as hearing a succession of interval roots in a melody. One can become more aware of these roots by experimenting with note clusters of various sizes. Many melodies include a succession of clusters. The next few examples suggest how to approach melodic cells to become more sensitive to their interval root content and closing effects.

Roots in Trichords

The step pattern 1-4-5 contains two root producing intervals, P4 and P5. In the next example, six different combinations were produced by changing the order of the notes. Perform each pattern. Is 1 always the root of the melodic cell? Do the closing effects of each rotation of the pattern differ?

The diamond-shaped notes mark the progressive shift to the left in each rotation. Any of these cells could be part of the surface details or the background skeleton of a melody.

Example 20. Three-note Melodic Cells

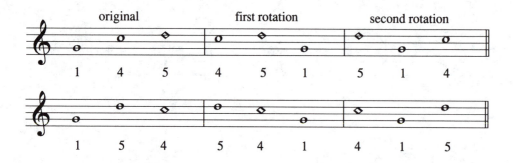

140

The patterns in the previous example were rotations of 1-4-5 or 1-5-4. There are six possible combinations of any three-note pattern. Because of changing closing notes and the order of intervals, 1 does not seem to be the root of each melodic cell. The raw order of the notes influences closing effects. One of the notes may have been the satellite of the remaining interval. What was the root of each cell?

Roots in Tetrachords

A pattern of four notes can be recombined in 24 different ways by changing the order of the notes. The patterns in example 21 were derived from the dominant tetrachord of the C major scale, steps 5-6-7-1. Rotations of the 6-1-7-5 and 1-6-5-7 combinations of this tetrachord were used in the example. Perform each pattern and determine which note is the root of the cell. Did you hear any of the notes as satellites? Interpretation is required to identify the root of each cell and to assess the strength of the cell's closure.

Compare the measures vertically (see arrows). The thirds in the second line are the inversions of the thirds in the first line. Does this have any effect on root tones or closure?

Example 21. Four-note Melodic Cells

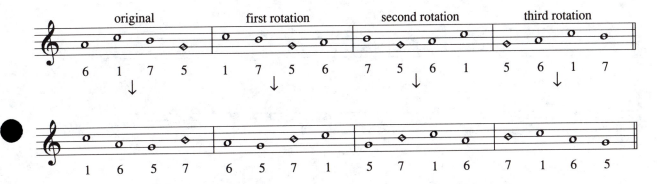

As you may have noted, one or two of the notes in a pattern serve as satellites of the notes of an interval. Did you hear two of the notes as satellites of an interval in any of the patterns? What was the root in each of the cells above? What was the closing effect of each cell?

Roots in Larger Melodic Cells

The possibilities increase as more notes are added to the patterns. For example, the notes in a pentachord like 1-2-3-4-5 can be recombined in 120 different ways. The notes in a hexachord like 1-2-3-4-5-6 can be recombined in 720 different ways. The roots and closing effects may differ depending on the order of the notes in each combination of these patterns. Thus, you must perform and consider each pattern individually to determine its root and closing effects.

Extended Tetrachords and Pentachords

Tetrachords and pentachords can be extended with upper and lower satellites. Satellites are shown with solid note heads. Their "gravitation" is shown by arrows.

Example 22. Extended Tetrachords and Pentachords

The upper, lower, or both satellites can be added to a tetrachord or pentachord. The dominant pentachord is commonly extended with an upper satellite. The extended pattern has the appearance of a hexachord, but, in context, the added tone functions as a satellite.

The folk tune "Old Grand Dad" is based on an extended tonic pentachord. The highest note (the sixth scale step A) acts as a satellite of G. If this upper neighbor tone is removed, the remaining notes form the tonic pentachord, C-D-E-F-G.

Example 23. "Old Grand Dad"

CHECKPOINT (Pitch and Rhythm Context)

1. Explain these terms:

focal pitch	satellite
background	skeleton melody
simplified melody	pitch recurrence
interval root	phrasing
pattern extremes	accent
dynamic accent	agogic accent
cadence	meter accent

parceling   duration accent

accent by serial position   extended pentachords and tetrachords

2. How can knowledge of pitch and rhythm focus help you

   a. interpret a melody?

   b. memorize a melody?

   c. learn a melody more accurately and quickly?

   d. improve your sight-singing and dictation skills?

3. Self-help Problems. Some of your solutions will depend on your interpretation of the pattern. These exercises were designed to be cut and dried, but differences in answers are likely to occur where interpretation is involved. If your solution differs from a sample solution, raise a question about it in class.

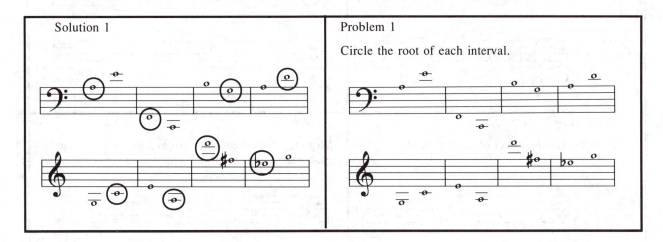

143

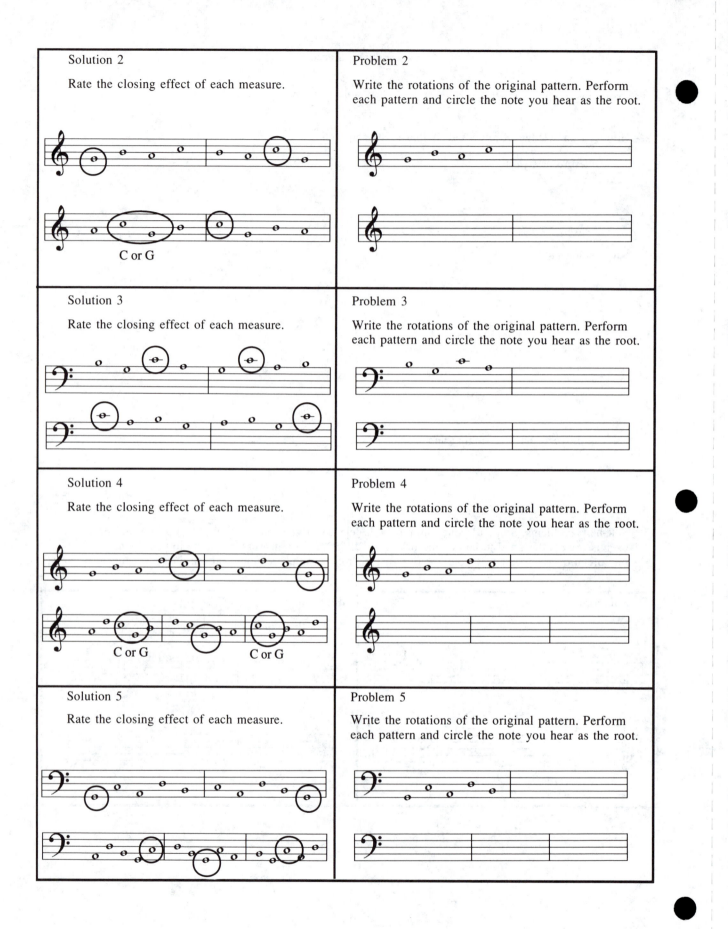

Solution 2

Rate the closing effect of each measure.

C or G

Problem 2

Write the rotations of the original pattern. Perform each pattern and circle the note you hear as the root.

Solution 3

Rate the closing effect of each measure.

Problem 3

Write the rotations of the original pattern. Perform each pattern and circle the note you hear as the root.

Solution 4

Rate the closing effect of each measure.

C or G   C or G

Problem 4

Write the rotations of the original pattern. Perform each pattern and circle the note you hear as the root.

Solution 5

Rate the closing effect of each measure.

Problem 5

Write the rotations of the original pattern. Perform each pattern and circle the note you hear as the root.

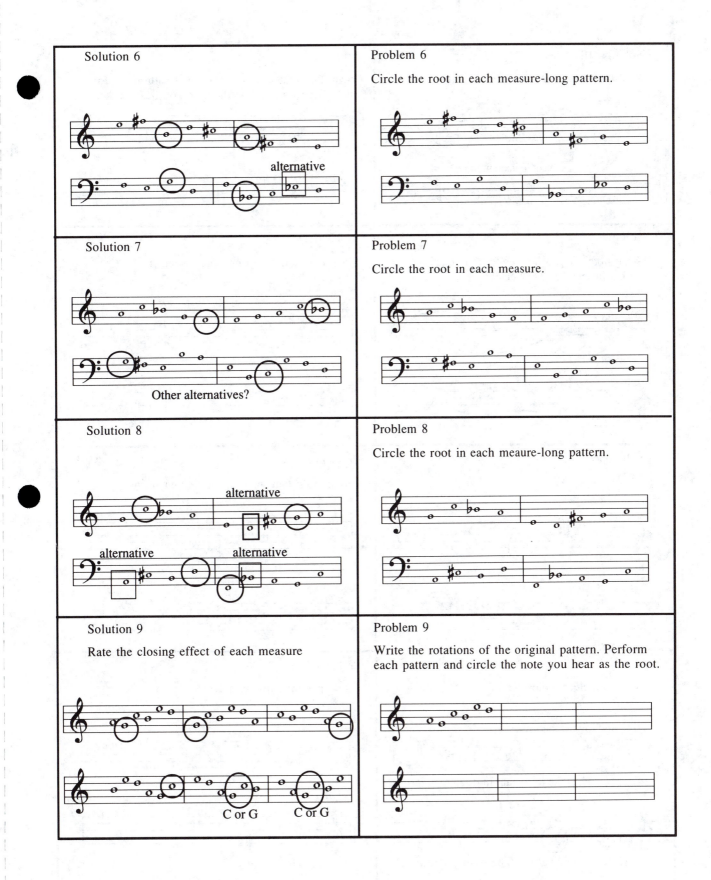

Solution 6

Problem 6

Circle the root in each measure-long pattern.

alternative

Solution 7

Problem 7

Circle the root in each measure.

Other alternatives?

Solution 8

Problem 8

Circle the root in each meaure-long pattern.

alternative

alternative   alternative

Solution 9

Rate the closing effect of each measure

Problem 9

Write the rotations of the original pattern. Perform each pattern and circle the note you hear as the root.

C or G   C or G

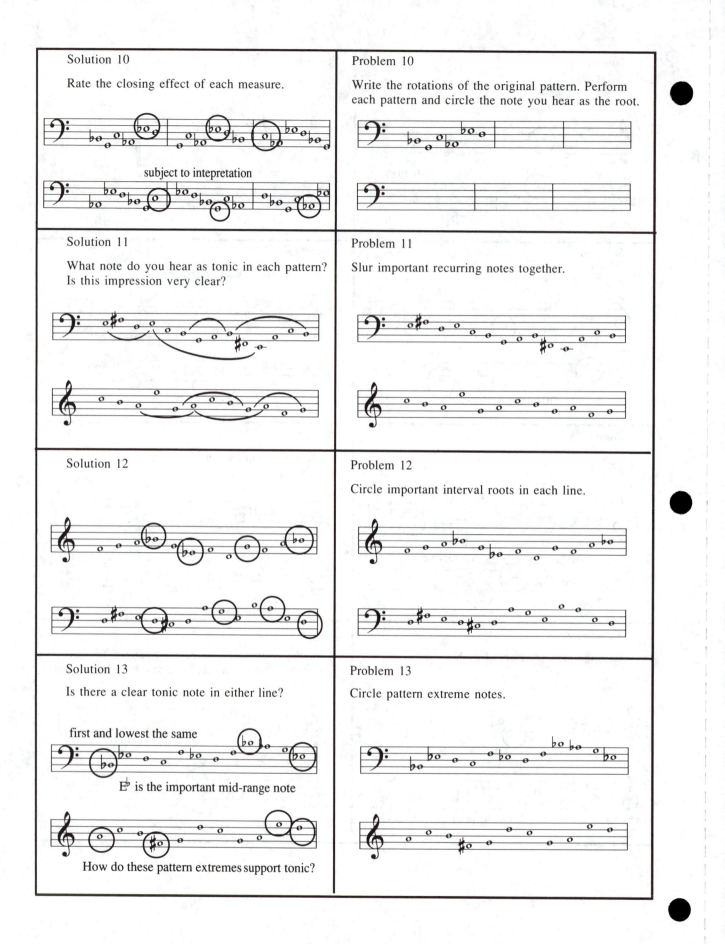

Solution 10

Rate the closing effect of each measure.

subject to intepretation

Problem 10

Write the rotations of the original pattern. Perform each pattern and circle the note you hear as the root.

Solution 11

What note do you hear as tonic in each pattern? Is this impression very clear?

Problem 11

Slur important recurring notes together.

Solution 12

Problem 12

Circle important interval roots in each line.

Solution 13

Is there a clear tonic note in either line?

first and lowest the same

E♭ is the important mid-range note

How do these pattern extremes support tonic?

Problem 13

Circle pattern extreme notes.

146

Solution 14

A is focal pitch

Problem 14

Is there a clear tonic note in either line? Use short slurs to connect satellites to their focal pitches.

APPLICATIONS

NAME _____ CLASS _____ DATE _____

1. Circle the the focal pitches in the next melody. Be prepared to justify your selection as recurring pitch, interval root, pattern extremes, or rhythmic accent. What note seems to be the root of the entire melody? Can you find any patterns that you can use as a reference to perform, memorize, and interpret this melody? Describe the contour and continuity features of the melody and relate this to other factors discovered in the melody.

Brandenburg Concerto No. 2   J. S. Bach

First Movement

Skeleton

2. Make a simplified version of the next melody. As indicated by the title, the theme is in C minor. Show how C is established as the root of this theme. Describe the contour and continuity features of the melody and relate this to other factors in the melody.

Passacaglia in C minor, Theme   J. S. Bach

Skeleton

3. Try a quick, on-the-spot analysis of the next melody as one might be required to do in a rehearsal. What pattern is formed by the focal pitches? Using focal pitches as a ''road map,'' see how quickly you can memorize this tune. How does this relate to the contour and continuity features of the melody?

from Academic Festival Overture, Op. 80   Brahms

Animato

4. What is the keynote of the next melody? How was it established? Describe the pattern made by the focal pitches. Do all the focal pitches in this melody have the same duration? How does this relate to the contour and continuity features of the melody?

Symphony No. 4 (''Italian''), Second Movement   Mendelssohn

Andante con moto

Skeleton

5. Make a skeletonized version of this melody. Justify each note in the skeleton. Verify this in your performance of the melody. Does an awareness of the skeleton help make this melody easier to learn? See how quickly you can memorize the melody. Describe the contour and continuity features of the melody and relate this to other factors in the melody.

Eine Kleine Nachtmusik, K. 525, Second Movement   Mozart

Andante

Skeleton

6. Make a skeletonized version of this melody. Explain how you selected the focal pitches. Is there any pattern to the satellite notes? Is there a pattern to the focal pitches? Describe the contour and continuity features of the melody and relate these features to other factors in the melody. How does knowledge of these patterns influence your interpretation of this melody?

Concert in A Minor, Op. 54 (Piano and Orchestra), First Movement, Second Theme   R. Schumann

Skeleton

Photocopy this page to produce your own manuscript paper.

8 HARMONY: PART 1

OVERVIEW   The *Harmony Path* begins in this chapter as part one of a two-part series on triads. The chapter contains instruction on tertian triads, parts of triads, types of triads, identification of triads, inversion, spacing of voices, interval roots in triads, and relative stability of each type of triad.

HARMONY

Triads

A **triad** is a three-note cluster of intervals. The bulk of Western music literature uses **tertian harmony** (chords made of thirds). Thus, a tertian triad is a stack of thirds. Its parts are a **root, third,** and **fifth** (3 + 3 – common tone = 5). For now, think of the root of the triad as the lowest note in the stack. The triad is **melodic** if its notes sound in a series and **harmonic** if its notes sound simultaneously.

Example 1. Tertian Triad

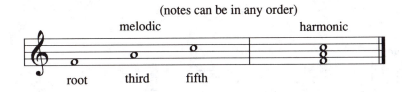

Triad Types

Major and minor thirds can be arranged in four triad pattern combinations. Each combination has a unique sound. The chart below shows the important features of each triad type. Compare this chart to the chords in the next example.

TRIAD TYPE	THIRDS	FIFTH	SPECIAL FEATURES
major	ma + mi	perfect	ma 3rd, P5 above root
minor	mi + ma	perfect	mi 3rd, P5 above root
augmented	ma + ma	augmented	all ma 3rds, +5 above root
diminished	mi + mi	diminished	all mi 3rds, o5 above root

Example 2. Triad Types

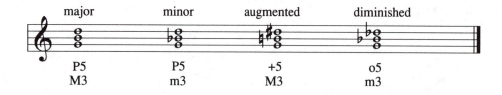

Triad Identification

A triad can be identified by its color and root name. This identification method resembles the chord notation used in popular sheet music, "lead sheets," jazz ensemble parts, guitar tablature, and song books.

Example 3. Triad Identification by Type

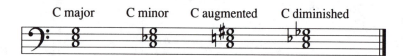

White-Key Major Triads

The roots of the white-key major triads are C, F, and G. These chords have the same roots as the white-key major thirds. These triads are members of the **primary triad** group and lie on the first, fourth, and fifth degrees of every major scale in the circle of fifths. The primary triads can be arranged so their roots are a perfect fifth apart, a strong harmonic relationship.

Example 4. White-Key Major Triads

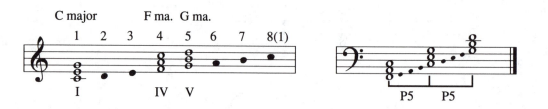

The chromatic transposition of white-key triads is a useful memory aid. For example, the C triad is major. Writing and identifying the C♯ and C♭ major triads is a simple matter of transposing ALL the notes in the triad up or down a chromatic half step. As shown in the next example, any of these chords can be changed to minor by lowering their thirds. This pattern applies to all of the white-key major triads.

Example 5. Changing Major to Minor

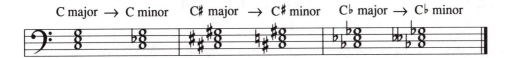

Major triads can be changed to augmented triads by raising their fifths a chromatic semitone.

Example 6. Changing Major to Augmented

Major triads can be changed to diminished triads by lowering their third <u>and</u> fifth a chromatic semitone.

Example 7. Changing Major to Diminished

White-Key Minor Triads

The roots of the white-key minor triads are A, D, and E. Like the white-key major triads, these chords can be arranged so their roots are a perfect fifth apart, a strong harmonic relationship. The three minor triads make up the primary triad group in natural minor (i, iv, and v).

Example 8. White-Key Minor Triads

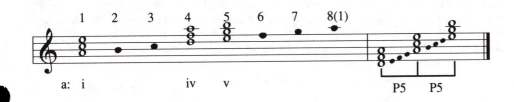

161

The chromatic transposition of these triads are A sharp, D sharp, and E sharp minor (ALL notes sharped), or A flat, D flat, and E flat minor (ALL notes flatted).

Example 9. Chromatic Transpositions of White-Key Minor Triads

Minor triads can be changed to major triads by raising their third a chromatic semitone.

Example 10. Changing Minor to Major

A minor → A major   A♯ minor → A♯ major   A♭ minor → A♭ major

Minor triads can be changed to diminished triads by lowering their fifth a chromatic semitone.

Example 11. Changing Minor to Diminished

D minor → D dim.   D♯ minor → D♯ dim.   D♭ minor → D♭ diminished

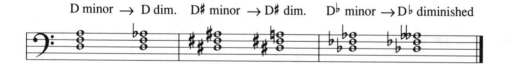

Minor triads can be changed to **augmented triads** by raising their third <u>and</u> fifth a chromatic semitone.

Example 12. Changing Minor to Augmented

E minor → E aug.   E♯ minor → E♯ aug.   E♭ minor → E♭ augmented

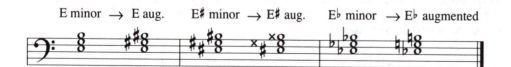

White-Key Diminished

There is only one white-key diminished triad. Its root is B and its chromatic transpositions are B flat and B sharp. Its fifth must be raised a chromatic semitone to convert it to a minor triad. Both notes of the diminished triad must be raised to change it to a major triad. What must one do to change a diminished triad to an augmented triad?

Example 13. The Diminished Triad and Its Chromatic Transpositions

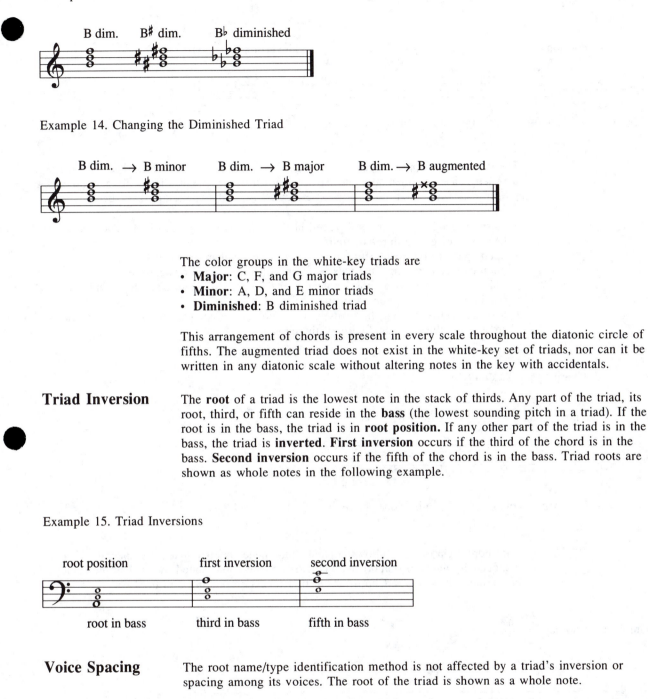

Example 14. Changing the Diminished Triad

The color groups in the white-key triads are
- **Major**: C, F, and G major triads
- **Minor**: A, D, and E minor triads
- **Diminished**: B diminished triad

This arrangement of chords is present in every scale throughout the diatonic circle of fifths. The augmented triad does not exist in the white-key set of triads, nor can it be written in any diatonic scale without altering notes in the key with accidentals.

Triad Inversion

The **root** of a triad is the lowest note in the stack of thirds. Any part of the triad, its root, third, or fifth can reside in the **bass** (the lowest sounding pitch in a triad). If the root is in the bass, the triad is in **root position.** If any other part of the triad is in the bass, the triad is **inverted. First inversion** occurs if the third of the chord is in the bass. **Second inversion** occurs if the fifth of the chord is in the bass. Triad roots are shown as whole notes in the following example.

Example 15. Triad Inversions

root position   first inversion   second inversion

root in bass   third in bass   fifth in bass

Voice Spacing

The root name/type identification method is not affected by a triad's inversion or spacing among its voices. The root of the triad is shown as a whole note.

Example 16. Root/Type Identification

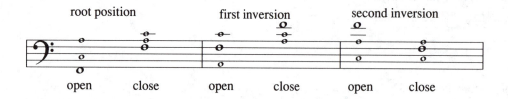

root position   first inversion   second inversion

open   close   open   close   open   close

The inversion of upper voices may change the distances among voices. The distance between voices is called **spacing**. Any changes in spacing will affect a triad's sound properties. Factors that have the most effect on a chord's sound are listed below.

- **close** spacing: Triad parts are placed in their closest possible position. The intervals between voices are thirds or fourths.
- **open** spacing: Intervals between voices are greater than thirds or fourths.
- **homogeneous** spacing: Intervals between voices are equal or nearly equal in size. This spacing emphasizes the wholeness of the chord's sound. Both close and open spacings can also be homogeneous.
- **heterogeneous** spacing: Intervals between voices are unequal in size. This spacing emphasizes the individual parts of the chord.

Example 17. Chord Spacing Conditions

homogeneous   heterogeneous

open   open   close   mixed open/close

The chordal phrase that follows contains homogeneous open and close spacings. This homogeneity tends to support the wholeness of the chord sound rather than the sound of the individual voices. Chords are in first inversion if third is in the bass.

Example 18. Chordal Passage

triad: A major D major E major A major B minor F♯ mi. B minor E major A major

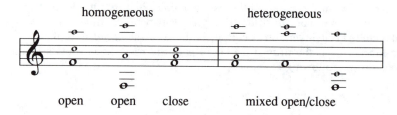

element
in bass: root   root   root   root   third   third   root   root   root

spacing: close open close open close open open close open

The next example features heterogeneous spacings. The bass is separated from the two upper voices by wide spacing. The two upper voices are coupled together by rhythm and continuous close spacing. The bass part stands out independently because of its more active rhythm and wide separation from the other voices.

Example 19. Sarabanda   A. Corelli

from Sonata Da Camera a Tres, Op. 4, No. 8

Interval Roots in Triads

Interval roots are most noticeable in major thirds, perfect fifths, and the inversions of these intervals. Focus on interval roots operates in clusters of intervals like chords. The major triad, for example, contains both the major third and perfect fifth. The roots of these two intervals are the same note as the root of the triad, the note common to both intervals. The root of a major triad can easily be identified regardless of how the parts of the chord are inverted.

Example 20. Interval Roots in the Major Triad

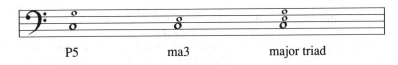

P5   ma3   major triad

Roots in Minor Triads

The minor triad (in close root position) consists of a minor third, a major third, and a perfect fifth (the sum of the two thirds). Two of these intervals, the major third and the perfect fifth, have strong roots. The root of the P5 is also the root of the triad. The root of the major third, however, lies on the third of the minor triad, making it a **secondary root** in the chord. This is especially noticeable if the third of the minor triad is in the bass. If so, the third can be mistaken for the root of the chord. Roots are shown by whole notes in the next example. Brackets show the root producing relationships among the intervals.

Example 21. Interval Roots in the Minor Triad

close   close   open   close   open

Interval Roots in Augmented Triads

The augmented triad consists of two major thirds and an augmented fifth (the sum of the two thirds). Every part of the chord is the root of a major third (or its inversion). The fifth of the chord is the root of the augmented fifth (the enharmonic equivalent of the minor sixth). Accordingly, every note in the augmented triad is an audible root of equal strength. Furthermore, the augmented triad divides the octave into three equal parts. The listener can only hear the augmented triad as a root position stack of thirds, regardless of how the chord is inverted or spelled. The "+" signifies augmented. Each inverted triad is respelled enharmonically to illustrate how the listener actually hears the chord.

Example 22. Enharmonic Augmented Triads

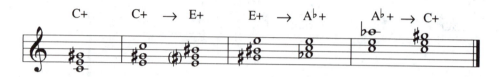

Roots and Diminished Triads

The diminished triad consists of two minor thirds and a diminished fifth (the sum of the two thirds). None of these intervals has a discernable root. In sound, the diminished triad is "rootless." The listener hears the root of the diminished triad only in the context of the arrangement of intervals in the chord. Inversions are detected by noting the arrangement of intervals.

Example 23. The Rootless Diminished Triad

Stable and Unstable Effects

Major and minor triads are perceived as **stable chords** because they both contain a perfect fifth, a strong root-producing interval. This stability makes these triads useful as closing chords in harmonic phrases. Diminished and augmented triads are **unstable** because of their root-tone ambiguity. Neither contains a perfect fifth. This instability makes these triads ineffective as closing chords in a phrase.

Example 24. Stable and Unstable Endings

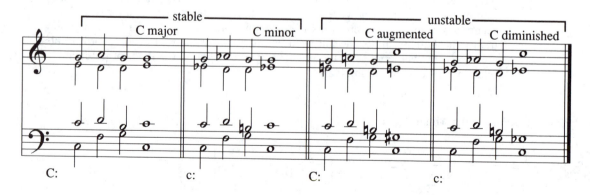

CHECKPOINT I (Triads)

1. Explain these terms:

triad	triad root
triad third	triad fifth
major triad	minor triad
augmented triad	diminished triad
tertian	bass
triad inversion	upper voice inversion
root position	first inversion
second inversion	spacing
close spacing	open spacing
homogeneous	heterogeneous
secondary root	stable chord
unstable chord	primary triads

2. Self-help Problems.

Solution 1	Problem 1
thirds root third fifth root	The tertian triad is so named because it is a stack of _____. The lowest tone in the stack is called the _____. The remaining parts of the triad are the _____ and the _____, so named because of their interval distance above the _____.

Solution 2	Problem 2
major minor perfect diminished augmented four	Triad thirds can have one of two qualities, _____ or _____. The fifth of the triad can have one of three qualities, _____, _____, or _____. These interval qualities can be combined to create the _____ types of triad.
Solution 3 major minor diminished augmented	**Problem 3** The two triads named according to the quality of their lowest third are the _____ and _____ triads. The two triads named according to the quality of their fifth are the _____ and _____ triads.

Solution 4

type	third	fifth
major	major	perfect
minor	minor	perfect
diminished	minor	diminished
augmented	major	augmented

Problem 4

Complete this table of triad elements.

type	third	fifth
major		
minor		
diminished		
augmented		

Solution 5	Problem 5
perfect major minor diminished diminished augmented augmented	Only one of the white-key fifths is not _____. Thus, only one of the white-key triads is not _____ or _____. This triad is _____ in quality because its fifth is _____. The _____ triad cannot be written exclusively with white keys because accidentals are required to spell the _____ fifth.

Solution 6	Problem 6
(in any order within each measure) major minor diminished 	Write the white-key triads. major minor diminished

Solution 7	Problem 7
cannot chromatically	When using accidentals to alter notes in a triad, the note names (can)(cannot) be changed. Thus, any part of a triad must be changed (chromatically)(diatonically).

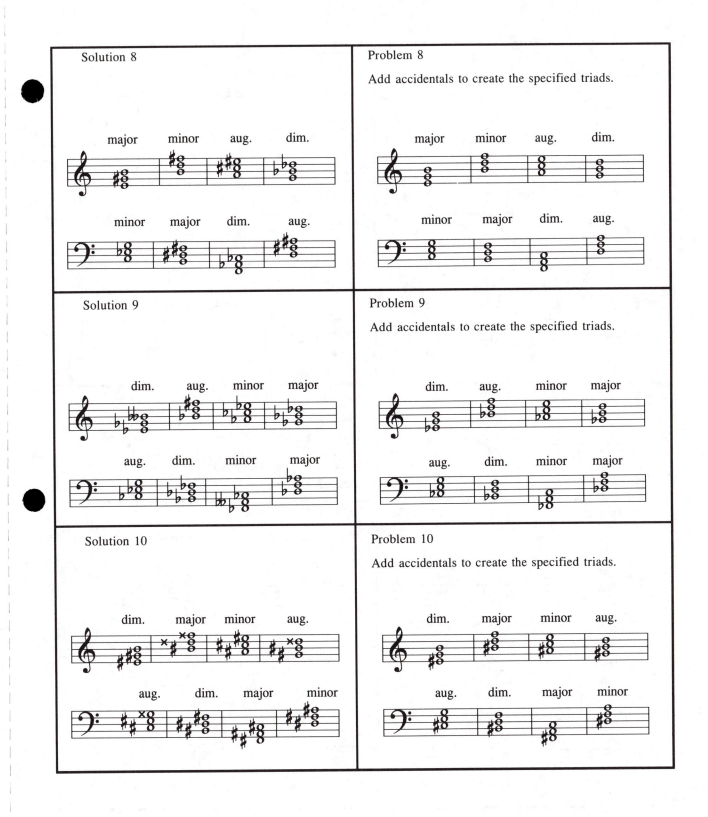

Solution 8

Problem 8

Add accidentals to create the specified triads.

Solution 9

Problem 9

Add accidentals to create the specified triads.

Solution 10

Problem 10

Add accidentals to create the specified triads.

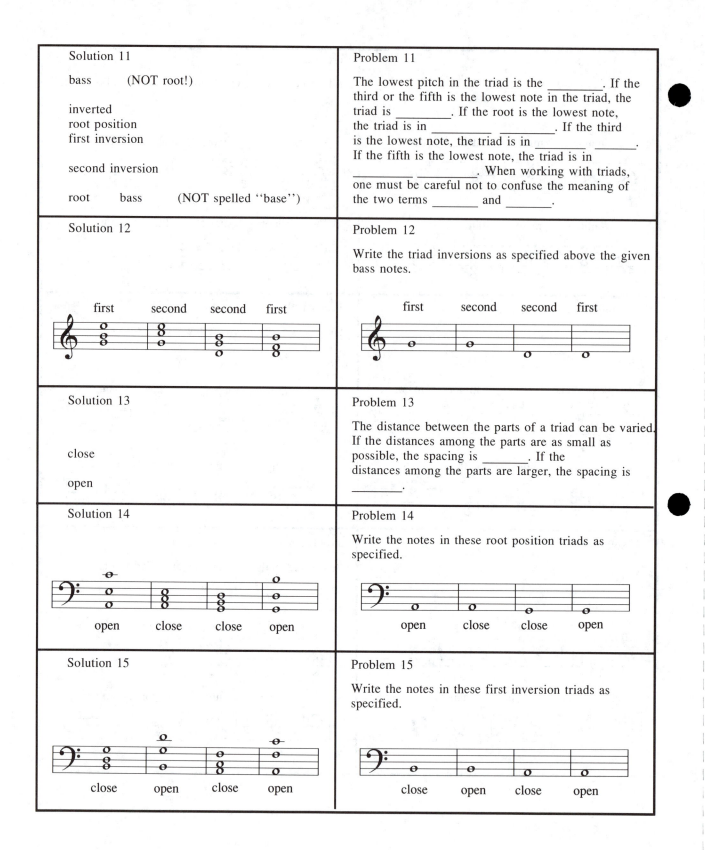

Solution 11

bass   (NOT root!)

inverted
root position
first inversion

second inversion

root   bass   (NOT spelled "base")

Problem 11

The lowest pitch in the triad is the _____. If the third or the fifth is the lowest note in the triad, the triad is _____. If the root is the lowest note, the triad is in _____ _____. If the third is the lowest note, the triad is in _____ _____. If the fifth is the lowest note, the triad is in _____ _____. When working with triads, one must be careful not to confuse the meaning of the two terms _____ and _____.

Solution 12

first   second   second   first

Problem 12

Write the triad inversions as specified above the given bass notes.

first   second   second   first

Solution 13

close

open

Problem 13

The distance between the parts of a triad can be varied. If the distances among the parts are as small as possible, the spacing is _____. If the distances among the parts are larger, the spacing is _____.

Solution 14

open   close   close   open

Problem 14

Write the notes in these root position triads as specified.

open   close   close   open

Solution 15

close   open   close   open

Problem 15

Write the notes in these first inversion triads as specified.

close   open   close   open

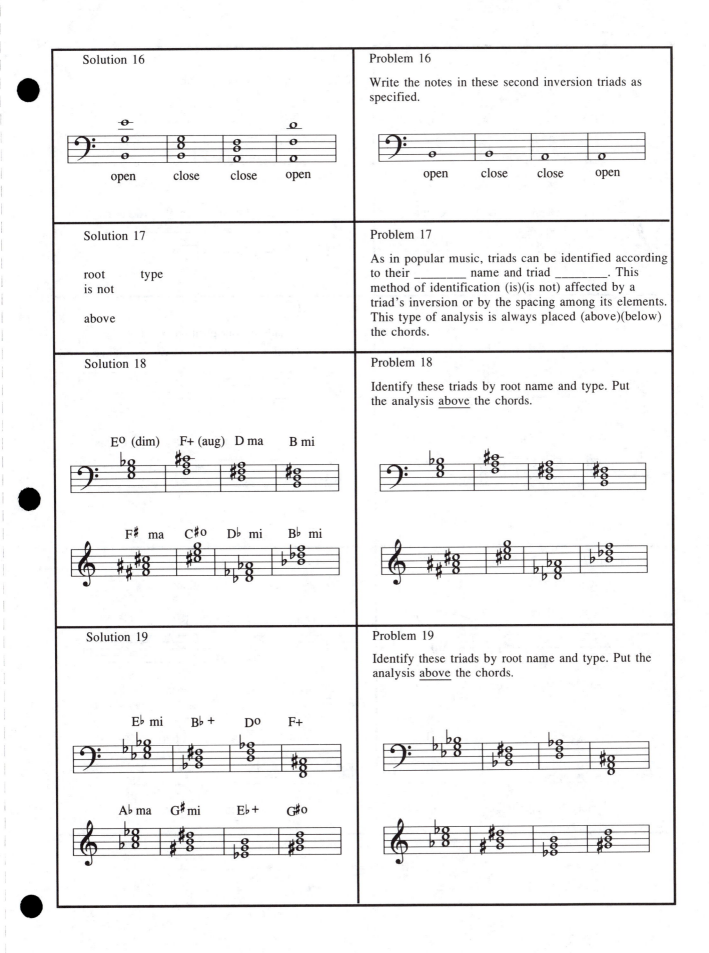

Solution 16

open   close   close   open

Problem 16

Write the notes in these second inversion triads as specified.

open   close   close   open

Solution 17

root   type
is not

above

Problem 17

As in popular music, triads can be identified according to their _____ name and triad _____. This method of identification (is)(is not) affected by a triad's inversion or by the spacing among its elements. This type of analysis is always placed (above)(below) the chords.

Solution 18

E° (dim)   F+ (aug)   D ma   B mi

F♯ ma   C♯°   D♭ mi   B♭ mi

Problem 18

Identify these triads by root name and type. Put the analysis <u>above</u> the chords.

Solution 19

E♭ mi   B♭ +   D°   F+

A♭ ma   G♯ mi   E♭ +   G♯°

Problem 19

Identify these triads by root name and type. Put the analysis <u>above</u> the chords.

171

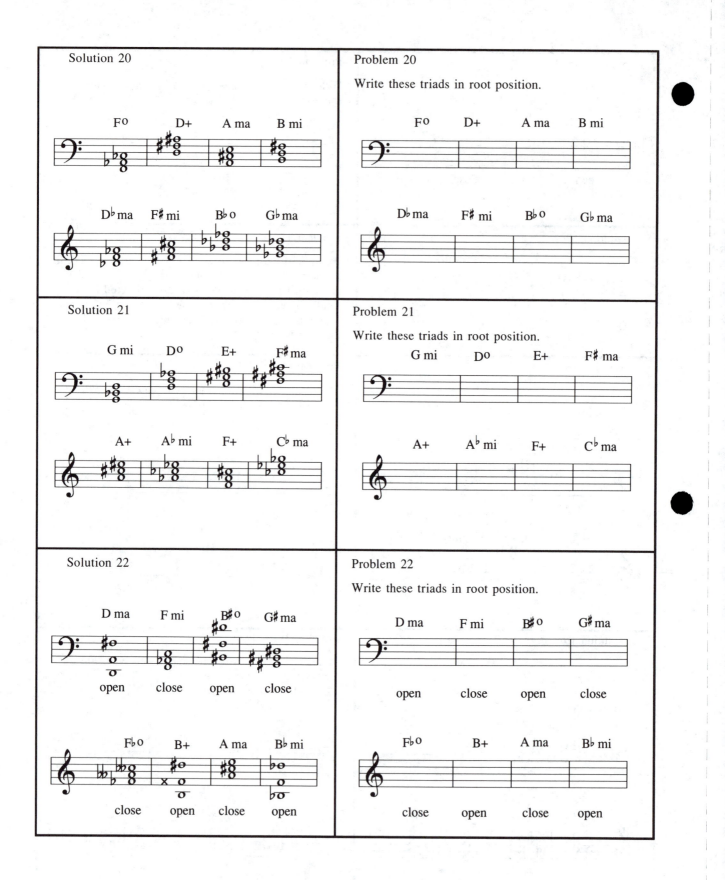

172

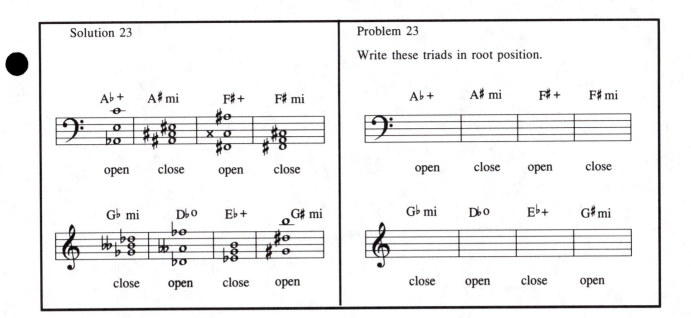

Solution 23

Ab+   A# mi   F#+   F# mi

open   close   open   close

Gb mi   Db o   Eb+   G# mi

close   open   close   open

Problem 23

Write these triads in root position.

Ab+   A# mi   F#+   F# mi

open   close   open   close

Gb mi   Db o   Eb+   G# mi

close   open   close   open

HARMONY APPLICATIONS

1. Sing-spell the primary triads in each scale in the major circle of fifths. Arpeggiate the chords in root position, close spacing as shown below.

    SAMPLE

C	E	G	E	C	F	A	C	A	F	G	B	D	B	G	C	E	G	E	C
1	3	5	3	1	4	6	1	6	4	5	7	2	7	5	1	3	5	3	1

2. Sing-spell the primary triads in each scale in the <u>harmonic</u> minor circle of fifths (the leading tone creates a major chord on the fifth step of the scale). Arpeggiate the chords in root position, closed spacing.

3. Play exercises 1 and 2 on a keyboard instrument.

4. Sing-spell the following above any note in the chromatic scale. Write them on music paper.

    a. Root position, closed spacing, major, minor, augmented, and diminished triads.

    b. First inversion, closed spacing, major and minor triads.

    c. Second inversion, closed spacing, major and minor triads.

5. Sing-spell the following below any note in the chromatic scale. Use the piano as a back-up to check your accuracy.

    a. Major and minor triads, closed spacing, using the root as the top (starting) note.

    b. Major and minor triads, closed spacing, using the third as the starting note.

    c. Major and minor triads, closed spacing, using the fifth as the starting note.

    NOTE: Any of the above exercises work well in group study.

9 INTERVAL TEXTURE, HARMONY: PART II

OVERVIEW

The *Interval Path* continues with the first part of a two-part series on intervals in texture. Ideas about intervals discussed in the chapter include consonance and dissonance, harmonic series and intervals, affect of register and spacing on intervals, tension patterns, and melodic satellites of focal intervals. The *Harmony Path* continues with the second of a two-part series on triads. Information is included on the harmonic series as the "chord of nature." The harmonic series provides models for spacing and doubling, and helps explain the effects of various spacings and doublings in different registers. The chapter concludes with an introduction to chord analysis and the functional grouping of chords in a key by type.

INTERVALS

Interval Inversion Pairs

An interval and its inversion are closely related. Inversions are octave complements of the original interval (original + inversion − common tone = octave). An interval and its inversion have similar sound effects. Thinking about intervals in octave complement pairs is a useful memory aid. Inversion pairs are

unison (octave)
minor second (major seventh)   **major second** (minor seventh)
minor third (major sixth)   **major third** (minor sixth)
P4 (P5)   **Tritone** ($^{+}4$, $^{o}5$)

A Smaller List of Intervals

As suggested in the previous list, the number of interval categories can be reduced by combining the major and minor intervals into larger family clusters. Thus, "seconds" include major and minor seconds and their inversions. "Thirds" include major and minor thirds and their inversions. These groupings help one organize information about the nature of intervals and their relationships to other intervals.

Consonant-Dissonant Continuum

Harmonic intervals can be placed in an order according to differences in their relative tension. This forms a **continuum** (graduated scale) ranging from low tension (**consonant**) to high tension (**dissonant**) intervals.

Example 1. Consonant-Dissonant Continuum

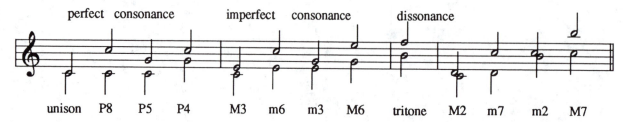

perfect consonance				imperfect consonance				dissonance				
unison	P8	P5	P4	M3	m6	m3	M6	tritone	M2	m7	m2	M7

Intervals in the Harmonic Series

The **harmonic series** is a natural phenomenon of great importance to all aspects of music. First indications of the importance of the harmonic series were documented observations of the harmonic series first made in ancient Greece. Pythagorus, also famous for founding geometry, did a great deal of research using a single string device called a *monochord*. Today, string, guitar, and harp players produce "harmonics" (pure, high pitched tones) by touching the strings at nodes (points at which the string divides into vibrating segments). This causes the strings to vibrate in fractions (halves, thirds, fourths, fifths, and so on). The next example represents a string vibrating as a whole, and in halves and quarters simultaneously. The nodes are located at the division points. A string player can be asked to demonstrate string harmonics for the class.

Example 2: String Vibrating Simultaneously as a Whole, in Halves, and in Quarters

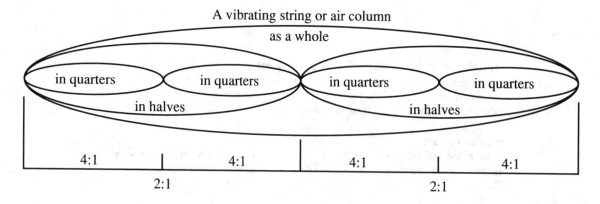

The fundamental pitch is caused by the string or column of air vibrating as a whole. Partial refers to "partial vibration" (a string or air column vibrating in segments rather than as a whole). The open tones on brass instruments lie in the pattern of the harmonic series. A brass player can be asked to demonstrate brass harmonics for the class.

Some sources call the note above the **fundamental** the first overtone or first partial instead of the second element in the harmonic series. These terms do not support the practice of numbering harmonics to express vibration ratios. In this book, the terms "fundamental" and "first harmonic" refer to the same part of the harmonic series. "First overtone" and "first partial" refer to the second harmonic. Two informative sources on the harmonic series and the acoustics of music are *The Acoustical Foundations of Music* by J. Backus and *The Musicians Guide to Acoustics* by M. Campbell and C. Greated. Campbell and Greated do not use the term "overtone" and carefully specify that "partial" has no implications regarding harmonic series ratios.

The harmonic series affects every pitched sound and combination of sounds in music. It is a factor in the construction of musical instruments (electronic or acoustical), sound reinforcement systems, concert halls, and other performance environments. You can hear some of the harmonics by completing the following experiment. (1) Depress (without sounding) a large group of piano keys with your right forearm. (2) Strike a very low note several times. (3) Listen for the after ring. The notes you hear are the undampened strings vibrating in sympathy with the harmonics of the notes you played.

The harmonic series influences our ideas on intonation, balance, timbre, and scoring. Changing standards for interval and chord usage through history roughly parallel an expanding awareness of the intervals in the harmonic series. The harmonic series is one of the roots of the science of sound (**acoustics**) and the psychology of musical perception. A detailed study of these fields reveals just how basic the harmonic series phenomenon is to all aspects of music making.

Any pitch in the audible spectrum can be the fundamental pitch of a harmonic series. Every harmonic series displays the same fixed pattern of intervals. Interval size gradually decreases from an octave to a minor second in the first sixteen harmonics. In harmonics 16 through 32, interval size gradually decreases from a minor second to a quarter tone (half of a half step). The pattern continues upward past the limits of human hearing, intervals becoming progressively smaller but never fully reaching a unison. Attempting to find a unison between adjacent harmonics is like trying to find the last decimal in a transcendental number like π (Pi).

The next example illustrates a harmonic series. The pitch C is the fundamental of this series, its root and lowest note. The fundamental is indicated by the numeral 1. Octaves of this note are numbered 2, 4, 8, and so on. These numbers are very important mathematically because they also represent **vibration ratios** among the notes in the series. For example, the notes in an octave can be represented by a 1:2 vibration ratio because the top note vibrates at twice the frequency of the bottom note (a string vibrating in halves). A double octave can be represented by a 1:4 ratio because the top note vibrates at four times the frequency of the bottom note (a string vibrating in quarters). Some pitches in the harmonic series do not match the tuning of the notes in the chromatic scale and can only be approximated by standard notation. In the next example, these "out-of-tune" notes are indicated by black notes.

Example 3. Harmonic Series on C

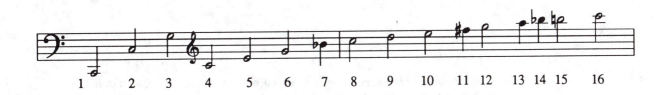

The Harmonic Series and Dissonance of Intervals

The order that intervals appear in the harmonic series closely resembles the order of the intervals in the **consonant-dissonant continuum** (see example 2). The lowest intervals in the harmonic series are the least dissonant intervals in the continuum. Notice that the roots of P5 (P4) and Ma3 (mi6) are always the same pitch (in higher octaves) as the fundamental of the harmonic series.

Example 4. Intervals in the Harmonic Series

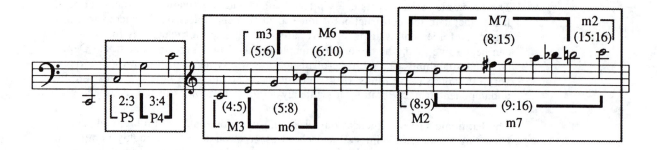

The tritone (°5 or +4) was not mentioned in the previous example. Unlike the other intervals, a close match for the sound of the tritone played on a piano cannot be found in the harmonic series. One pitch only roughly matches a note in the chromatic scale (see the 11th harmonic). This may explain why the tritone is melodically unstable and difficult to classify. The tritone has been treated as an enigma for centuries. Its ancient nickname is *Diabolus in Musica*, the Devil in Music. In a more favorable light, we can view the tritone as nature's "transcendental" interval because we cannot determine its last decimal in a musical sense.

Register and Spacing Effects

The tension of a given harmonic interval seems to decrease as it is moved to higher **registers.** In the next example, a minor second and its inversion seem to have the least amount of "bite" in high registers. This effect changes as the intervals are moved downward. Listen to the example. Can you hear a change of tension? Can you see a connection between this change and a pattern in the harmonic series?

Example 5. Effect of Register

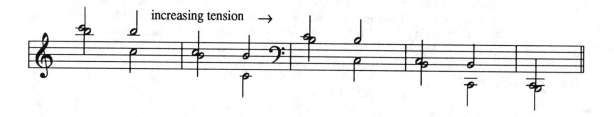

Interval tension decreases as distance is added between the notes of an harmonic interval. Listen to the next example. Can you hear a change in tension? Is there a connection between this change and the pattern of the harmonic series?

Example 6. Effect of Spacing

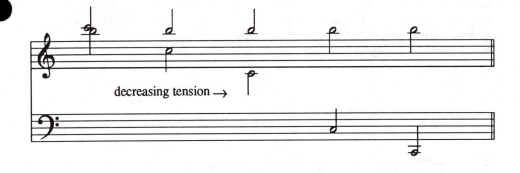

In a series of harmonic intervals, different interval tensions can be arranged in patterns. In the next example, intervals with like or similar tension properties were arranged to create **tension norms.** A *norm* is a steady or fixed state.

Example 7. Harmonic Interval Tension Norms

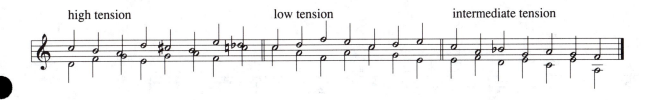

In the next example, interval tensions were arranged to create a **tension crescendo,** diminuendo, and **wave.**

Example 8. Tension Dynamic Patterns

The tension changes in the previous example were gradual because intervals moved to adjacent intervals in the consonant-dissonant continuum (example 2). Tension change is abrupt if an interval in the continuum is skipped.

Example 9. Abrupt Tension Changes

179

Interval Satellites   In a stream of harmonic intervals, notes in an interval can be decorated by melodic **satellites.** In the next example, the first measure in each line represents a basic movement of harmonic intervals. The rest of each line illustrates ways to decorate the basic pattern. In two-part music, dissonant intervals are treated as satellites. P4 is treated as a dissonance in two-part music. If there is no dissonance, rhythmically weaker notes are considered satellites.

Example 10. Interval Satellites

CHECKPOINT I (All Interval Review)

1. Explain these terms:

interval inversion pairs   dissonant interval

consonant interval   imperfect consonant (see examples 1 and 4)

perfect consonant (see examples 1 and 4)   acoustics

harmonic series   fundamental pitch

vibration ratio   tension wave

register effect   spacing effect

tension norm   tension crescendo

interval satellite   consonant-dissonant continuum

2. Self-help Problems.

Solution 1	Problem 1
complementary inversion (complement) common dissonance (or tension)	An interval and its inversion form a _____ pair. An interval and its _____ have certain characteristics of sound in _____. Intervals can be placed in a graduated series of increasing _____.
Solution 2	Problem 2
sound (or acoustics, or music) fundamental harmonics ratios decreases perfect imperfect	The harmonic series is to _____ what the spectrum is to optics. The lowest pitch in the harmonic series is called the _____. The parts of the series are called _____. The numbering of the notes in the harmonic series also represents vibration _____ between pitches. Starting at the fundamental pitch, interval size _____ as one moves higher in the series. The intervals included in harmonics 1 through 4 belong to the category of _____ consonance. The intervals included in harmonics 4 through 6 belong to the category of _____ consonance.

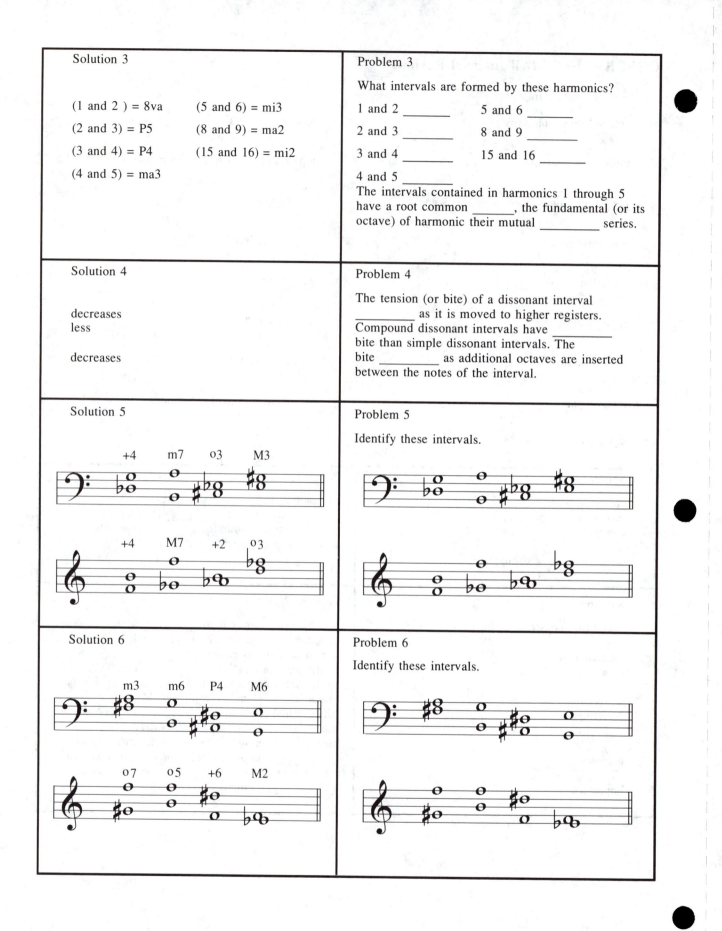

Solution 3

(1 and 2) = 8va   (5 and 6) = mi3

(2 and 3) = P5   (8 and 9) = ma2

(3 and 4) = P4   (15 and 16) = mi2

(4 and 5) = ma3

Problem 3

What intervals are formed by these harmonics?

1 and 2 _____   5 and 6 _____

2 and 3 _____   8 and 9 _____

3 and 4 _____   15 and 16 _____

4 and 5 _____

The intervals contained in harmonics 1 through 5 have a root common _____, the fundamental (or its octave) of harmonic their mutual _____ series.

Solution 4

decreases
less

decreases

Problem 4

The tension (or bite) of a dissonant interval _____ as it is moved to higher registers. Compound dissonant intervals have _____ bite than simple dissonant intervals. The bite _____ as additional octaves are inserted between the notes of the interval.

Solution 5

Problem 5

Identify these intervals.

Solution 6

Problem 6

Identify these intervals.

Solution 7

Problem 7

Write these intervals above the given notes.

Solution 8

Problem 8

Write these intervals above the given notes.

Solution 9

Problem 9

Write these intervals below the given notes.

Solution 13

Problem 13

Circle the interval satellites.

Solution 14

low tension

abrupt changes, tension contrasts

Problem 14

Identify these interval tension patterns.

Solution 15

wave (high-low-high)

decrease (high-to-low)

Problem 15

Identify these interval tension patterns.

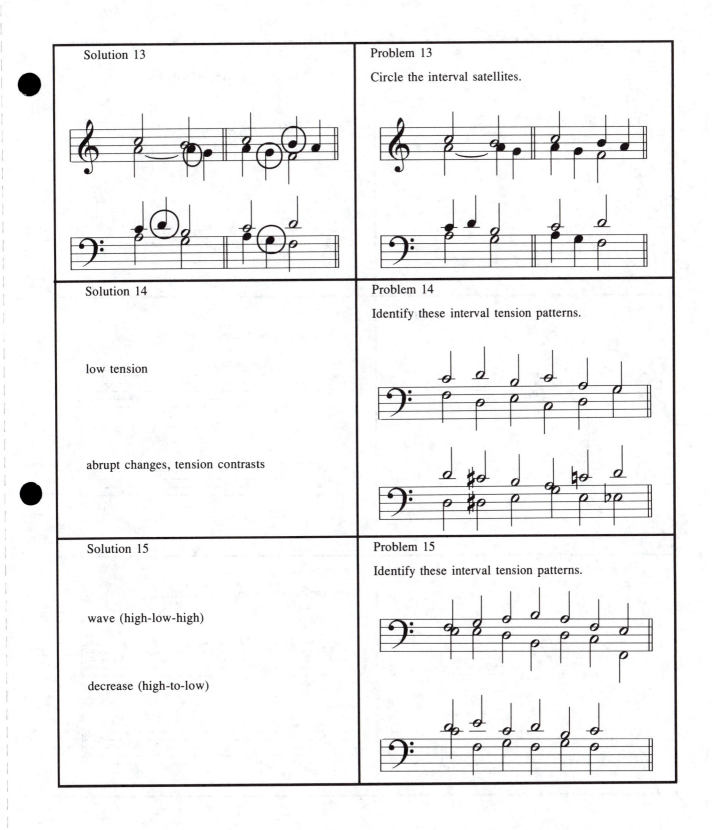

185

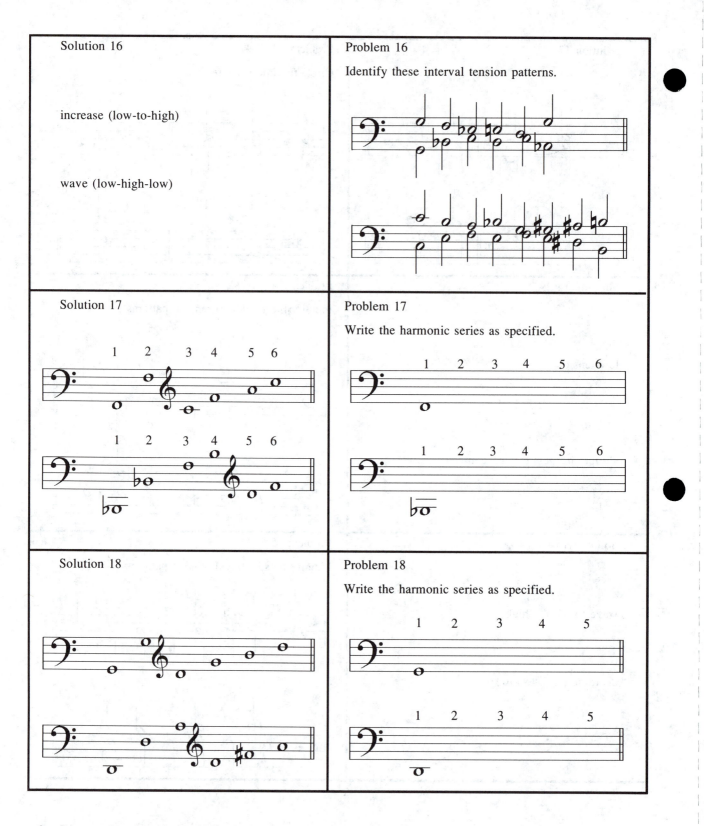

Solution 16

increase (low-to-high)

wave (low-high-low)

Problem 16

Identify these interval tension patterns.

Solution 17

Problem 17

Write the harmonic series as specified.

Solution 18

Problem 18

Write the harmonic series as specified.

3. Discuss the advantages of knowing the
    a. order of intervals in the harmonic series
    b. pairings and larger groupings of intervals and their inversions
    c. relative tension, ordering of intervals according to relative tension
    d. affects of spacing and register on interval tension

APPLICATIONS

1. Make a chart of the consonant-dissonant continuum of simple intervals.

2. Write an harmonic series through the 16th harmonic on the fundamentals G and E♭. Show the first time each interval (simple) of the dissonance-consonance continuum appears in the series. Give the vibration ratio of each interval.

3. Be able to write and sing-spell any simple interval above or below any note in the chromatic scale.

HARMONY

Chords and the Harmonic Series

The **harmonic series** is sometimes called the **chord of nature** because it is a natural phenomenon in the form of a chord. In the next example, the first few harmonics form a major triad. Notice the distribution of the triad parts in the example. How many roots, thirds, and fifths of the major triad are present here?

Example 11. The First Six Harmonics

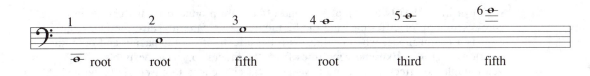

Doubling

The recurrence of a chord part in another voice or in another octave is called **doubling**. The distribution and recurrence of chord parts in the harmonic series is a model for doubling in scoring writing. In music literature (as in the harmonic series), the root is the most frequently doubled chord tone. The third is the least doubled part of the triad. Unless special effects are sought, composers and arrangers usually score chords so the larger intervals are at the bottom and smaller intervals are at the top.

Doubling, Spacing, and Register

Doubling, spacing, and **register** are interrelated factors that determine the sound effects of a particular chord. In a broad sense, the sound effect of a chord can be predicted by how the distribution of its parts matches or deviates from the harmonic series pattern. The next example shows how the sound of a chord is effected by closing the low spacing. Sound these chords and compare them to the harmonic series chord given at the beginning of the example.

Example 12. The Harmonic Series Model (harmonics 1 through 6)

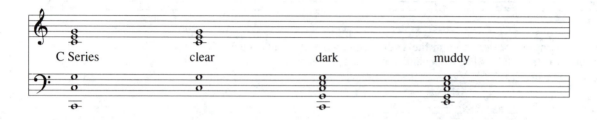

The next example shows how the sound of a chord is affected by increasing the distances between high voices. Compare these effects to the harmonic series chord given at the beginning of the example.

Example 13. The Harmonic Series Model (harmonics 1 through 16)

As shown in the last two examples, sound effects are produced by the chords in a score resembling or differing from the harmonic series pattern. Thus, the harmonic series is a useful model when dealing with the effects of chord spacing and doubling in various registers. Extreme departures from the model can have desirable effects even though the effect may create new technical challenges in ensemble blend and tuning.

Beethoven used closely spaced, low register triads to create a drum-like, rhythmic effect.

Example 14. Compact Low Spacing from Piano Sonata No. 21 in C major Beethoven

Allegro con brio

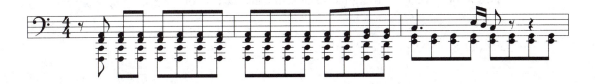

Functional Analysis

Functional analysis is a way to indicate information about the inversion of a chord and its role in a key. This is indicated by various combinations of Roman and Arabic numbers. Chord inversion is indicated by Arabic numerals that show the interval between the bass and other parts of the chord. These numerals always refer to simple intervals. Compound intervals in a chord are identified with simple interval expressions. Doubled tones are not indicated by this analysis. Triad inversion is determined by the part of the chord in the bass voice.

Example 15. Analysis of Chord Position

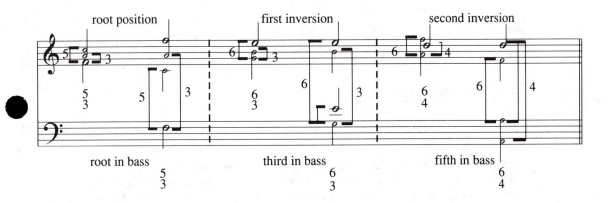

As shown in the next example, the interval analysis of triads can be **abbreviated.** In analysis "shorthand," no numbers are needed to indicate root position and only one number is used to indicate first inversion. The analysis of second inversion is not abbreviated.

Example 16. Analysis Abbreviation

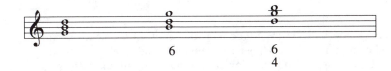

189

A chord's role in a key is indicated by Roman numerals. The Roman numerals show which scale step is being used as the root of the chord. The functional names of the scale steps are given in the next example. If a triad root is located on the first step of a scale, it is called a one chord because it is indicated by a Roman I. It can also be called a tonic triad (by using the scale step name instead of the scale step number).

Example 17. Functional Names of Scale Steps

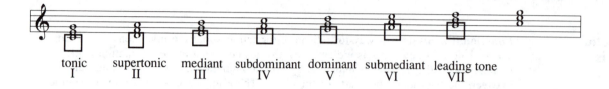

| tonic | supertonic | mediant | subdominant | dominant | submediant | leading tone |
| I | II | III | IV | V | VI | VII |

Function Names   The prefixes **super** and **sub** refer to the position of a note above (super) or below (sub) the tonic pitch. The **supertonic** is a whole step <u>above</u> tonic. The **subtonic** note is a whole step <u>below</u> tonic in natural minor. The **leading tone** is a half step below tonic as found in major, harmonic minor, and melodic minor.

Example 18. Supertonic and Subtonic

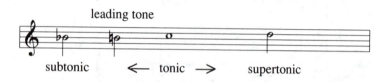

In the next example, the **dominant** is a fifth above tonic and the **subdominant** is a fifth below tonic. The **mediant** lies midway between the tonic and the dominant (a third *above* the tonic). The **submediant** lies midway between the tonic and the subdominant (a third *below* the tonic).

Examples 19. Subdominant and Submediant

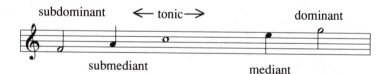

Roman numerals can be used to indicate triad type and triad root. In the next example, lower case numerals indicate minor triads. Upper case numerals indicate major triads. Diminished is indicated by adding an "o" to a lower case numeral. Augmented is indicated by adding a plus sign (+) to an upper case numeral.

190

Example 20. Triad Type Indication

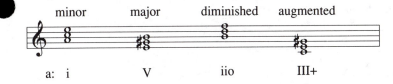

The next example shows how these signs are used to complete a functional analysis of a chord progression. Notice the amount of information about each chord that is communicated through each sign.

Example 21. Functional Analysis

C: I   IV6   I   V6   I 6   vi   iii   ii 6   I 6   V   I
        4   4   4

Chord Color Groups, Primary and Secondary Triads

In major keys, the major triads are I, IV, and V, and are called **primary triads**. Chords in this group can be easily arranged to promote focus on the tonic pitch. In major, the minor chords are vi, ii, and iii. The chords in this group are called **secondary triads.** In a major key, the secondary group of triads lies a diatonic third below the primary group of triads. The secondary triads can be easily arranged to promote focus on the sixth step of the scale (the submediant, the tonic of relative minor).

Example 22. Triad Color Groups in Major

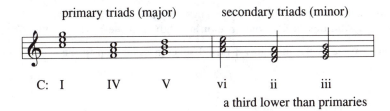

Chord Color Groups in Minor

In natural minor, the **primary triads** are minor—i, iv, and v. The major chords are III, VI, and VII (the secondary triads in minor). In natural minor, the major chords lie a diatonic third above the primary triads. The chords in this group can be arranged to place focus on the third step of the scale (the mediant, the tonic of relative major).

191

Example 23. Triad Color Groups in Natural Minor

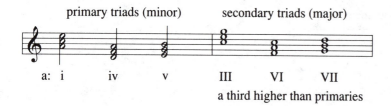

primary triads (minor)　　　secondary triads (major)

a:　i　　　iv　　　v　　　III　　　VI　　　VII

a third higher than primaries

A major key and its relative natural minor share a single diminished triad.

Example 24. The Diminished Triad in Major and Relative Minor

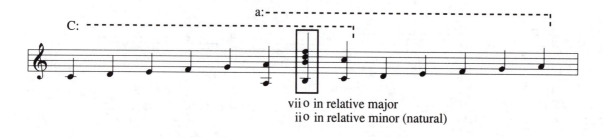

C:　　　　　　　　　　　　　　　a:

vii o in relative major
ii o in relative minor (natural)

In all the forms of minor, any chord not included in the primary group is regarded as a secondary chord. Since the leading tone chord can be used in place of the dominant chord, it (viio) can function as either a primary or secondary chord in major or minor.

Example 25. Diminished Triads in Major and Minor Keys

natural　　melodic
or　　　　　or
harmonic　harmonic　　melodic

C:　vii o　　c:　ii o　　　vii o　　　vi o

The accidentals used in harmonic and melodic minor keys increase the chord color possibilities. The added possibilities in harmonic minor are shown in the next example. "#$\hat{7}$" written above a chord indicates a raised seventh scale step in the chord.

Example 26. Effect of Accidentals on Chord Colors in Harmonic Minor

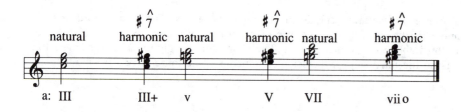

　　　　　#$\hat{7}$　　　　　　#$\hat{7}$　　　　　　#$\hat{7}$
natural　harmonic　natural　harmonic　natural　harmonic

a:　III　　III+　　v　　　V　　VII　　　vii o

The added possibilities in melodic minor are shown in the next example. "#6̂" written above a chord indicates a raised sixth scale step in the chord. Since melodic minor includes two altered steps, #6̂ and #7̂, the altered chords of harmonic minor are also available to melodic minor.

Example 27. Affect of Accidentals on Chord Colors in Melodic Minor

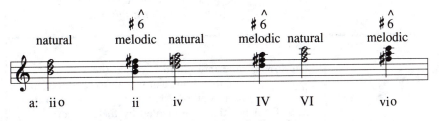

*III+ is only available in harmonic and melodic minor.

CHECKPOINT II (Triads)

1. Explain these terms:

harmonic series and spacing	chord of nature
harmonic series and doubling	harmonic series and register
harmonic	functional analysis
inversion analysis	inversion abbreviation
tonic	doubling
overtone	subtonic
mediant	subdominant
supertonic	dominant
leading tone	submediant
chord color groups	primary triads
secondary triads	natural minor
altered minor	harmonic minor
melodic minor	

193

2. Self-help Problems.

Solution 1	Problem 1
functional root scale intervals	The use of Roman and Arabic numerals to analyze chords is called _____ analysis. Roman numerals identify the position of the chord _____ in _____ degrees. Arabic numerals indicate what _____ are present above the bass.
Solution 2 bass Any root 5 (and) 3 third 6 (and) 3 fifth 6 (and) 4	**Problem 2** The lowest note in a chord is called the _____. _____ part of the chord can be the lowest note in the chord. In a root position triad, the _____ is in the bass. Root position is indicated by the numbers _____ and _____. In a first inversion triad, the _____ is in the bass. First inversion is indicated by the numbers _____ and _____. In a second inversion triad, the _____ is in the bass. Second inversion is indicated by the numbers _____ and _____.
Solution 3 tonic super tonic mediant submediant subdominant dominant	**Problem 3** Supply the functional names of the scale degrees. step name step name 1 2 3 6 4 5
Solution 4 tonic leading tone subtonic	**Problem 4** The term "keynote" has the same meaning as the term _____. If the seventh steps lies a half step below the keynote, it is called the _____. If the seventh step lies a whole step below the keynote, it is called the _____.

194

Solution 5 major minor augmented diminished	Problem 5 Special signs indicate triad color (quality). An upper case Roman numeral indicates _____. A lower case Roman numeral indicates _____. A "+" added to an upper case Roman numeral indicates _____. A "o" added to a lower case Roman numeral indicates _____.

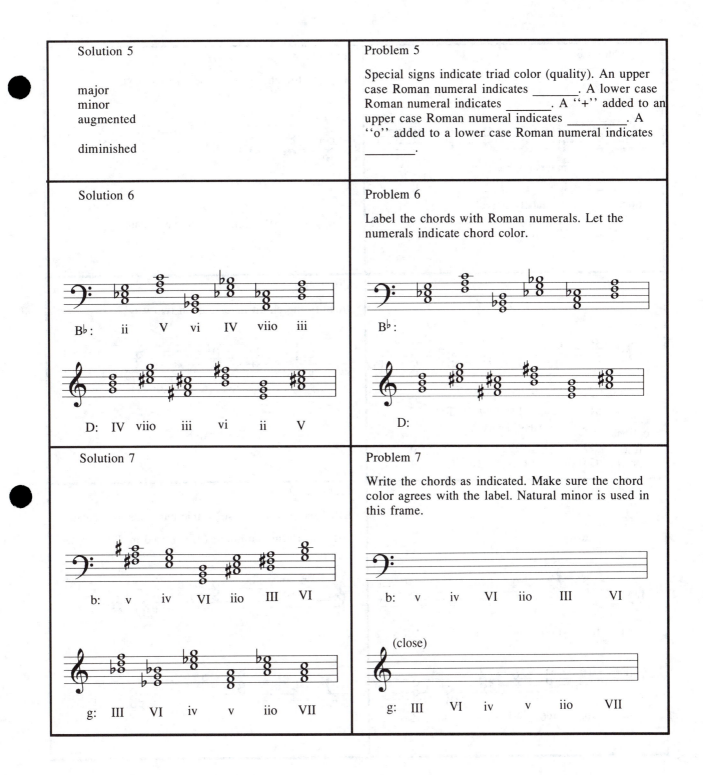

Solution 6

Bb: ii V vi IV viio iii

D: IV viio iii vi ii V

Problem 6

Label the chords with Roman numerals. Let the numerals indicate chord color.

Bb:

D:

Solution 7

b: v iv VI iio III VI

g: III VI iv v iio VII

Problem 7

Write the chords as indicated. Make sure the chord color agrees with the label. Natural minor is used in this frame.

b: v iv VI iio III VI

(close)

g: III VI iv v iio VII

Solution 8

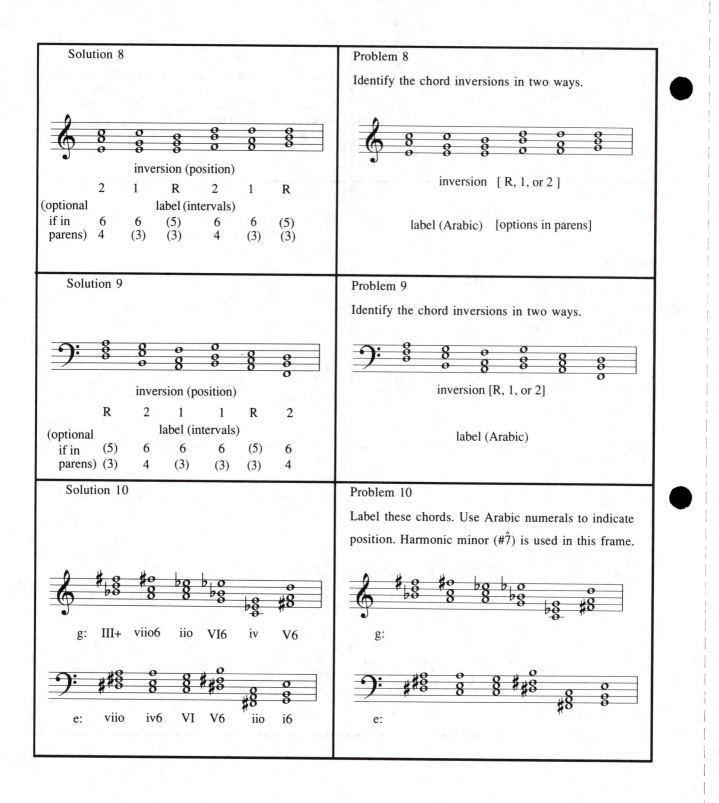

inversion (position)

	2	1	R	2	1	R
(optional			label (intervals)			
if in	6	6	(5)	6	6	(5)
parens)	4	(3)	(3)	4	(3)	(3)

Problem 8

Identify the chord inversions in two ways.

inversion   [R, 1, or 2]

label (Arabic)   [options in parens]

Solution 9

inversion (position)

	R	2	1	1	R	2
(optional			label (intervals)			
if in	(5)	6	6	6	(5)	6
parens)	(3)	4	(3)	(3)	(3)	4

Problem 9

Identify the chord inversions in two ways.

inversion [R, 1, or 2]

label (Arabic)

Solution 10

g: III+   viio6   iio   VI6   iv   V6

e: viio   iv6   VI   V6   iio   i6

Problem 10

Label these chords. Use Arabic numerals to indicate position. Harmonic minor (#$\hat{7}$) is used in this frame.

g:

e:

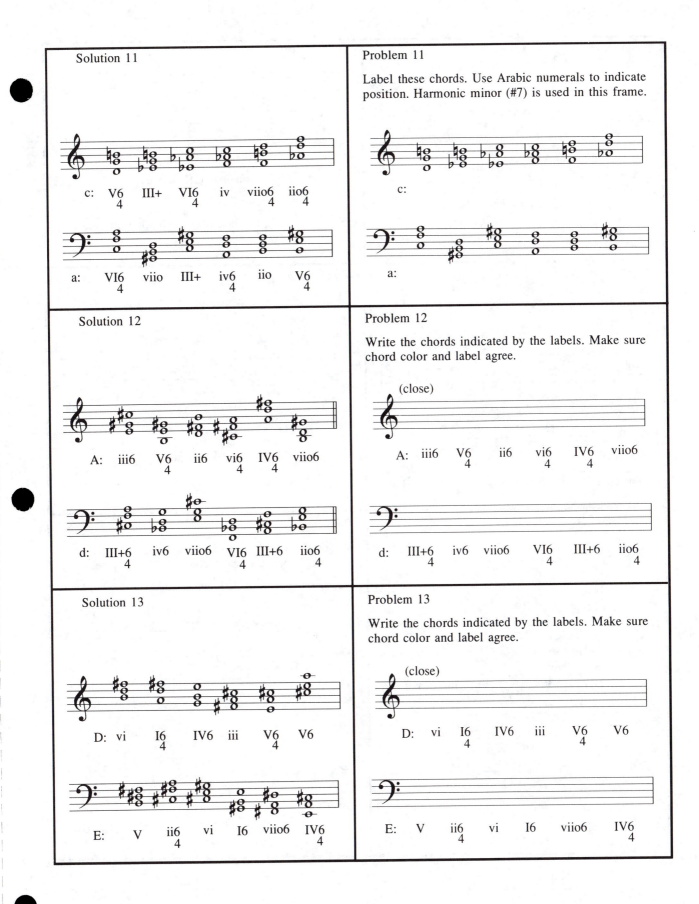

Solution 11

c: V6/4 III+ VI6/4 iv viio6/4 iio6/4

a: VI6/4 viio III+ iv6/4 iio V6/4

Problem 11

Label these chords. Use Arabic numerals to indicate position. Harmonic minor (#7) is used in this frame.

c:

a:

Solution 12

A: iii6 V6/4 ii6 vi6/4 IV6/4 viio6

d: III+6/4 iv6 viio6 VI6/4 III+6 iio6/4

Problem 12

Write the chords indicated by the labels. Make sure chord color and label agree.

(close)

A: iii6 V6/4 ii6 vi6/4 IV6/4 viio6

d: III+6/4 iv6 viio6 VI6/4 III+6 iio6/4

Solution 13

D: vi I6/4 IV6 iii V6/4 V6

E: V ii6/4 vi I6 viio6 IV6/4

Problem 13

Write the chords indicated by the labels. Make sure chord color and label agree.

(close)

D: vi I6/4 IV6 iii V6/4 V6

E: V ii6/4 vi I6 viio6 IV6/4

197

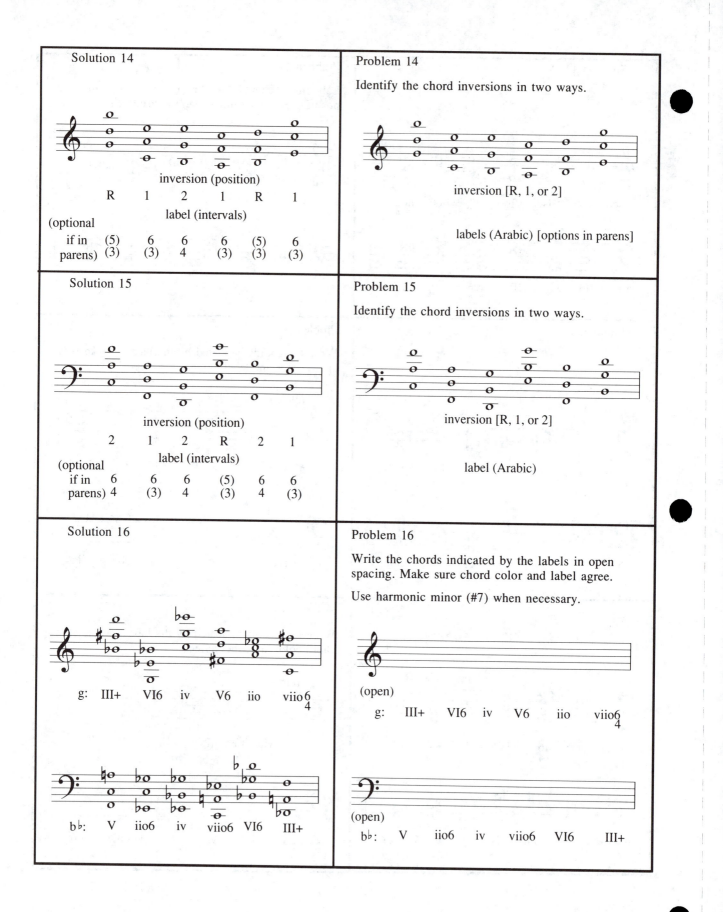

Solution 14

inversion (position)

| R | 1 | 2 | 1 | R | 1 |

label (intervals)

(optional
if in   (5) 6   6   6   (5) 6
parens)   (3) (3) 4   (3) (3) (3)

Problem 14

Identify the chord inversions in two ways.

inversion [R, 1, or 2]

labels (Arabic) [options in parens]

Solution 15

inversion (position)

| 2 | 1 | 2 | R | 2 | 1 |

label (intervals)

(optional
if in   6   6   6   (5) 6   6
parens) 4   (3) 4   (3) 4   (3)

Problem 15

Identify the chord inversions in two ways.

inversion [R, 1, or 2]

label (Arabic)

Solution 16

g: III+   VI6   iv   V6   iio   viio6
                                       4

bb: V   iio6   iv   viio6   VI6   III+

Problem 16

Write the chords indicated by the labels in open spacing. Make sure chord color and label agree.

Use harmonic minor (#7) when necessary.

(open)

g: III+   VI6   iv   V6   iio   viio6
                                       4

(open)

bb: V   iio6   iv   viio6   VI6   III+

198

Solution 17

f: VI6   viio   iv6/4   III+6/4   iio   V6/4

b: iio6/4   III+6/4   viio   i   iv6/4   V6/4

Problem 17

Write the chords indicated by the labels in open spacing. Use harmonic minor (#$\hat{7}$) when necessary.

(open)

f: VI6   viio   iv6/4   III+6/4   iio   V6/4

(open)

b: iio6/4   III+6/4   viio   i   iv6/4   V6/4

Solution 18

F: IV   viio6   iii6/4   vi   ii6/4   V6   I

Problem 18

Label the chords. Let the chord signs show both chord color and inversion.

F:

Solution 19

e: V   ii6   III6/4   IV6   vio   viio6   i6

Problem 19

Label the chords. Use #$\hat{6}$ or #$\hat{7}$ when necessary.

e:

Solution 20

A♭: vi   V   ii6   viio6/4   iii6/4   IV6   I

Problem 20

Label the chords.

A♭:

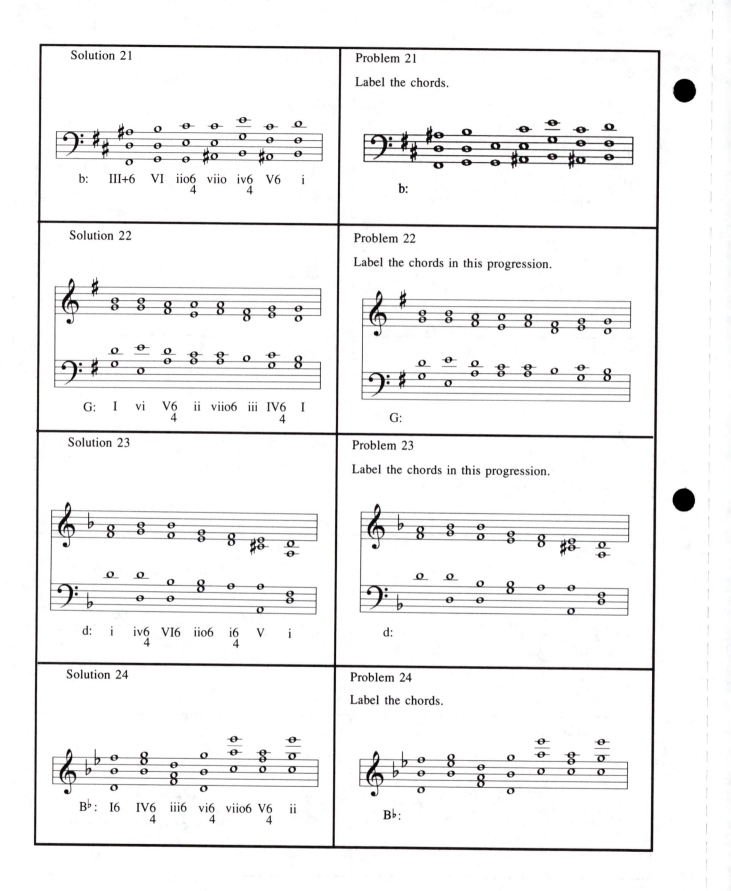

Solution 21

b: III+6   VI   iio6   viio   iv6   V6   i
                      4   4

Problem 21

Label the chords.

b:

Solution 22

G: I   vi   V6   ii   viio6   iii   IV6   I
                 4   4

Problem 22

Label the chords in this progression.

G:

Solution 23

d: i   iv6   VI6   iio6   i6   V   i
            4   4

Problem 23

Label the chords in this progression.

d:

Solution 24

Bb: I6   IV6   iii6   vi6   viio6   V6   ii
             4   4   4

Problem 24

Label the chords.

Bb:

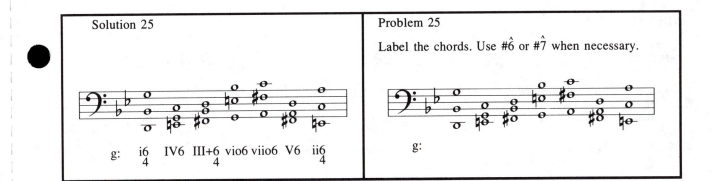

Solution 25

g: i6   IV6 III+6 vio6 viio6 V6   ii6
         4   4   4

Problem 25

Label the chords. Use #$\hat{6}$ or #$\hat{7}$ when necessary.

g:

3. Explain how to use the harmonic series as a model for:

    a. doubling chord parts

    b. spacing chord parts

4. Write two versions of each triad as specified, one in close spacing and one in open spacing.

A♭ Ma: V6   vi6   I6   iii6   viio6   IV6   ii6
          4   4   4

B mi: i6   V6   III+   vio6   iv6   viio6   iio6   III6
                                    4   4

201

NAME _____ CLASS _____ DATE _____

1. Complete a functional harmonic analysis of the following Colonial hymn. Satellites are present in some beats and are labeled ''nct.'' These notes should not be regarded as chord tones. Chord durations vary between half and quarter notes. Satellites are generally in values smaller than the chord rhythms.

Chester (1778)   William Billings

Let ty - rants shake their I - ron rods   And Slav' - ry

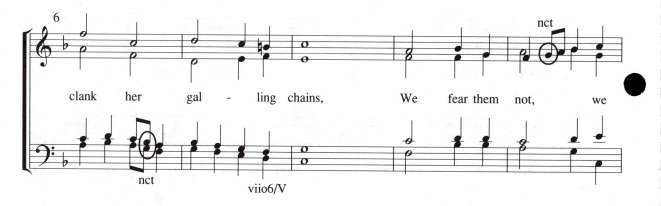

clank her gal - ling chains,   We fear them not, we

trust - in God,   New Eng-land's God for ev - ver reigns.

2. Complete a functional analysis of this chorale. Satellites are circled and should not be considered part of the harmony. Key changes are indicated beneath the music. At each key change, change the basis for Roman numerals.

Ermuntre dich, mein schwacher Geist from 371 Four-Part Chorales (No. 102)   J. S. Bach

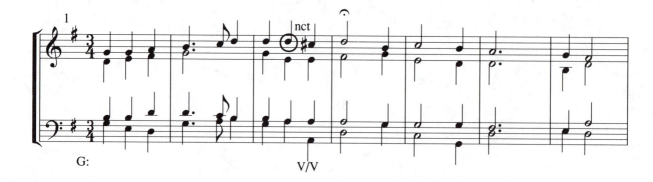

10 TWO-PART TEXTURE

OVERVIEW

The *Interval Path* continues with information about intervals in two-part texture. The chapter includes ideas about relative motion (parallel, similar, oblique, and contrary) and its application in two-part writing. A survey of two-part music written between the 11th and early 20th centuries is incorporated. Exercises in two-part writing are presented at the end of the chapter to prepare for the four-part writing activities in later chapters.

TWO-PART TEXTURE

Motion Relationships

A stream of harmonic intervals produces two melody lines. The individuality of these lines depends in part on how the melodies move relative to each other. The melodies will have the least individual impact if both lines move to the same rhythms and in the same directions. Under these circumstances, the listener will be more aware of the stream of interval sounds than the details of the separate melodies.

If the parts of a texture use a common rhythm pattern, the texture is **monorhythmic** (note against note). **Parallel motion** means that the parts move in the same direction interval for interval (i.e., in fifths, thirds, tenths, etc). The next example includes passages that are monorhythmic and in parallel motion. Listen to the example. Do you notice the individuality of the two melodies, or the stream of interval sounds? Does one melody in each passage seem to be more important than the other?

Example 1. Parallel Motion

parallel twelfths   parallel tenths

Other **motion relationships** include **similar**, **oblique**, and **contrary** motion. The patterns shown in the next example are below.
• **similar motion**: Parts move in the same direction but to dissimilar intervals.
• **oblique motion**: One line remains stationary but the other moves in any direction.
• **contrary motion**: Lines move in opposite directions.

Example 2. Similar, Oblique, and Contrary Motion

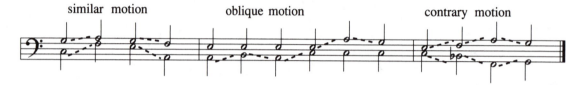

similar motion   oblique motion   contrary motion

The individuality of the lines in a texture can be stressed by the varied use of motion factors and by the rhythmic independence of each line. The next example illustrates how this separateness is achieved. Perform the example. It is <u>not</u> monorhythmic. The contour peaks and valleys of the two melodies occur at different times (**contour independence**). What motion factors are used? Where do they occur and how do they coincide with accents and differences in contour? Are you more aware of the passing of interval sounds or the movement of individual lines? How do you account for your impression? Does one melody seem more important than the other, or are they equal partners? What do the lines have in common?

Example 3. Ave Maria (ca. 1500) Des Pres

A - ve Ma - ri - a,

A - ve Ma - ri - a, gra - ti - a - ple

Parallelism

Parallelism refers to a texture based exclusively on lines that always move together in the same direction. The next example illustrates **parallel organum**, one of the earliest kinds of part music. **Composite** versions, the result of singing one or more of the parts in octaves, are shown at the right. What intervals were used? What effect does this have? Does one line seem more important than the other? How do you account for this impression?

206

Example 4. from Scholia Enchiriades (ca. 850 A. D.)

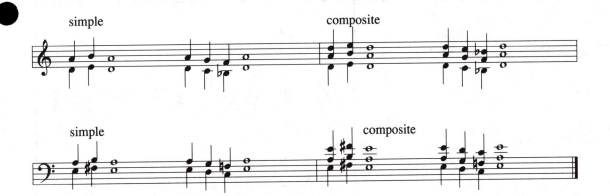

CHECKPOINT (Two-Part Texture)

1. Explain these terms:

monorhythmic	motion relationship
parallel motion	oblique motion
similar motion	contrary motion
contour independence	parallelism
parallel organum	composite organum

2. Self-help Problems.

Solution 1	Problem 1
contrary parallel	Identify the motion patterns.
oblique similar	

Instruction: Parallel thirds will include a mixture of major and minor thirds if the pitches comply to the key signature. This is called **tonal parallelism.** If the pitches are altered by accidentals to make the thirds all one type (i.e., all major), the result is a **real parallelism.**

Solution 3	Problem 3
tonal real	Write the words "real" or "tonal" to identify the parallel motion.
real tonal	

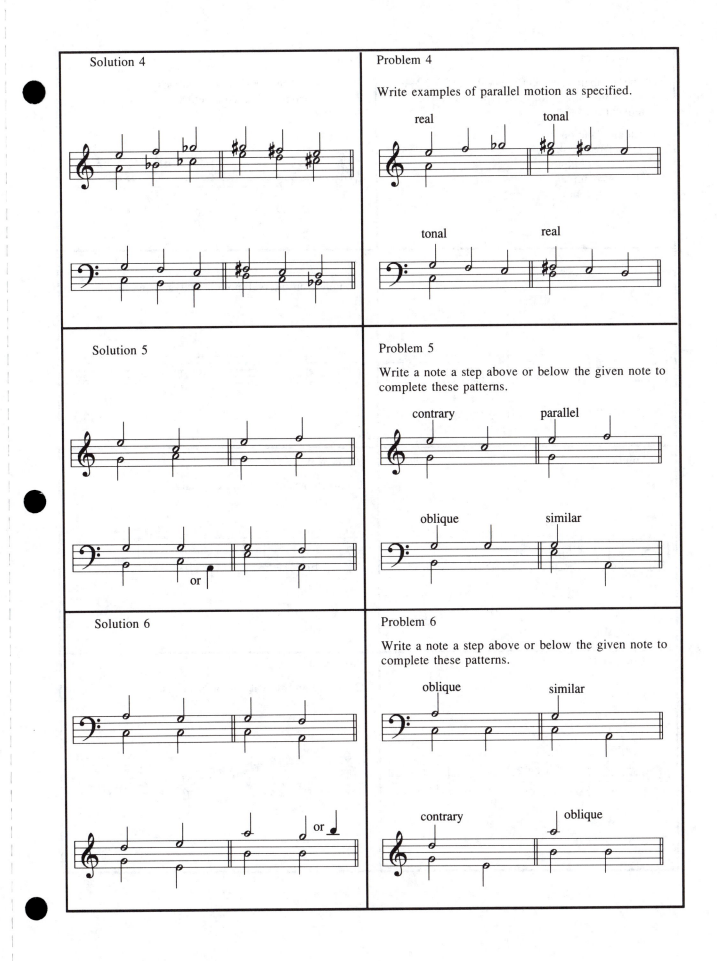

Solution 4

Problem 4

Write examples of parallel motion as specified.

real   tonal

tonal   real

Solution 5

Problem 5

Write a note a step above or below the given note to complete these patterns.

contrary   parallel

oblique   similar

or

Solution 6

Problem 6

Write a note a step above or below the given note to complete these patterns.

oblique   similar

or

contrary   oblique

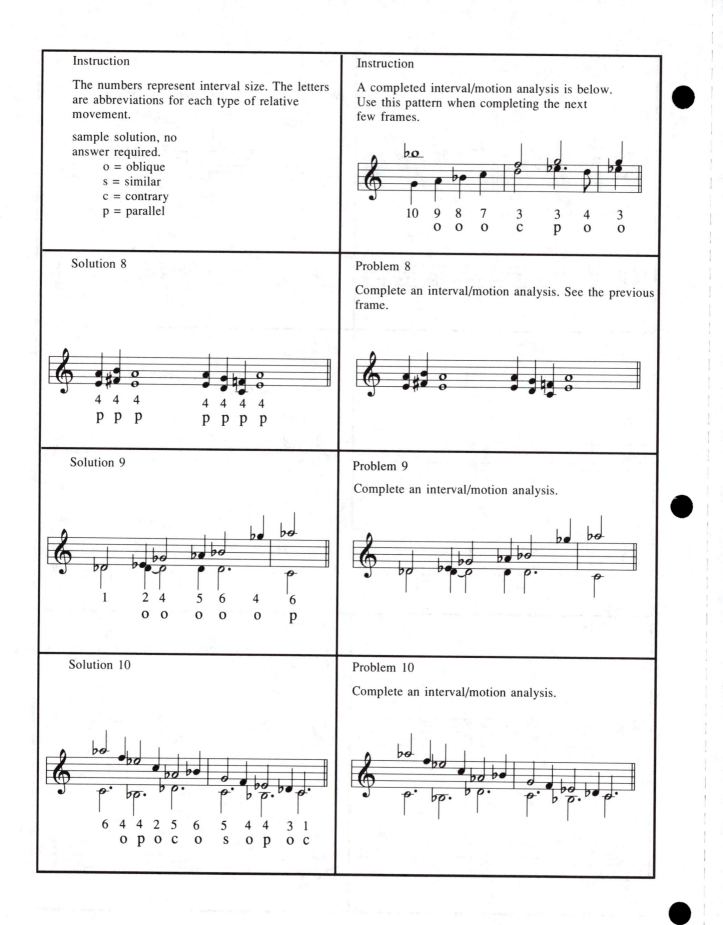

Instruction

The numbers represent interval size. The letters are abbreviations for each type of relative movement.

sample solution, no answer required.

    o = oblique
    s = similar
    c = contrary
    p = parallel

Instruction

A completed interval/motion analysis is below. Use this pattern when completing the next few frames.

10 9 8 7   3   3   4   3
o   o o c   p   o   o

Solution 8

4 4 4   4 4 4 4
p p p   p p p p

Problem 8

Complete an interval/motion analysis. See the previous frame.

Solution 9

1   2 4   5   6   4   6
     o o   o   o   p

Problem 9

Complete an interval/motion analysis.

Solution 10

6 4 4 2 5 6 5 4 4 3 1
o p o c o s o p o c

Problem 10

Complete an interval/motion analysis.

210

APPLICATIONS

I. Analytical Survey of Two-Part Music

An historical/analytical overview of two-part music follows. Each example embodies ideas about accepted writing practices that were in effect when the music was written. Some of the "rules" of good writing for each historic period can be inferred from the study of these examples. Perform each example and evaluate its effects. Compare one excerpt to others, using the following checklist as a guide.

How to Approach Excerpts

a. What kinds of intervals were allowed in the excerpt?
b. Which intervals were treated as satellites, and in what kinds of patterns?
c. How much individuality do the lines have? Are they relatively independent or dependent on each other in regard to:
  • rhythm (monorhythmic, polyrhythmic)
  • contour (coincidence of highs and lows)
  • motion (parallel, contrary, similar, oblique)
  • idea relationships between lines
d. What is the comparative importance of each line? Is one dominant over the other? Are they equal in importance?

1. The next excerpt is taken from early polyphony (**polyphony** or **polyphonic** texture contains two or more active melodies. In contrast to homophony, emphasis is placed on the interplay between lines rather than on a single melody or a stream of chord sounds. The interplay of contour, motives, continuity features, and rhythms are important factors in polyphonic texture). What kinds of intervals seem favored? What motion factors seem preferred? Are certain intervals approached in particular ways? Can you find any cases of parallel or similar motion? If so, what intervals are involved? How do the contours of the two lines compare? How do the rhythms compare? Does one line seem more important than the other?

Cunctipotens Genitor　　　　11th Century (Medieval)

2. The numbers below this excerpt indicate an interval analysis. Interval satellites are circled. The lines connecting notes show motion relationships between parts. What is the ratio between melodic step and skip? What are the contour and rhythmic relationships between the parts? Does one line seem more important than the other? How does this compare with the previous excerpt?

Virelai (14th Century)　　　　Machaut (Medieval)

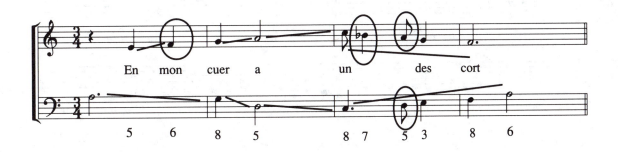

3. In this excerpt, an optional middle voice is indicated by cue notes. How does the middle voice relate to the top voice? Perform the excerpt with and without the middle voice. What does the middle voice contribute? When the middle voice is added, do you perceive two or three separate parts? How do you account for this? How do the two versions of this example compare to the previous excerpts?

from Missa Sancti Jacobi (15th Century)   Dufay (Medieval-Renaissance)

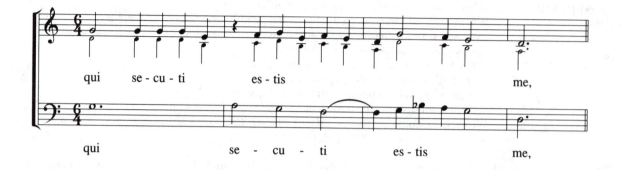

4. Perform this excerpt at about 120 half notes per minute. Complete an interval analysis by writing numbers under the music. Apply the checklist to this example (see *How to Approach the Excerpts* at the beginning of this survey). What makes the lines independent? What binds them together? What does the change in rhythmic pace contribute to this excerpt?

from Cantiones Duarum Vocum

No. 1 (pub. 1577)   Orlandus Lassus (Renaissance)

5. The next excerpt is taken from 18th century keyboard literature. There are less constraints on the ranges of the parts and on the size of melodic intervals than in the previous excerpts. Is this because of differing media (i.e., instrumental versus vocal music)? Is this excerpt more difficult to sing than the others? How do you account for this? What is the comparative importance of the two lines? What ties them together? How do they contrast? Make a simplified version that contains only the accented intervals. Briefly discuss this simplified version in terms of prevalent intervals and rhythm, motion, and contour relationships between the two simplified parts.

from English Suite No. 3 (BWV 808)   Bach (1685–1750) (Baroque)

Gavotte I

6. The next excerpt is in four voices. Can you conceive of it as a two-line texture? Make a simplified two-part version of this excerpt using only accented intervals. How do the two parts relate to each other? How does the simplified version compare to other simplified versions?

from String Quartet in D minor   Haydn (Classical)

Menuetto (Allegro, ma non troppo)

7. Can you see one part as a mirror image of the other in this excerpt? The two lines skip and step simultaneously. How does the rhythmic off-setting starting in bar three affect this? Describe the relationship between the first and second halves of this excerpt. What is the comparative importance of the two lines? Does this status vary? If so, where—and why?

from Piano Sonata No. 8 in C major, Op. 13 (1798)   Beethoven (Classical-Romantic)

8. Mentally reduce the next excerpt to a quarter note skeleton. In this simplified version, is one voice more important than the other? How does the simplified version compare to the previous example? What factors make the simplified versions different?

from Album for the Young, Op. 68 (1848) Schumann (Romantic)

mm = 90

9. Although the next excerpt is in six parts, it can be seen as a two-part texture with organum-like doublings. Isolate the two basic lines. How do the rhythm and contour of these lines relate? How does the melodic interval continuity of these lines differ?

La Cathedrale Engloutie (1910)   Debussy (early 20th Century)

from Claude Debussy, *Complete Preludes, Books 1 and 2*. Copyright © 1989 Dover Publications, Inc., Mineola, NY. Used with permission of the publisher.

10. Write a short paper to show your understanding of differing attitudes about intervals as illustrated in the preceding excerpts. What are the significant similarities and contrasts in practice between the different time periods? State, support, and illustrate your points.

11. As an alternative, write a short, two-part composition that applies some of the ideas shown in the previous excerpts.

II. Two-Part Writing

The two-part writing exercises at the end of this chapter have been simplified so students can concentrate on the basics of part-writing. Follow the prescription below to complete the exercises. Use ideas from this chapter in your solutions.

Prescription for Writing Traditional Two-Part Texture

- Use <u>only</u> consonance (i.e., perfect unison, P8, P5, thirds, sixths. DO NOT use P4, T, seconds or sevenths).
- Approach perfect intervals <u>only</u> by contrary motion.
- Use no more than three parallel thirds or sixths in succession.
- Use mainly <u>simple</u> intervals.
- Keep the low voice <u>below</u> the high voice.
- Change direction after a skip (or soon after).
- Use more steps than skips.

1. Self-help Problems. Apply the above prescription to two-part texture writing. Avoid skips in the framed exercises, but allow oblique approaches to P5.

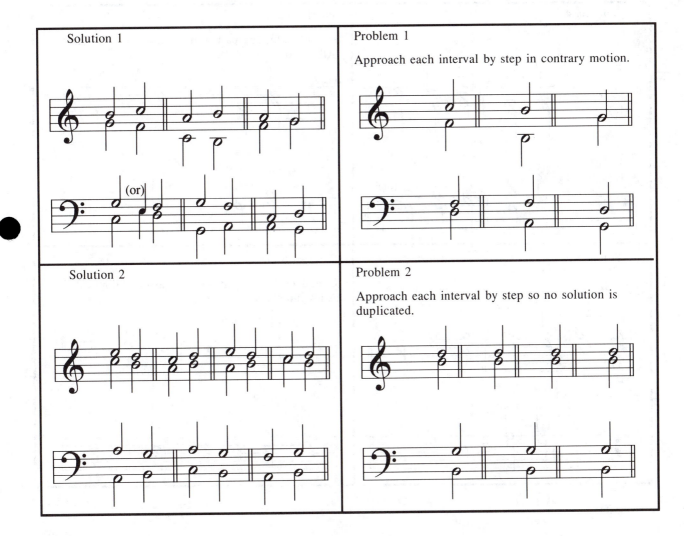

Solution 1

Problem 1

Approach each interval by step in contrary motion.

Solution 2

Problem 2

Approach each interval by step so no solution is duplicated.

Solution 3

Problem 3

Complete the top part so no measure is duplicated. Allow no skips.

Solution 4

Problem 4

Complete the top part so no measure is duplicated. Allow no skips.

(or)

Solution 5

Problem 5

Complete the top part so no measure is duplicated. Allow no skips.

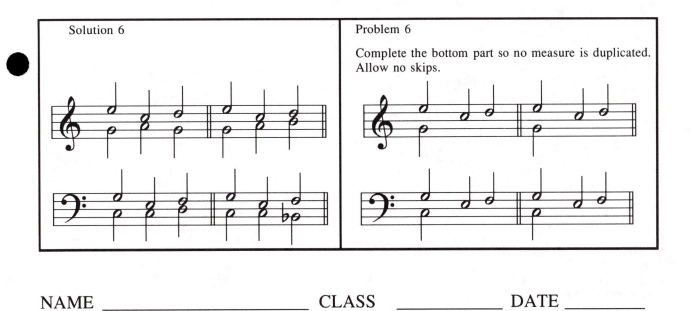

Solution 6

Problem 6

Complete the bottom part so no measure is duplicated. Allow no skips.

NAME _____ CLASS _____ DATE _____

2. Writing Two-Part Phrases

Apply the prescription for two-part writing to the letter in the first few phrases. Allow melodic skips of consonant intervals only (P5 or smaller). Change direction after a skip.

1. Add the bottom voice (monorhythmic: note against note).

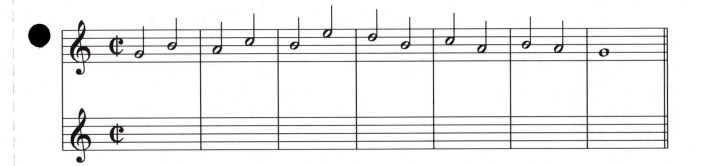

2. Add the bottom voice (monorhythmic: note against note).

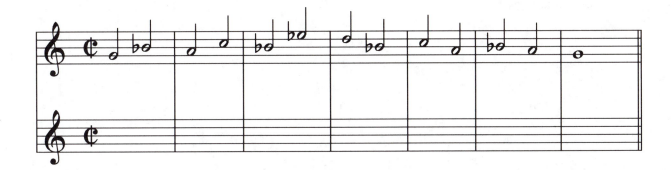

3. Add the top voice (monorhythmic: note against note).

4. Add the bottom voice in quarter notes (two against one). Limit your use of intervals. Perfect intervals may be approached by <u>both</u> oblique and contrary motion (except the unison).

5. Add the top voice in quarter notes (two against one). Limit your use of intervals. Perfect intervals may now be approached by <u>both</u> oblique and contrary motion (except the unison).

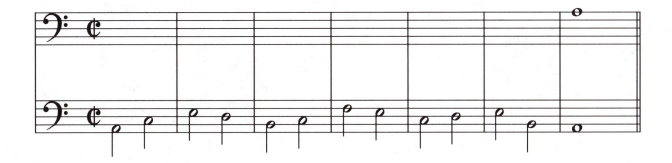

In what time period(s) would the above specifications for two-part writing be considered rules for ''good and proper'' composition? In what musical styles do these same ''rules of good compositional conduct'' not apply?

CHAPTER

11 HARMONIZING MELODY: BASICS

OVERVIEW

The *Harmony* and *Melody* paths merge in this chapter to form the first of a two-part series on harmonizing melody. Basics of harmonizing melody are introduced. A method is presented for choosing chords based on melodic skeleton, harmonic rhythm, tonic focus, key change, typical harmonizations of cadences, inversion effects, and consideration of the bass as a secondary melody.

Harmonization

A **harmonization** is a series of chords that support and accompany a melody. An effective harmonization agrees with and reinforces patterns in a melody and in its background structure.

Nonchord Tones

Any note in a melody can be treated as any part of a chord (root, third, fifth, etc). Any note in a melody that is not part of the current chord is treated as a **nonchord tone**. Focal pitches are usually treated as chord tones. Satellites are usually treated as nonchord tones.

Choosing Chords

Often, a single chord can harmonize a succession of two or more melody tones. Any melodic interval can be harmonized with one chord. As shown in the next example, melodic thirds or sixths can be harmonized with either of two chords. Melodic fourths and fifths can be harmonized with only one chord. Why is the harmonization of fourths more limited than the harmonization of thirds?

Example 1. Chording Melodic Intervals

Sketching

A **sketch** or working draft begins with a trial harmonization based on first impressions of a melody. Try some sketching with the next examples. First, quickly scan the next melody for melodic intervals. These intervals often suggest the use of particular chords. A chord is outlined in bar 9, leaving no doubt about chord selection. Identify your chord choices by root name and write them above the melody. Carefully align the chord labels with the melody so that the rhythm of chord changes is clear to the viewer.

Example 2. A Melody for Sketching

Drink to Me Only With Thine Eyes (text by Ben Jonson, 1615)   Traditional English

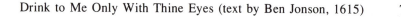

Harmonic Rhythm

Harmonic rhythm refers to chord rhythms and the timing of chord changes. In addition to revealing essential pitches, a simplified version of a melody (skeleton) can be used to determine **harmonic rhythm**.

A simplified version of this melody in included in the next example. Sample chord choices are given below the music. How does this compare to the harmonization you wrote in example 2? The simplification (skeleton) reveals certain background melodic intervals. The skeleton also provides a rhythmic outline of the melody, useful for deciding what rhythm to use for each chord. In this case, the melodic skeleton indicates the use of dotted quarter rhythms. Preference was given to the I, IV, and V chords to strengthen tonal focus (to be discussed in a few pages).

Example 3. A Harmonized Version of *Drink to Me Only With Thine Eyes*

Scan the next melody. Circle notes that belong to its skeleton. Sketch in some chord choices based on patterns outlined in this melody. Look at the harmonic rhythm of your sketch. How does it compare to the rhythmic skeleton of the melody?

Example 4. Another Tune for Sketching Earlie One Morning (Traditional)

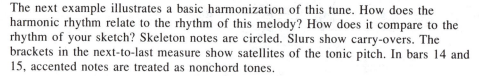

The next example illustrates a basic harmonization of this tune. How does the harmonic rhythm relate to the rhythm of this melody? How does it compare to the rhythm of your sketch? Skeleton notes are circled. Slurs show carry-overs. The brackets in the next-to-last measure show satellites of the tonic pitch. In bars 14 and 15, accented notes are treated as nonchord tones.

Example 5. A Simple Harmonization

Tonal Focus

An effective harmonization supports the tonal organization of a melody. This **tonal focus** occurs when a particular note (tonic) becomes the primary focal pitch of the melody. Focus on the tonic note happens through a network of relationships contained in a melody, often most evident in a simplified version of the melody. Look at the next melody and its skeleton. Which notes are pattern extremes? Which notes recur most often? Which are interval roots? Which notes appear to have greater rhythmic weight?

Example 6. Agnus Dei   Gregorian Chant

Ag - nus   De - i,   qui   tol - lis

skeleton

pec - ca mun - di: mi - se - re re no - bis:

The next example includes a melody, its skeleton, and a sample harmonization. Chord choices are placed at the downbeat of each measure and chord labels are placed beneath the bass line. Only root position chords are used. Hear the bass line as a simple melody that accompanies the principal melody. The first part of the melodic skeleton is a descending scale. The bass notes connected by slurs form a background scale pattern that points to the dominant pitch. How does the harmonic rhythm relate to the rhythm of the melodic skeleton? Spell the chords given in the example. How do these chords relate to intervals in the melody? Are any of the chords completely outlined in the melody?

Example 7. Sarabande   Corelli

melody

skeleton

bass

F: I   V   vi   iii   IV   I   V   I

Cadence Harmonization

Cadences mark the ends of phrases with varying degrees of finality, just as commas or periods mark the ends of clauses or sentences in language. Cadences provide strong harmonic focal points because of their punctuating function. The use of the I and/or V chord(s) to end phrases is a common, effective way to confirm the focus on the tonic pitch, or to **tonicize**. The roots of these chords furnish one or both of the notes of the tonicizing interval 5–1. The root of the I chord is also the root of this melodic interval. The most commonly used cadence progressions are shown in the next example.

Example 8. Common Cadence Progressions

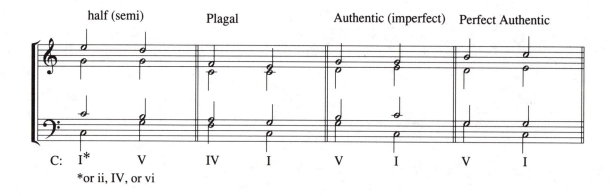

Develop an explanation for each type of cadence based on example 8. Note the chords used in each cadence progress, and the notes in the soprano and bass of the two types of authentic cadence.

In the **perfect authentic** cadence (V→I), the tonic note is placed in the outer voices of the closing chord, that is, the tonic pitch is in both the soprano and bass of the I chord. Both chords of the progression are in root position, thus the perfect authentic cadence is the most conclusive of all the cadences.

Tonicizing Progressions

To tonicize means to create focus on the tonic pitch. This is accomplished in chord progressions through repetition of the tonic and dominant notes. The next example shows how tonicizing works in chord progressions.

• The tonic is the focal pitch in V-I progressions. The roots of these chords form the 5-1 interval (1 is the root of the interval).
• The tonic and dominant notes are imbedded in the voices of the harmony and recur frequently.
• Melodic patterns imbedded in the voices of the harmony often point to the tonic and dominant notes.
• The IV chord often functions as a satellite chord of the V, enhancing focus on V.

Example 9. Tonicizing Factors

Modulation

The processes of *tonicizing* a note to make it the tonic pitch can be applied to any pitch. Tonicizing can be used to shift focus to a new tonic pitch, a process called **modulation**. Modulation is an extensive topic and will be covered in volume 2. The following material is a brief introduction to the subject, placed here to illustrate the tonicizing process in general. This introduction should help students cope with modulation until they make a detailed study of the subject.

The change to a new tonic is usually accompanied by a change in accidentals. Because of their strategic importance, cadences are important places to look for evidence that a modulation has occurred. Other evidence includes focus changes in melodic skeleton and tonicizing progressions.

A modulation occurs in the second phrase of the next example. The first phrase (bars 1–2) is in the key of C major. The second phrase (bars 3–5) ends in G major.

An analysis of the harmony is written below the music. One chord in bar 3 is labeled in both keys. This dual analysis indicates a "pivot chord," a chord that is common to both keys and occurs just before the dominant chord in the new key.

Harmonic satellites (nonchord tones) are enclosed in boxes. Bach used these tones to create step-wise motion in the voices. Bars 1 and 3 can be analyzed more than one way. If one assumes harmonic rhythm is half notes, the chords and nonchord tones will be labeled differently than shown.

Example 10. Meinen Jesum laß ich nicht. (No. 348)   Bach

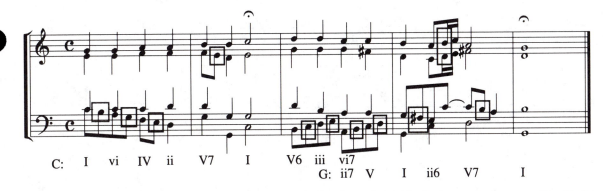

C: I   vi   IV   ii   V7   I   V6   iii   vi7
                                G: ii7   V   I   ii6   V7   I

The '7' beside a Roman numeral indicates a seventh chord, a triad with the interval of a seventh added.

More About Example 10

Factors that establish C as tonic in bars 1–2 are below.
- Top voice (soprano) traverses the dominant tetrachord of C major.
- Bottom voice (bass) traverses a descending C major scale (with a detour through G the dominant pitch).
- First phrase closes with a perfect authentic cadence in C major.

Factors that establish G as tonic in bars 3–5 are below.
- Discounting the sixteenth note satellites in bar 4, the top voice traverses the tonic pentachord of G major.
- A melodic skeleton of the pitches B, A, and G occurs in the bass in bars 3–4 (on beats 1, 3, and 1).
- F is replaced by F♯ (the leading tone of G) in bars 3–4.
- The second phrase closes with a perfect authentic cadence in G major.

Chord Inversion Effects

Exclusive use of root position triads creates a disjunct bass line. Inverted chords can be used to create a more conjunct bass line. This helps establish the bass as a secondary melody.

Example 11. Chord Inversion and Bass Line

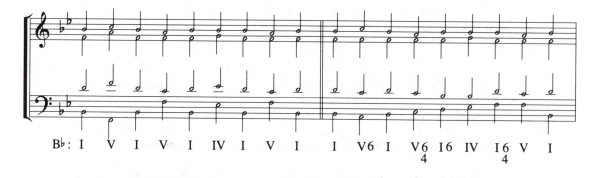

Bb: I V I V I IV I V I   I V6 I V6/4 I6 IV I6/4 V I

Inverted triads are less stable and resonant than root position triads. Because of their instability, inverted chords are less effective as closing chords. Second inversion is the least stable position and the least effective inversion for a closing triad.

Example 12. Unstable Endings

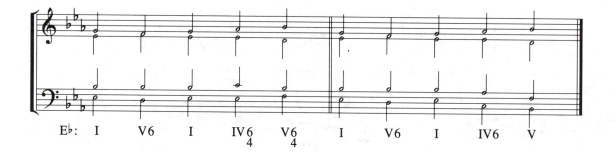

Eb: I V6 I IV6/4 V6/4 I V6 I IV6 V

Bass Line as Melody

The bass notes of a harmonization form a skeleton-like melody that accompanies the principal melody. The interaction between the melody and the bass line produces a two-part texture. This texture is apparent regardless of the simplicity or complexity of the setting. An effective harmonization shows that motion relationships between the melody and bass line have been controlled so both lines will remain independent. Persistent parallel motion defeats this independence. The independence of these two lines is more pronounced if the peaks and valleys of their contours do not coincide. Rhythms in bass line tend to support the rhythmic highlights in the melody.

The next example contains a seventeenth century two-part setting of the melody. Complete an interval/motion analysis of the example. How are the motion, contour, and rhythmic factors in the two-part texture handled? How does the bass line enhance the focus on the tonic pitch?

Example 13. Old 100th (Bay Psalm Book, Boston, 1698)

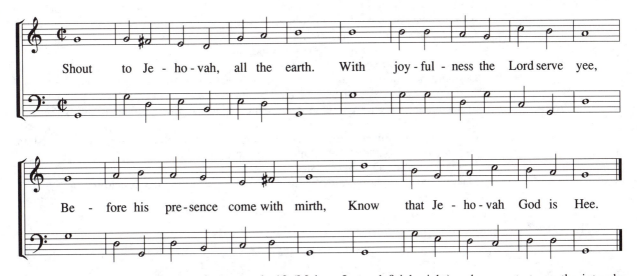

Shout to Je-ho-vah, all the earth. With joy-ful-ness the Lord serve yee,

Be - fore his pre-sence come with mirth, Know that Je-ho-vah God is Hee.

Re-examine example 10 (Meinen Jesum laß ich nicht) and concentrate on the interplay between the soprano and bass parts. Complete an interval/motion analysis of the two voices. How are the motion, contour, and rhythmic factors in the two-part texture handled?

Summary

An important objective of a harmonization is to select chords that support the design of the melody. For example, the tonal design of the melody is supported through the repeated use of primary triads. Cadences, because they provide musical punctuation, should close on stable chords and be harmonized with standard chord progressions that reinforce the key.

Clues about the design of the melody can be discovered through analysis. When analyzing, one should seek out patterns in the pitch and rhythm background of a melody to help decide which chord to use and when to use it.

Many melodies can be harmonized with primary triads alone—especially simple folk melodies that feature strong tonal focus. Sometimes the simple clarity of primary triads is the best solution.

229

GUIDELINES FOR HARMONIZING MELODY

1. Plan
   - Simplify the melody to reveal background pitch and rhythm patterns. Look for patterns that focus on the tonic pitch.
   - Look for intervals or triads outlined in the melody.
2. Sketch
   - Select chords implied by outline patterns.
   - Select chords that support tonic focus.
   - Design a harmonic rhythm that supports the melody's rhythmic background.
   - Harmonize cadences with the standard progressions (V-I, IV-I, x-V).
3. Test
   - Test your setting on a chording instrument like a piano or a guitar. LISTEN AND EVALUATE!
   - Change chord choices and harmonic rhythms if needed. Retest until you are satisfied.
4. Polish
   - Use inversions to add melodic interest to the bass line.
   - Use root position to enhance harmonic focus.
   - Make changes to improve the independence between the melody and the bass line.

CHECKPOINT

1. Define these terms:

   harmonization   nonchord tone

   sketching   tonal focus

   modulation   harmonic rhythm

   Plagal cadence   half (semi-) cadence (example 8)

   authentic cadence (example 8)   tonicize

   unstable inversion   perfect authentic cadence (example 8)

   disjunct bass   stable inversion

   melodic bass   conjunct bass

2. Self-help Problems.

Solution 1

Problem 1

Write all the white-key triads that can be used to harmonize each note.

Solution 2

Problem 2

Write all the white-key triads that can be used to harmonize each interval.

Solution 3

Problem 3

Write all the white-key triads that can be used to harmonize each interval.

Solution 4

E major

Problem 4

Circle the notes that contribute to tonic focus. Mark satellites with slurs.

The key is _____ .

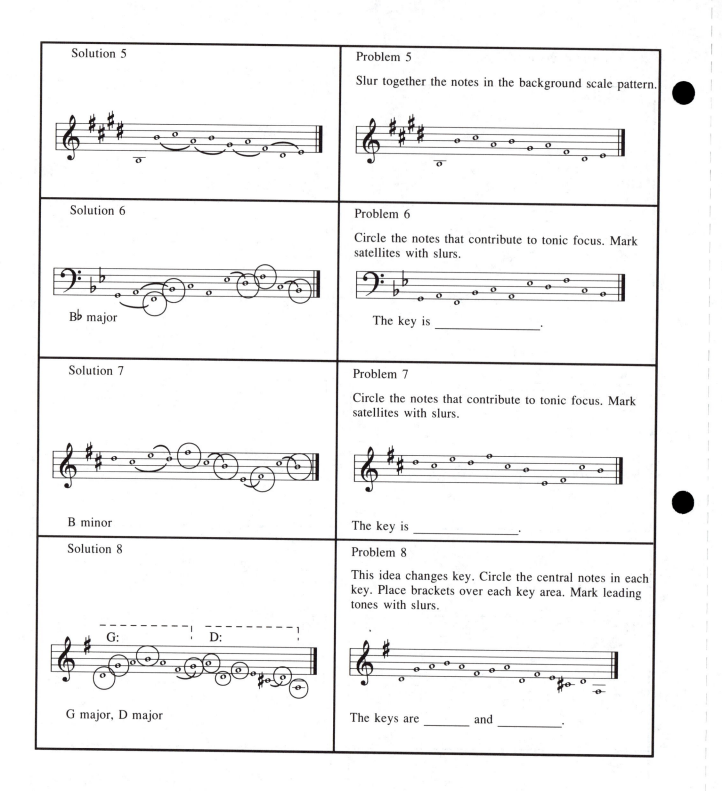

Solution 5

Problem 5

Slur together the notes in the background scale pattern.

Solution 6

Bb major

Problem 6

Circle the notes that contribute to tonic focus. Mark satellites with slurs.

The key is _____.

Solution 7

B minor

Problem 7

Circle the notes that contribute to tonic focus. Mark satellites with slurs.

The key is _____.

Solution 8

G major, D major

Problem 8

This idea changes key. Circle the central notes in each key. Place brackets over each key area. Mark leading tones with slurs.

The keys are _____ and _____.

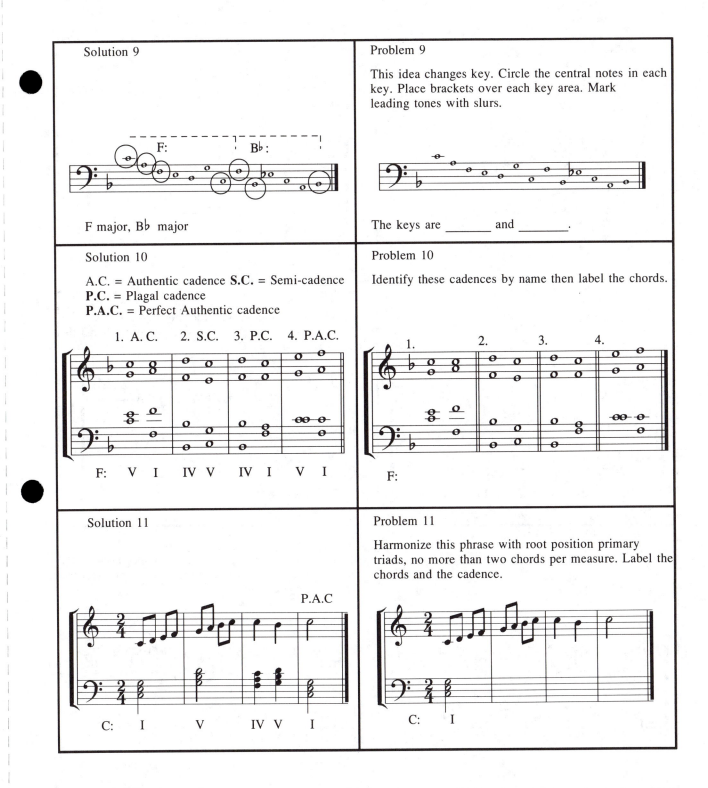

Solution 9

F major, B♭ major

Problem 9

This idea changes key. Circle the central notes in each key. Place brackets over each key area. Mark leading tones with slurs.

The keys are _____ and _____.

Solution 10

A.C. = Authentic cadence S.C. = Semi-cadence
P.C. = Plagal cadence
P.A.C. = Perfect Authentic cadence

1. A.C.   2. S.C.   3. P.C.   4. P.A.C.

F: V   I   IV   V   IV   I   V   I

Problem 10

Identify these cadences by name then label the chords.

1.   2.   3.   4.

F:

Solution 11

P.A.C

C: I   V   IV   V   I

Problem 11

Harmonize this phrase with root position primary triads, no more than two chords per measure. Label the chords and the cadence.

C: I

233

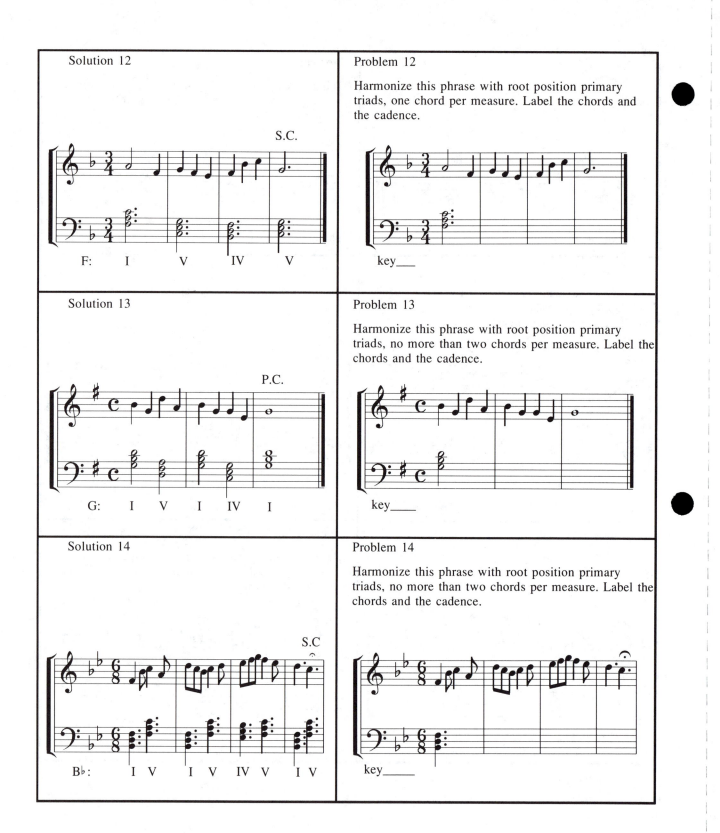

Solution 12

S.C.

F: I   V   IV   V

Problem 12

Harmonize this phrase with root position primary triads, one chord per measure. Label the chords and the cadence.

key___

Solution 13

P.C.

G: I   V   I   IV   I

Problem 13

Harmonize this phrase with root position primary triads, no more than two chords per measure. Label the chords and the cadence.

key___

Solution 14

S.C

B♭: I V   I V   IV V   I V

Problem 14

Harmonize this phrase with root position primary triads, no more than two chords per measure. Label the chords and the cadence.

key___

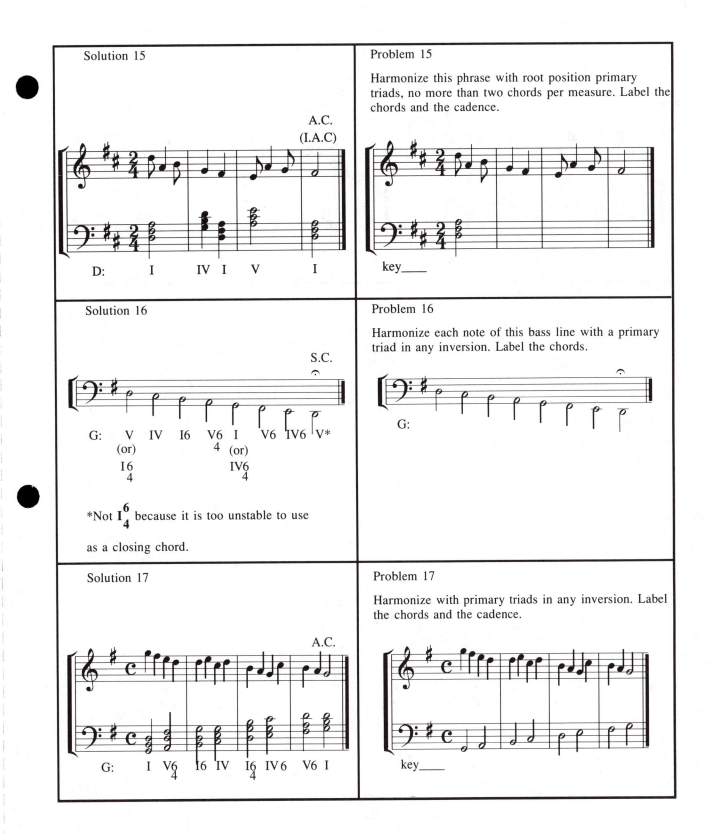

Solution 15

A.C.
(I.A.C)

D: I   IV I   V   I

Problem 15

Harmonize this phrase with root position primary triads, no more than two chords per measure. Label the chords and the cadence.

key____

Solution 16

S.C.

G: V   IV   I6   V6   I   V6   IV6   V*
      (or)   4   (or)
       I6   IV6
        4   4

*Not I$^6_4$ because it is too unstable to use

as a closing chord.

Problem 16

Harmonize each note of this bass line with a primary triad in any inversion. Label the chords.

G:

Solution 17

A.C.

G: I   V6   I6   IV   I6   IV6   V6   I
           4   4

Problem 17

Harmonize with primary triads in any inversion. Label the chords and the cadence.

key____

235

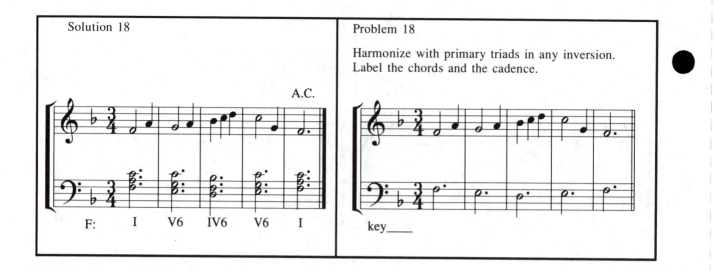

Solution 18

A.C.

F: I V6 IV6 V6 I

Problem 18

Harmonize with primary triads in any inversion.
Label the chords and the cadence.

key____

NAME _____ CLASS _____ DATE _____

3. Below are deliberately flawed harmonizations. Explain what is wrong with each (refer to the Harmonizing Guidelines (p. 230). Supply an improved harmonization for each melody.

Problem 1.

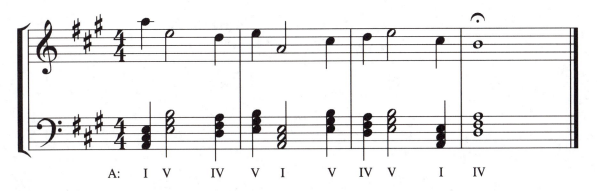

Problem 2.

Problem 3.

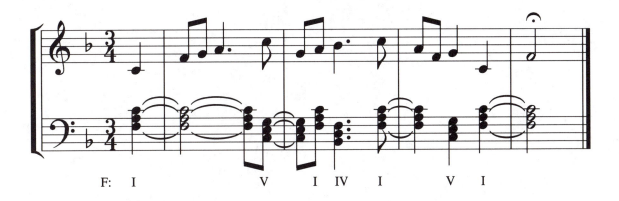

Problem 4.

G: I   IV   I   IV   V   IV

Problem 5.

Bb: IV   V   I   V   IV   V   IV   I V   I

Problem 6.

D: V   I V   I   V   I   IV   I   IV   viio

1. Use only primary triads to harmonize this melody. Indicate your chord choices by writing chord labels under the notes. Be sure the chords and harmonic rhythm agree with factors already in this melody. Align the chord signs to show the rhythmic position of chord changes.

from Academic Festival Overture, Op. 80   Brahms

Allegro (second theme)

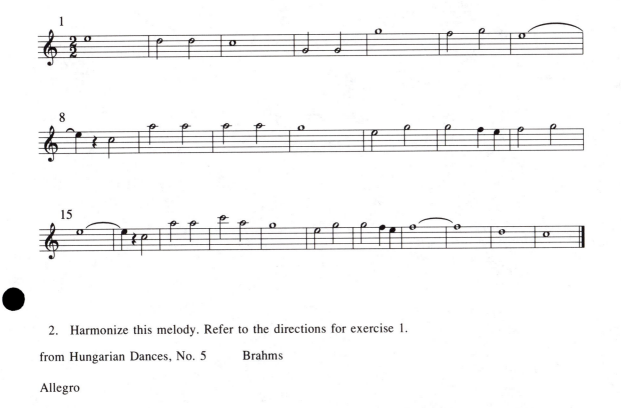

2. Harmonize this melody. Refer to the directions for exercise 1.

from Hungarian Dances, No. 5   Brahms

Allegro

3. Supplemental Application: Harmonize several folks songs using only primary triads. Make the harmonic rhythm agree with the rhythmic skeleton of the melody. Folks song collections are available in most libraries. Some melodies may not be suited to a harmonization based exclusively on primary triads. Save these for work in later chapters. Submit your work as specified by your instructor.

12 MELODIC SEGMENTS

OVERVIEW   The *Melody Path* continues with an exploration of the organization of melody in segments. Details are included on motives, phrases, and phrase groups. Instruction is provided on closure and cadence, motive rhythm, and motive variation. Material on the organization of phrase groups includes information on parallel and symmetrical construction and phrase extension techniques. The chapter ends with the presentation of criteria for analyzing and describing the segment organization of melodies.

MELODIC SEGMENTS

Segment Types; The Motive

Most melodies are made of a series of segments of various lengths. The shortest of these segments is called a **motive**. The motive is a brief pitch/rhythm idea, repeated in various forms to make longer segments in the melody. The motive is a thematic primitive used to build melodies and to add pattern to accompaniments.

Consider this idea:

A single note has little thematic impact. Consider the idea with another note added. Does this two-note idea remind you of other musical ideas? Are you tempted to add to or complete this idea?

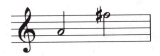

Perhaps the next idea was the one you were expecting. The two notes probably led you to think about some other idea that you may have completed in your own imagination. The expectation, sensing, or creation of an ending is called **closure**.

This three-note idea has all the properties of a motive. It is short but complete. This motive was used to create the next example. Note the recurrences of the motive. Can you hear where each motive ends (its closure) in the stream of motives? Does the whole stream of motives have its own closure?

Example 1. A Stream of Motives

In the next example, brackets are placed over the motives and longer segments. Every note of the melody is included in one motive or another. Motive ideas and their recurrences are identified by the lower case letters "a" and "b." In this particular melody, the two ideas are always paired to make **subphrases**. The subphrases are paired to make **phrases**. The phrases make a longer melodic unit called a **period**. As in many melodies, the segments form a "wheels-within-wheels" relationship. You might think of this process as pattern **nesting** (complete patterns residing within larger patterns).

Example 2. Symphony No. 8   Schubert

Andante

Motive Continuity

A stream of motives forms a **motive continuity**. The nature of this continuity is affected by the ways the ideas are connected. For example, the separation between motives is easy to hear in some melodies. In other melodies, motive endings are not as apparent. In the next melody, the separation between motives is very noticeable. Motive closure is quite obvious, helped by the quarter note at the ends of the even numbered measures (a recurring "beat-beat-beat-close" pattern).

246

Example 3. from "Surprise" Symphony   Haydn

Andante

In contrast, the motives in the next example are joined in an almost inseparable flow of sound. Motive closure is ambiguous, less definite, more difficult to pin point.

Example 4. from Symphony No. 4   Tchaikovsky

Andantino in modo di canzona

Closure

Closure results from our awareness of the completion of a musical idea. Our perception of closure gives dimensions and boundaries to musical ideas. As shown in previous examples, the intensity of motive closure affects how we hear individual motives in a stream of motives. In example 3, endings were very pronounced. In example 4, endings were indistinct, making it difficult to sense where one idea stopped and the next began. Now, go back to example 3 and perform it again. Compare the motive closures. Did the endings all have the same intensity, or did some seem stronger than others? Now perform example 4. Compare closure effects in examples 3 and 4.

Segments and Attention

We can use music to provide a pleasant background while we attend to something else, homework, for example. We also listen to music actively. When listening actively, we allow the details of the music to hold our interest and attention.

If we pay attention to the music, we hear motives as streams of figures against a sonic ground. These motives have "boundaries" that make them stand out from the ground. As we listen, we note any changes in the status of individual parts (voices, lines). For example, an inner part in a chorus may attract and hold our attention momentarily because the part has gained some properties that make it more vivid to our senses.

We view melodic segments like motives, subphrases, and phrases as thematic figure-on-ground. Making sense of music has something to do with how we listen to a stream of figures, note and recall particular features of this stream, note similarities and differences among the figures, and detect emerging new figures. Music often consists of two or more interwoven streams of ideas. Our attention shifts from stream to stream as we compare ideas and weave these ideas together into unified wholes. If we learn how attention is attracted to these figures, we can form a better understanding of how musical compositions are organized. This knowledge helps us to realize how we make sense out of music and respond to it in our own minds.

CONSIDER THIS: If you direct your attention to these two dots,

• •

they will hold your attention, even out of the "corner" of your eye. You may have trouble reading the rest of this page comfortably until you cover them up. Why do these dots become interesting, even captivating? Is it because they contrast sharply with the other characters on the page? Does an awareness of these dots do something to your attention that interferes with your normal reading process? There are obvious visual differences between the dots and the alphabetical characters on the page. One could say that the boundaries of the dots are "sharp." Can you make a connection between this visual illustration and how boundaries, figure, and ground operate in music?

A stream of ideas that seems coherent is made of a series of figures that have similar features. We tend to track similar figures automatically. [Did you put the two dots together in a short stream because they had the same features?] Yet, our attention may wander from a stream of figures that are too alike (do you really pay attention to every picket in a fence?). Some variation is needed to hold our attention, but we can also lose interest when there are so many differences among the figures that they have no common elements to link them in a logical sequence. In this case, the stream becomes chaos, a perceptual "junk pile" that makes no sense.

When listening to melody, we tend to complete or "close" a pattern if it contains enough elements to remind us of a shape we have heard before. A motive stream becomes more intelligible if we know what to expect (what to look for, where to look for it, and where it's going). When it makes sense, we know how and when to supply closure. When rehearing a familiar composition, we have a memory of its overall pattern that we reconstruct and "savor" as the composition unfolds in time. We enjoy this process like sonic gourmets. We become more aware of both the structure (the plot) and the details (the motives). We hear music as sonic data in flux. As we develop attention skills, compositions become sharper, richer, and more alive for us.

Our attention is drawn to figures that seem intense or vivid in comparison to the ground. We notice the sharpness of the boundaries between figure and ground. As attention intensifies, our feelings about the objects become more vivid. Anything that is highly interesting stands out spontaneously and our response to it is stronger. The more interesting a figure, the more responsive we are to it. These responses are often physical in nature.

In music making, mental and physical states seem extremely interrelated. For example, Harrer and Harrer obtained pulse graphs from the conductor Herbert von Karajan while he was conducting Beethoven's Leonora No. 3, and later while he was shooting landings in his jet. Changes in these pulse graphs closely paralleled the sequence of both events. Von Karajan's feelings about the music as reflected in his heart and respiration rates were drawn as a dramatic plot of the composition [Harrer, G. and H. Harrer. "Music, Emotion, and Autonomic Function." In *Music and the Brain*, edited by Critchely and Henson, pp. 204–205. Springfield, IL: Charles C. Thomas, 1977.]

Motive Rhythm

A **motive rhythm** is a foundation idea (a primitive) that can be repeated to build ideas of longer duration. Beethoven's use of the rhythmic idea " ○ ○ ○ ═══ " throughout his Symphony No. 5 is a classic example of the use of a recurring figure to create a large thematic structure. [Leonard Bernstein discusses this in a recorded analysis of Beethoven's Fifth Symphony, Columbia Records. Peter Schickele (also known as P. D. Q. Bach) recorded a "play by play" analysis of the first movement of the same symphony . Both versions are instructive.]

The essential **motive rhythm features are**
a. Length—as brief as two notes
b. Closure —conclusiveness of its ending
c. Comparative weight of first and last notes
d. Location of primary accent(s) within the motive

In the next example, the meter has a strong influence on the comparative weight of the notes in the motive rhythm. When performing the example, be especially aware of the basic ingredients of motive rhythms. The arrows represent weak (up) and strong (down) points.

Example 5. Types of Motive Rhythm

The next melody is based on the repetition of a single idea. Pay close attention to the motive rhythms as you perform the melody. Notice a change in the rhythm of the closing note midway through the melody. How does this change affect your perception of closure? How does it affect your perception of pace?

Example 6. A Single-Motive Phrase

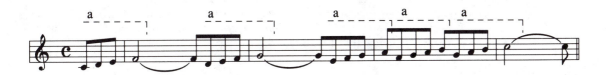

Motive Variation

Although repetition is necessary in the organization of music, unvaried, unrelenting repetition can be dull. To avoid monotony, recurring motives can be varied to hold the listener's interest. Several motive variation techniques are used by composers and arrangers that must be recognized by players, singers, and conductors for appropriate interpretation of a work.

The next melody is based on repetitions of one idea. Each recurrence is varied by **transposition** (the transferring of an idea to a new pitch level). Each transposition exhibits a slight change in rhythm or interval pattern. Perform this melody and its simplified version. Compare the motive patterns of both versions. Notice the simplicity of this melody, and the effectiveness of Puccini's use of variation techniques.

Example 7. from Madame Butterfly   Puccini
Copyright 1904–1907 by G. Ricordi and Co., S.P.A. Milan. Used with permission of Hendon Music, Inc. A Boosey & Hawkes Company.

Andante molto calme

simplified version

PERSON TO PERSON: In the Puccini melody, the relationship between motive changes and the two-note motives in the skeleton is significant. Timbre and dynamics can be intensified where the background intervals are largest to promote a sense of growth. How do you respond to these factors? Does your awareness of Puccini's writing techniques contribute to your appreciation and enjoyment of this melody?

Classic Motive Variants

A motive can be varied by turning it upside-down (**inversion**), backwards (**retrograde**), or both backwards and upside-down (**retrograde-inversion**). When using the term "inversion," be aware of the difference between **interval inversion** and **melodic inversion**. If a melody is inverted, the intervals remain the same size although their directions reverse. For example, a downward third when melodically inverted becomes an upward third. On the other hand, the interval inversion of a third is a sixth, the octave complement of the original interval.

Example 8. Melodic Inversion, Retrograde

250

A motive can be varied by increasing or decreasing all of its rhythm values by the same amount. If its values are made larger, the motive is in **augmentation**. If its values are made smaller, the motive is in **diminution**.

Example 9. Rhythmic Diminution and Augmentation

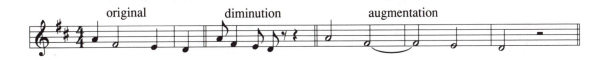

Phrase

A **phrase** is made of a series of motives and sometimes subphrases. Unlike its component parts (motives), the phrase ends in a **cadence**, a special kind of closure. The cadence in music is like punctuation in language. A cadence can be conclusive (like a period) or less conclusive (like a comma). A period-like closure is produced by a **full cadence** (V–I) and a comma-like closure by a **half cadence** (x–V) or a *deceptive cadence* (V–vi). The full (or authentic) cadence ends on a note in the tonic chord. The half (or semi-) cadence ends on a note in the dominant chord.

Subphrase

The **subphrase** is a division of the phrase. Subphrases can be unusually long motives with unusually strong closure, or a group of motives that ends with relatively strong closure. Subphrase closure is not intense enough to qualify as musical punctuation, and thus as a cadence. Subphrases are not always present in a phrase.

The next example shows a phrase that contains two subphrases. The first subphrase breaks down to two motives. The second does not. This difference provides an element of contrast between the two halves of the phrase. How does this break down and contrast relate to a simplified version of this melody?

Example 10. from Sonata in A (Piano), K.331   Mozart

Allegro con spirito

Phrase Group

The **phrase group** is the musical version of a compound sentence. It contains two or more phrases, each punctuated by cadences. These phrases are like independent clauses in language. The pattern of the phrase group is determined by the motive content of its constituent phrases, the length relationships among its phrases, and the relative effect of each closure in the stream of events.

Phrase Group Content

The term **parallel construction** means that two phrases being compared contain the same or closely similar motive ideas. **Contrasting construction** means that the motives in the two phrases are dissimilar.

251

Symmetry

Length relationships among motives, subphrases, and phrases are an important factor in the rhythmic organization of the phrase group. If ideas are about equal in length, the construction is **symmetrical**. If the parts are not equal, the construction is **asymmetrical**.

The phrase group shown in the next example is made of two phrases based on the same motive ideas. The pattern is labeled "a + a" because its two phrases are parallel. The phrases are of equal length so the construction is symmetrical.

Example 11. from Symphony No. 4   Tchaikovsky

Finale, allegro con fuoco

Period

The **period** is a special case of a phrase group. It contains two phrases; one ends on a half cadence (harmonically "open"), and the second phrase ends on a full cadence (harmonically "closed"). This open and closed harmonic effect sets up a *question/answer* or *antecedent/consequent* pattern, a special feature of the period.

Example 12. Period in Parallel Construction   Greensleeves (first two phrases)   Traditional

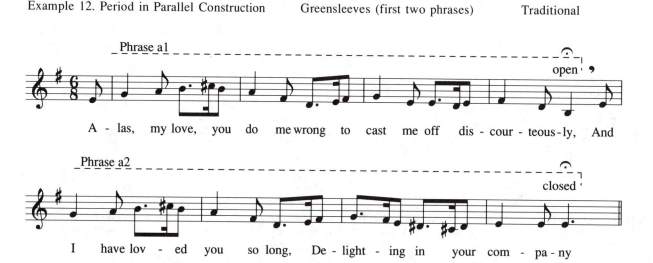

A two-phrase group is shown in the next example. The phrases are labeled "a" and "b" because each is based on different motive ideas. Closures are emphatic in this melody. The extra stems in motive "d" mark the notes of motive "a" that are imbedded in this idea. The first cadence (bar 4) is harmonically "closed." A contour arch is completed in the first four measures, so the first phrase is not dependent on the second phrase for completion. This eliminates the question/answer "feel" one associates with a period.

Example 13. from Symphony No. 5, Op.67   Beethoven

Allegro

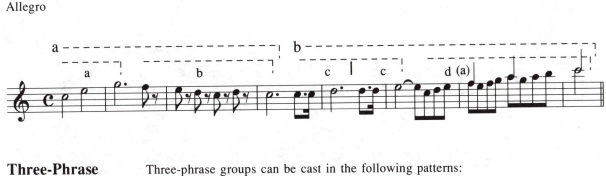

Three-Phrase Groups

Three-phrase groups can be cast in the following patterns:

a + a + a   a + a + b   a + b + a   a + b + b   a + b + c

The structure of the next example is described as ''a+b+c'' because of significant differences in the content of each phrase. However, material in phrases ''b'' and ''c'' is derived from phrase ''a.'' Notice how the ends of phrase ''a'' and ''c'' rhyme. Phrase ''c'' lacks the clear subphrase closure of the other phrases.

Example 14. Three-Phrase Group

from Le Nozza di Figaro, K. 492   Mozart

Andante con moto

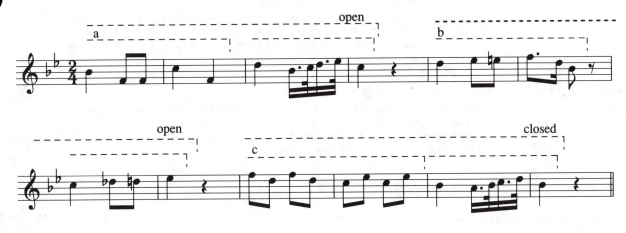

Four-Phrase Groups

Even more possibilities exist for four-phrase groups. A few of the possibilities are listed below.

a + a + a + a   a + a + a + b   a + b + a + b   a + b + a + c   a + b + c + d

The next melody is a four-phrase group labeled ''a + a + b + b.'' The two halves of this group have contrasting content. The first three cadences are open, not conclusive (see bars 3, 7 and 11). The last cadence is more conclusive because it closes on the tonic pitch and is rhythmically stronger than the other cadences.

Example 15. Sovejg's Song (from Peer Gynt)   Grieg

Poco andante

Through Composition

In previous examples, melodies were made of varied repetitions of one or two motives. Occasionally, a melody flows from one idea to the next without repetition. This musical version of free association is called **through composition**. In the next example, the succession of motives is through composed in the first two phrases. Although the motives have something in common, each is a new idea. The second two phrases are a repetition of the first two phrases.

Double Period

This melody is a **double period** because
• A period (phrases one and two) is repeated in phrases three and four (nearly verbatim) but
• phrase two ends on a half-cadence, not the full cadence required to "close" the first Pair of phrases as an independent period

Example 16. from Midsummer Night's Dream   Mendelssohn

Nocturne, andante tranquillo

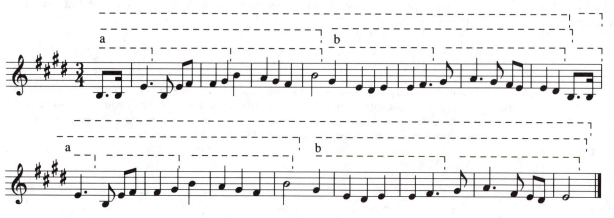

Phrase Extension

Phrase lengths in multiples of two measures are common (i.e., 2 × 2 = 4, 2 × 2 × 2 = 8 measures). Other phrase lengths also occur in music literature. The total number of accents in a phrase is as important as the total number of measures. For example, phrases span fewer measures in slow tempi because there are more accents per measure as one approaches a divided beat. This tendency reverses in fast tempi. Often, "normal" phrase length is established by the composer at the beginning of a composition. "Norm" is probably a better term for this than "normal." Once this norm is established in a composition, the composer can add or take away material for variation or effect.

The next melody is made of two five-bar phrases. Closure in the fourth measure is emphatic, yet the cadence figure is restated in the next bar. This **re-cadencing** is one way to extend a phrase. Notice how this cadence repetition and the following silences set one phrase apart from the other.

Example 17. from Scheherazade   Rimsky-Korsakov

Allegro non troppo

In the next melody, the brackets show a phrase **extension by augmentation.** Phrase duration is extended by stretching time rather than by adding or repeating material.

Example 18. from Symphony No. 5   Tchaikovsky

Andante

The bracket in the next melody shows an extension to the beginning of the second phrase, called an **extended upbeat** or **anacrusis**. This extension creates an impression of delayed motion.

Example 19. from Symphony No. 5　　　Sibelius

Andante mosso, quasi allegretto

Points of View

The analysis of music is seldom cut and dried. Analysis is a process in which one brings the sum of one's experience to bear on a composition to gain a better understanding of it. Because experiences vary, differences in point of view and interpretation are expected. Furthermore, most compositions contain elements of ambiguity that make more than one solution possible. Differing interpretations of ambiguous passages (''shades of gray'') are commonplace. One's reason for analyzing a particular composition is another factor that can result in a unique solution. In view of these possible differences, one's primary concern should be for a well structured approach that contains logically supported conclusions (a well supported point of view). A ''blow-by-blow'' report of every item noticed by the analyst may not reveal much about the nature of a composition, but details that illustrate a unique quality in a work can contribute a great deal to one's understanding of a composition.

Often you must share your findings about a composition with someone else, so communication is an important aspect of an analysis. You must be able to verbalize or use graphics effectively to illustrate your thoughts. Active musicians analyze music continuously, often ''on the fly'' during a rehearsal or performance. They use the information obtained from analysis to develop interpretations, uncover something that needs to be shared with fellow musicians, or pass on an understanding to one of their own students.

The next example is a gray situation that shows how differing points of view might develop. The example is cast in three symmetrical segments and could be seen as a three-phrase group, ''a + a + b.'' The second and third segments begin with the strong upbeat-to-downbeat pattern, 𝅘𝅥𝅭 𝅘𝅥𝅯 𝅘𝅥 . Closure at the end of the two ''a'' segments, however, might not be strong enough to rate as a cadence. If these segments do not close with cadences, they cannot be analyzed as phrases. Under these circumstances, the melody could be seen as a phrase made of three clearly articulated subphrases. Which point of view do you favor?

Example 20. from Concerto No. 5   Beethoven

Allegro

The next melody is through composed, but each idea is restated before the melody progresses to a new idea. Notice how closures become less distinct as the melody unfolds and the ideas get progressively longer. Compare the lengths of the first five segments. The third segment is made of a series of two-note fragments. Considering the tempo, is this segment a phrase or a sub-phrase? What is the phrase pattern here? Can you see how the ideas in segments 2, 3, and 4 are derived from the first motive? Can you see how the rhythm in segment 5 was derived from other segments? Note how the rests help produce an initial declamation. What contributes to the drama of this excerpt?

Example 21. from Symphony in D minor   Franck

From César Franck, "Symphony in D minor, Opus 48 (1886–88)" *Symphonie pour Orchestre par César Frank.* Originally published by J. Hamelle, Paris. Reprinted with permission of Dover Publications, Inc.

Allegro non troppo

SEGMENT ANALYSIS GUIDELINES

Think of the segment organization of a melody as musical sentence and paragraph structure. Find the germ idea or ideas and look for recurrences of them. Note motive rhythm patterns and motive variation devices. Observe closure and punctuation effects. Use the marks provided below to label the different kinds of segments.

UNITS WITHIN THE PHRASE

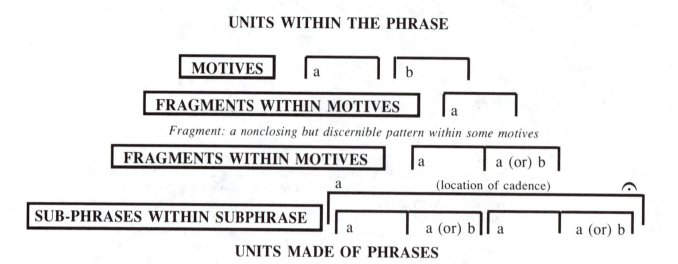

Fragment: a nonclosing but discernible pattern within some motives

UNITS MADE OF PHRASES

[P = partial closure (half, deceptive, nonconclusive authentic cadence), H = half cadence, and F = full cadence. The analysis of motives and other segments within a phrase can be omitted where brevity is desired.]

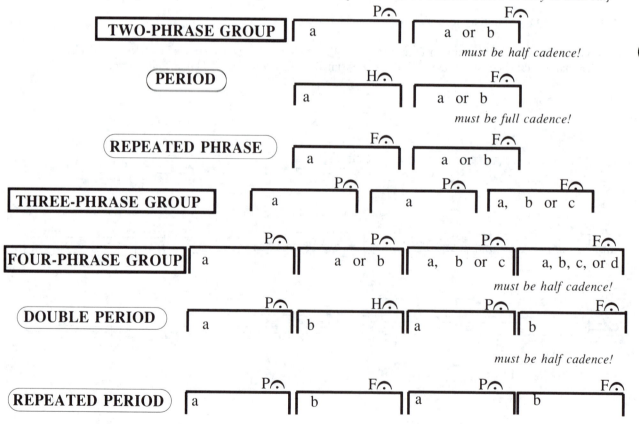

258

CHECKPOINT

1. Explain these terms:

motive	closure
motive rhythm features	phrase group
motive rhythm (4 types)	motive continuity
transposition	melodic inversion
interval inversion	retrograde
augmentation	retrograde-inversion
diminution	subphrase
phrase	nested patterns
cadence	full cadence
half cadence	period
double period	parallel construction
extension by augmentation	symmetrical construction
through composition	contrasting construction
re-cadencing	asymmetrical construction
extended upbeat (anacrusis)	

2. Self-help Problems. Solutions to these problems are subject to interpretation. Be prepared to discuss in class any differences between your answers and the sample solutions.

Solution 4

Problem 4

Mark each motive with a bracket. Every note must be included in a motive.

Solution 5

original   transposition

retrograde   diminution

Problem 5

Write each variation of the original motive.

original   transposition

retrograde   diminution

Solution 6

original   inversion

augmentation   change fragment order
                sample

Problem 6

Write each variation of the original motive.

original   inversion

augmentation   change fragment order

261

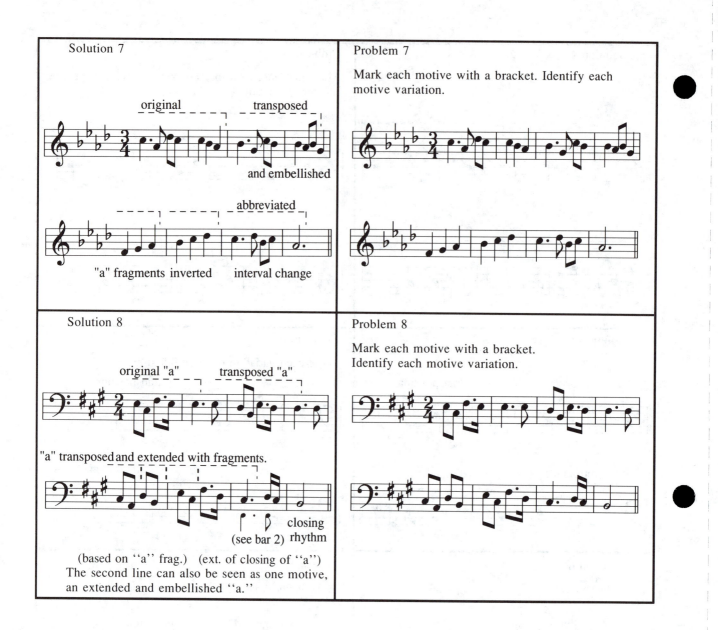

Solution 7

original · · · · · transposed

and embellished

"a" fragments inverted · · · · · abbreviated · · · · · interval change

Problem 7

Mark each motive with a bracket. Identify each motive variation.

Solution 8

original "a" · · · · · transposed "a"

"a" transposed and extended with fragments.

closing (see bar 2) rhythm

(based on "a" frag.)   (ext. of closing of "a")
The second line can also be seen as one motive, an extended and embellished "a."

Problem 8

Mark each motive with a bracket. Identify each motive variation.

262

ANALYSIS APPLICATIONS

NAME _____ CLASS _____ DATE _____

1. Complete a segment analysis of this melody following the Segment Analysis Guidelines (page 258). Describe the overall pattern and any special features. Label each cadence.

from Sonata in A flat, Op. 26   Beethoven

Andante (theme for variations)

2. Find the closures then discuss their relative intensity. How does this affect how you hear the motive continuity? How does this influence your styling of this melody? Label each cadence.

from Symphony No. 2   Brahms

Allegretto grazioso (third movement)

3. What is the overall structure of this melody? Describe its construction patterns (i.e., asymmetrical, contrasting, and so on). Label each cadence.

from Symphony in E minor, Op. 93   Dvorak

Largo

4. Mark each motive with a bracket. Include all notes in a motive. Describe the relative lengths of ideas and the relative strengths of the closures. Identify the overall pattern. Label each cadence.

from Eine Kleine Nachtmusik   Mozart

Andante

5. Mark each motive with a bracket. Include all notes in a motive. Comment on the closures, especially their changing position in the meter. What affect does this have on segment continuity? How does this information affect your interpretation and performance of this melody?

Traumerei from Scenes from Childhood, Op. 75   Schumann

Andante

6. Identify the overall pattern. Briefly discuss the scheme of contrasting phrases. Symmetry, implied harmonic rhythm, and change of pace are factors in this contrast. Circle notes that belong in the skeleton of this melody. How does this information affect your performance of this melody?

Waltz of the Flowers from Nutcracker Suite, Op. 71   Tchaikovsky

7. Mark segments with brackets so that motives, sub-phrase, phrases, and phrase groups can be seen. What variation devices are used on recurring motives? Locate closures. Label cadences. Compare the relative lengths of segments and relate this to the tonal organization of the melody (i.e., key changes). What makes you expect phrase closure? How does the idea of varied repetition apply to this melody? Classify the overall structure of the melody. Circle notes that belong to the skeleton of the melody. Compare this skeleton and its harmonic implications with the segment analysis.

Waltzes, Op. 39 (No. 15)   Brahms

Although the following exercises emphasize phrase and phrase-group construction, a successful melody must also possess effective contour, continuity, and skeleton features. These exercises provide an opportunity for you to synthesize these factors in successfully written melodies. Try different contour and continuity patterns for each melody. See the Guidelines for Contour and Continuity Analysis, Skeletonizing, Segment Analysis, and Harmonizing.

Harmonize each melody. You will find it helpful to develop a harmonic sketch as you develop each melody. If you have not done much writing before, you will be pleasantly surprised at your ability to create an interesting melody. Please set aside the notion that creativity is a rare, mystical gift.

There is no mystery to the creative process. Creativity comes from a desire to originate material and from the motivation to work. Writing is like practicing—the more one does it, the better one gets. Most individuals have the ability to work imaginatively with all manner and sorts of ingredients. Once these ingredients and their natures have been identified, ways to play with and combine them will be discovered. Frankly, you will discover more possibilities than you can use. Composition is more a job of editing, of deciding which possibilities go best together. Learn to discard unused possibilities (or put them in a sketch book for future reference).

WRITING APPLICATIONS

1. Write original motives that complete each of the rhythmic movements below. Remember that a motive (a) can be as brief as two notes, (b) has closure, and (c) contains one primary accent.

   (a) weak-strong

   (b) strong-strong

   (c) weak-weak

   (d) strong-weak

2. Use varied repetitions of one of your original motives to build a four-bar phrase. Concentrate on variants based on transposition and minor rhythm and pitch changes. Begin by choosing clef, key signature, and meter.

3. Use varied repetitions of one of your original motives to build a four-bar phrase. Concentrate on transposed inversion and retrograde variants. Begin by choosing clef, key signature, and meter.

4. Use one of the above phrases as a basis for an eight-bar period in parallel, symmetrical construction. Begin by choosing clef, key signature, and meter.

5. Use any of the above material as the basis for an eight-bar period in contrasting, symmetrical construction. Begin by choosing clef, key signature, and meter.

6. Modify the period created in the previous exercise so it becomes a double period (| a | b | a | b ||).

7. Write a two-phrase group in asymmetrical, contrasting construction.

13 HARMONIZING MELODY: STRATEGIES FOR VARIETY

OVERVIEW

This chapter emphasizes adding variety to a basic harmonization. Details are presented on root tone relationships, chord substitution, non-tonic focus, triad and seventh chord color resources, series-of-fifths progressions, and harmonic sequence.

Review

As suggested in the previous chapter, chords selected to harmonize a melody should support and complement its rhythmic and pitch design. A harmonization will complement a melody if

- the key is supported by repeated use of V and I and
- cadences are harmonized with stable chords and standard chord progressions that reinforce the key

Patterns in the pitch and rhythm background of a melody help one decide what chord to use and when to use it. Sometimes, the simple clarity of primary triads is the best solution to harmonize a melody.

Balance Between Variety and Tonal Structure

The exclusive use of primary triads is not always appropriate or desirable. Patterns in the melody may call for the use of non-primary triads (i.e., chords other than I, IV, or V). When relief from the continual use of primary triads is desired, devices for harmonic variety are brought into play. Even though variety is required, simplicity remains an important principle in the arts. Too much emphasis on variety can cloud the purpose of a harmonization. Do *enough* and no more to get a point across. [Listen to Satie's "Gymnopedies" for a musical illustration of this principle of simplicity.]

Root Tone Relationships

Chord progressions can be categorized by the interval formed between the roots of adjacent chords. Progressions can be arranged in three root-interval classes; seconds, thirds, or fifths. If the interval between chord roots is a second, the progression is called a **second relation**. If the interval is a third, it is called a **third relation**—if a fifth, a **fifth relation**. Each class of chord progression has its own unique effect and motion characteristic. *These classes also include the inversions of these intervals.*

Example 1. Interval Relationships Between Roots of Chords

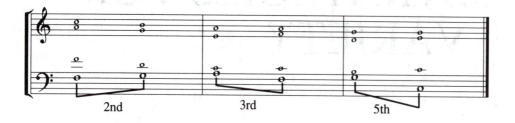

Second Relations

In **second relations**, the melodic interval of the m2 and M2 between the roots of chords produces no distinct root. Thus, by itself, the second relation cannot tonicize. Color changes may or may not occur from chord to chord in a second relation. In the next example, different note characters indicate different colors. The second chord of a second relation contains ALL new pitches and the voices move mainly by step to the second chord. The bass and the upper voices move in contrary motion. This gives second relations considerable melodic thrust, the principal feature of this progression class.

Example 2. Second Relations

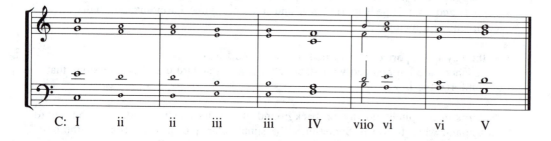

C: I   ii   ii   iii   iii   IV   viio vi   vi   V

Third Relations

The two chords of a **third relation** always have two notes in common. Because of these common tones, this progression is melodically and harmonically static. Unless alterations are added, third relations <u>always</u> involve a change of chord color, so the principal effect of third relations is color variation. Chord color differences are shown in the example by different note characters.

Example 3. Third Relations

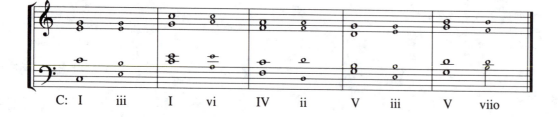

C: I   iii   I   vi   IV   ii   V   iii   V   viio

Fifth Relations

The perfect fifth (and P4) is a root producing interval. Accordingly, **fifth relations** produce a progression root, the root of the melodic fourth or fifth between chord roots. Chord colors may or may not change in a fifth relation. The principal effect of this progression is a generation of harmonic focus. There is a marked difference between a melodic fifth down and a fifth up. A fifth relation down **tonicizes** because it sharpens the focus on the bottom note of the fifth. What is the effect of a fifth up progression, movement <u>away</u> from the progression root? Play these patterns forwards and backwards to evaluate this effect. What is the difference in effect of the fifth up and the fifth down?

Example 4. Fifth Relations

C: V   I   vi   ii   viio   iii   ii   vi

Chord Substitution

Triads in a third relation share two pitches (common tones). Only one note changes in a third relation of triads. Because of this kinship between the triads, chords a third relation apart can be used in place of one another with minimum harmonic and melodic impact.

The process of replacing a chord by its third relation is called **chord substitution**. The chord that replaces another in this process is called a **substitute chord**. A chord can be preceded by or followed by its substitution, or can be replaced by it entirely. The principal effect of a chord substitution is a change of chord color.

The first part of the next progression is made of primary triads. Substitute chords were inserted between the original chords in the second part of the progression. The substitutions add color and variety to the progression without disturbing its underlying tonicizing function. The ii chord, a common substitute for IV, adds to the closing tonicizing effect by setting up a short series-of-fifths progression, ii–V–I.

Example 5. Downward Substitutions

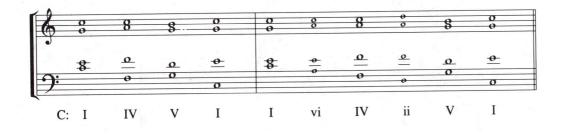

C: I   IV   V   I   I   vi   IV   ii   V   I

Systematic chord substitution can create alternating colors in a progression. In the next example, the substitutions are upward. Near the end of the example, the "viio" is used as a substitute for the V chord without disrupting the dominant function of the local harmony. The viio chord does not stand in a P5 relation to I but does contain the leading tone. *The leading tone movement produces melodic focus on tonic.*

Example 6. Upward Substitutions

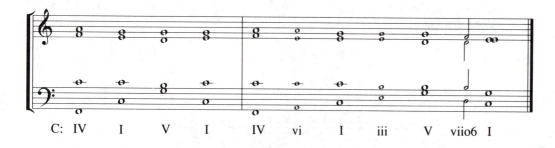

C: IV   I   V   I   IV   vi   I   iii   V   viio6   I

Deceptive Cadence

The **deceptive cadence** is an authentic cadence in which vi is used as a substitute for I. It is called a deceptive cadence because it is ordinarily used in places where the listener expects to hear the tonic chord in an authentic cadence. The listener, expecting a I chord, is literally deceived by the substitution of the vi chord. Also, the iii chord can replace the V chord in a **deceptive semi-cadence**.

Example 7. Deceptive Cadences

C: V   I   V   vi   vi   V   vi   iii

In the next example, a deceptive cadence is used to close a phrase. Were you led to expect an authentic cadence because of the **domino effect** of a series-of-fifths relations? Were you deceived by this cadence? How conclusive was the punctuation effect of this cadence?

Example 8. Deceptive Cadence

C: I   IV   viio   iii   vi   ii   V   vi

Chord Color Groupings

The **primary triads** (I, IV, V) support the mode of major or minor keys and are used to define the keynotes. The primary triads are major in a major key and minor in a natural minor key. Every major and natural minor key contains a group of secondary chords that contrasts in color with the primary triads. These two groups of chords are equal in size (three chords) and both groups have the same internal relationships (i.e., chord roots are a P5 apart). In major, the diminished triad viio is a frequent substitute for V. While not of the primary color group, viio has a dominant function when it replaces V.

Example 9. Chord Color Groups in Major, Relative, Minor, and Parallel Minor

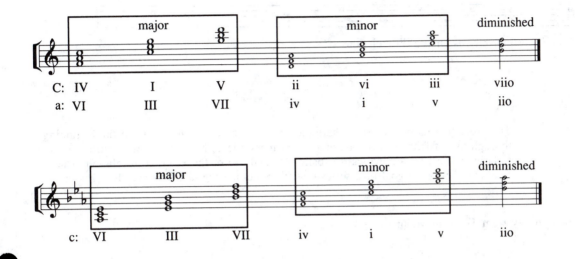

One way to give variety to a harmonization is to shift focus away from the primary triads temporarily. For example, one can tonicize a chord within the secondary color group by using the fifth relations among these chords repeatedly. The most likely note to tonicize is the keynote of the relative mode since it is the substitute for tonic. The secondary chords can be substituted as a block for the primary triads of the key.

In the next example, the first harmonization contains primary triads only. This defines the tonic pitch and supports the major mode of the melody. The second harmonization includes secondary chords. These minor triads are used in a block to contrast with the mode and tonality established in the first bar (see bars 2 and 3). Later, the minor triads are used to create a pattern that alternates between major and minor colors (see bars 5 and 6). The rhythmic pacing is more rapid in the second version.

Example 10. I Know Where I'm Going   Traditional

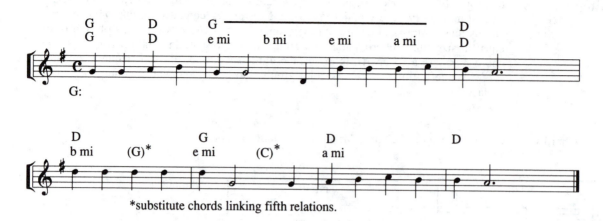

*substitute chords linking fifth relations.

The procedure used in the next harmonization established tonic focus at the beginning through use of fifth relations among the primary triads. Next, focus was shifted to vi (relative minor) by a downward substitution and use of the vi –ii fifth relation. The final chord was the goal of a series-of-fifth relations (the last four chords).

Example 11. Focus Away from Tonic in Major

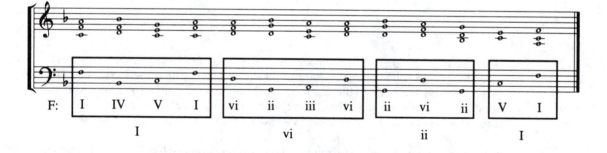

In the previous example, no new accidentals were used but focus was shifted to various notes in the key. The focus areas of vi and ii stand in a fifth relationship to each other. This creates a background movement of fifths with the tonic pitch as the eventual goal.

This variation process is equally effective in a minor key. In the next harmonization, attention was shifted to the major chord color group via an upward substitution. This shift was reinforced through tonicizing fifth relations within the contrasting chord color group (III–VII). Natural minor (no altered tones) was used to intensify the focus of III (chords 5–8). As in the previous example, a series-of-fifth relations pattern underlies the progression. The goal of the background progression is the tonic pitch. The leading tone, indicated by ♯7̂, is brought back into play to sharpen focus on the pitch D.

Example 12. Focus Away from Tonic in Minor

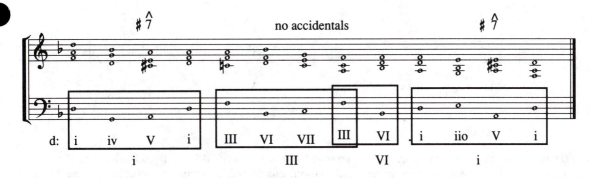

Non-Tonic Focus in Melody

Non-tonic focus can be an integral part of the design of a melody. This can be seen in the next example after the repeat sign in the melody (bars 5–8). During this time, the G-D fifth momentarily replaces the E-B fifth in the melodic skeleton. This shift is so definite that one could argue this is really a change of key rather than a simple change of focus.

Example 13. Built-in Shift of Focus

Traditional melody

Chord Color Resources in Minor

The raised sixth and seventh steps in melodic and harmonic minor greatly increase the chord color vocabulary in minor keys. These alterations are shown in the next example (♯6 means "raised sixth"; ♯7 means "raised seventh"; and ♯3 means "raised third"). The major tonic triad (Picardy Third) is sometimes used to make a cadence more conclusive in a minor key. Generally, melodic motion continues in the direction of the alteration. If a note is raised, the melody continues upward, and if the note is lowered, the melody continues downward. *The raised accidentals in minor generally intensify the focus on tonic.*

Example 14. Additional Chord Colors in Minor

C mi: I   ii   III+   IV   V   vio   viio

Series-of-Fifths Progressions

The chords in a key can be arranged into a series-of-fifth relation. Because of the tonicizing function of the fifth relation, this particular arrangement of chords creates a domino effect among the chord roots. If the tonic pitch is the last root in the "row of dominos," tonic comes into even sharper focus because it is the goal of this strong pattern. Four background step movements are also imbedded in a series-of-fifths progression. These **step progressions**, marked by slurs, proceed toward the notes of the tonic triad. The tonic chord becomes the goal of all melodic lines in a downward series-of-fifths.

Example 15. Series-of-Fifths Progression

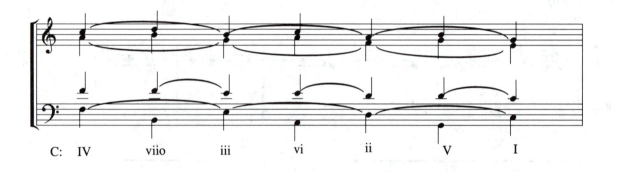

C: IV   viio   iii   vi   ii   V   I

A **series-of-fifths progression** heightens tonal focus both melodically and through a root-tone domino effect. It can provide a systematic way to use all the chord colors within a key. This pattern is very common in all kinds of music—folk, popular, jazz, and art music. The series-of-fifths provides the harmonic foundation for the next melody, the classic popular song, "Autumn Leaves."

Example 16. Autumn Leaves (Les Fevilles Mortes) English Lyric by Johnny Mercer. French Lyric by Jacques Prevert. Music by Joseph Kosma. © 1947, 1950 Enoch Et CIE. © Renewed 1975, 1978 ENOCH ET CIE. Sole Selling Agent for U.S. and Canada: MORLEY MUSIC CO., by arrangement with Enoch et Cie. International Copyright Secured. All Rights Reserved. Reprinted by permission of Enoch and Cie and Morley Music Co.

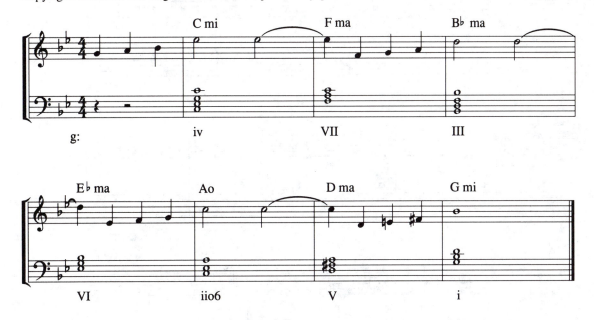

Numerous melodies are based on a series-of-fifths scheme. This scheme does not require that all the steps in a key be used. For example, the progression vi–ii–V–I is long enough to produce the series-of-fifths domino effect. Remember that cues for chord selection can be found in the pitch and rhythm skeleton of the melody. If "Autumn Leaves" was based on a series-of-fifths, its background patterns will show evidence of series-of-fifths thinking. **Step progressions** (background scales) often indicate the use of a series-of-fifths plan. In "Autumn Leaves," the closing notes of each motive form a descending background scale.

The next example is also based on a series-of-fifths pattern. The simplified version of the melody is written in bass clef. Notice that the tonic pitch is not emphasized until the end of the melody. Interval root is the most significant focusing factor in this melody. Interval roots are shown in the simplified version with normal note characters. Satellites are indicated with cue note characters.

Example 17. Ich grolle nicht   Schumann

A portion of the series-of-fifth pattern can be seen in the skeleton of "Ich grolle nicht." A complete series-of-fifths is included in the next example for comparison. Step progressions in the series-of-fifths are marked with slurs. The numbers written below the skeleton indicate scale degrees. How does the skeleton of "Ich grolle nicht" compare to the complete series-of-fifths scheme? Do you see a relationship between the two halves of the melodic skeleton? Notice that the first half does not close $\hat{1}$. In contrast, the close on $\hat{1}$ in the second half is strengthened through repetition.

Example 18. Ich grolle nicht, skeleton

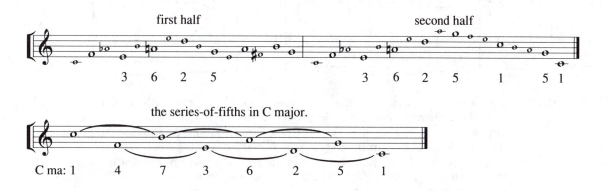

the series-of-fifths in C major.

Harmonic Sequence

A **harmonic sequence** results from the systematic transposition of a progression and its voice leading patterns. Ordinarily, a progression of two chords is transposed repeatedly in seconds. The next example shows harmonic sequences based on fifth relations. The result is very similar to a series-of-fifths progression. Notice that the melodic patterns contained in each voice of the original progression are preserved in each transposed repetition.

Listen for the difference in effect between the upward and the downward sequence-of-fifths. How does this relate to movement towards or away from the progression root? [Some authorities refer to movement away from the root of the progression as "retrogression."]

Example 19. Sequence-of-Fifths

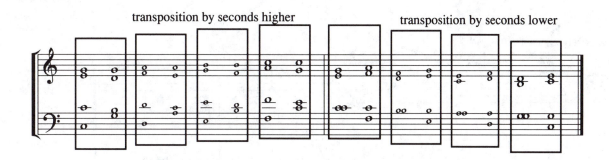

285

A harmonic sequence can be based on any of the three root-relation intervals (seconds, thirds, or fifths). Sequences based on seconds or thirds are not used very often, perhaps because they do not establish a harmonic goal as does a sequence of downward fifths.

Example 20. Sequence of Seconds, Thirds

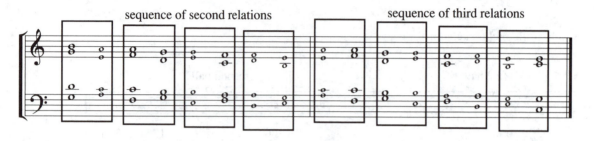

Melodic Sequence   The harmonic sequence-of-fifths is often used to support a **melodic sequence**. A **melodic sequence** is based on a series of transpositions of a motive, usually a chain of transpositions of a second. Two different harmonizations of a phrase are given in the next example. Each melodic sequence is marked with a bracket. The second version uses all of the available triads in the key. The voice movement in each transposed progression is repeated literally. The sequence of downward fifths brings strong focus to the final chord.

Example 21. Angels We Have Heard On High   Traditional

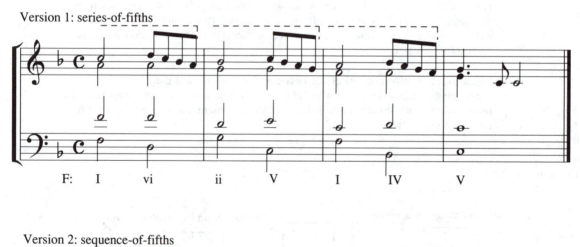

286

CHECKPOINT I (Harmonic Variety Devices)

1. Define these terms:

   chord color group   chord color resources

   second relation   third relation

   fifth relation   progression root

   domino effect   series-of-fifths format

   substitute chord   deceptive cadence

   harmonic sequence   melodic sequence

   secondary triad   non-tonic focus

   primary triad   deceptive semi-cadence

   step progressions

2. Short Answers

   Use Roman numerals to answer (a) and (b).

   a. In major, the minor triads are:

   b. In natural minor, the major triads are:

   Use chord root/quality signs to answer (c) through (h).

   Sample: In B major, the major triads are: <u>B ma, E ma, F#ma</u>.

   c. In E major, the major triads are:

   d. In E major, the minor triads are:

   e. In E major, the diminished triad is:

   f. In F#minor (nat.), the diminished triad is:

   g. In F#minor (nat.), the minor triads are:

   h. In F#minor (nat.), the major triads are:

3. Self-help Problems. Problems are in the right column, solutions in the left.

Solution 1 second (up or down) none melodic, linear	Problem 1 Supply the requested information about second relations. Interval of chord roots: _____ common tones? _____ general effect: _____
Solution 2 third (up or down) two color change	Problem 2 Supply the requested information about third relations. Interval of chord roots: _____ common tones? _____ general effect: _____
Solution 3 fifth (up or down) one harmonic focus, tonicize	Problem 3 Supply the requested information about fifth relations. Interval of chord roots: _____ common tones? _____ general effect: _____
Solution 4 (I) IV vii° iii vi ii (V)	Problem 4 Arrange all the triads of a key in series-of-fifths order. I __ __ __ __ __ V
Solution 5 third (never)	Problem 5 Chord substitution occurs if a chord is replaced by another a _____ relation lower or higher. Unless accidentals are added, a substitute chord is (always) (sometimes)(never) the same color as the original chord.

Solution 6 I IV V vi ii iii third substituted	**Problem 6** What are the chords in each group in a major key? Major Color Group: ___ ___ ___ Minor Color Group: ___ ___ ___ Because one group lies a _____ away from another, one whole group can be _____ for the other.

Solution 7
 	
i   iv   v
 	
III   VI   VII
 	
relative
	Problem 7
	
	What are the chords in each group in a natural minor key?
	
	  Minor Color Group: ___ ___ ___
	
	  Major Color Group: ___ ___ ___
	
	If one group is substituted for the other, the music will seem to be in the _____ mode.

Solution 8 sequence second harmonic	**Problem 8** If a chord progression is transposed literally and systematically, the result is called a harmonic _____. The transposition interval is usually a _____. Melodic sequences are usually underscored by _____ sequences.

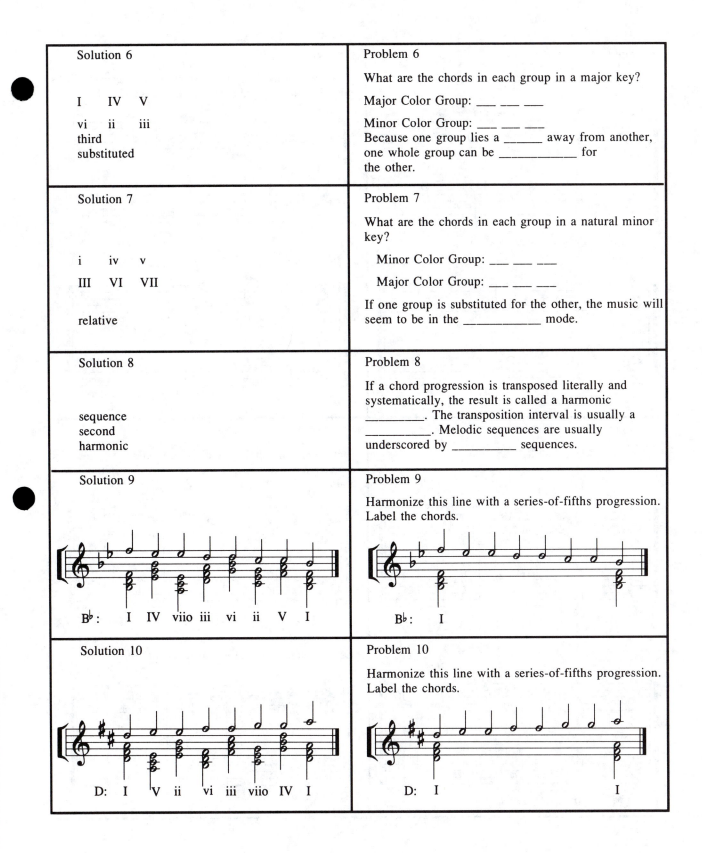

Solution 9

B♭: I IV viio iii vi ii V I

Problem 9

Harmonize this line with a series-of-fifths progression. Label the chords.

B♭: I

Solution 10

D: I V ii vi iii viio IV I

Problem 10

Harmonize this line with a series-of-fifths progression. Label the chords.

D: I   I

Solution 11

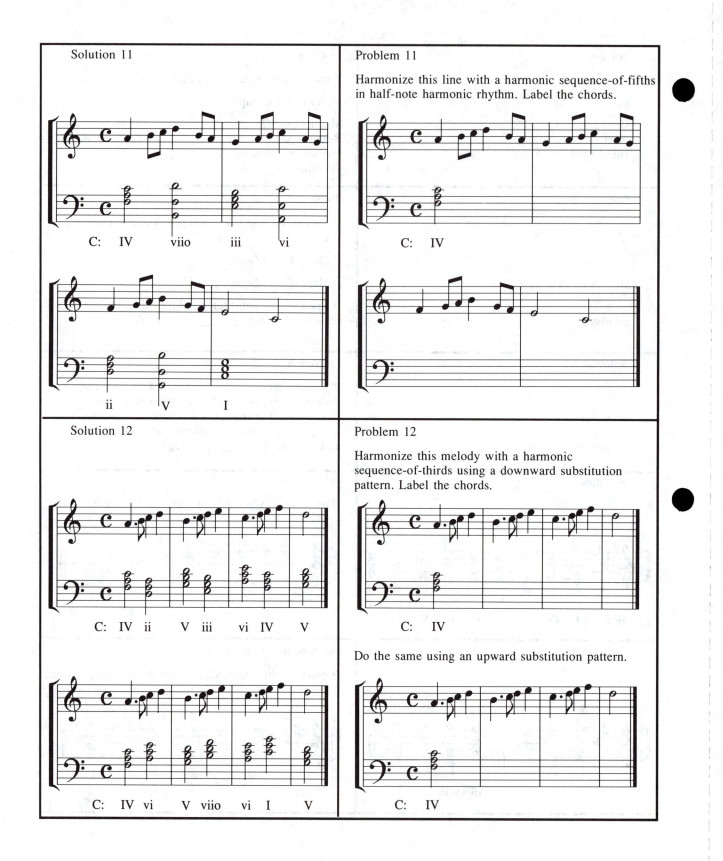

C: IV   viio   iii   vi

ii   V   I

Problem 11

Harmonize this line with a harmonic sequence-of-fifths in half-note harmonic rhythm. Label the chords.

C: IV

Solution 12

C: IV ii   V iii   vi IV   V

C: IV vi   V viio   vi I   V

Problem 12

Harmonize this melody with a harmonic sequence-of-thirds using a downward substitution pattern. Label the chords.

C: IV

Do the same using an upward substitution pattern.

C: IV

290

Solution 13

F: I vi7 iii vi iii vi ii V

Problem 13

Create a momentary focus on vi (submediant) in measures 3 and 4. Label the chords.

F:

Solution 14

G: I vi ii vi ii vi V

Problem 14

Create a momentary focus on ii (supertonic) in measures 3 and 4. Label the chords.

G:

Solution 15

g: i V VII

III iv V i

Problem 15

Create a momentary focus on III (mediant) in measures 3 and 4. Label the chords. Use #7 in dominant chords.

g:

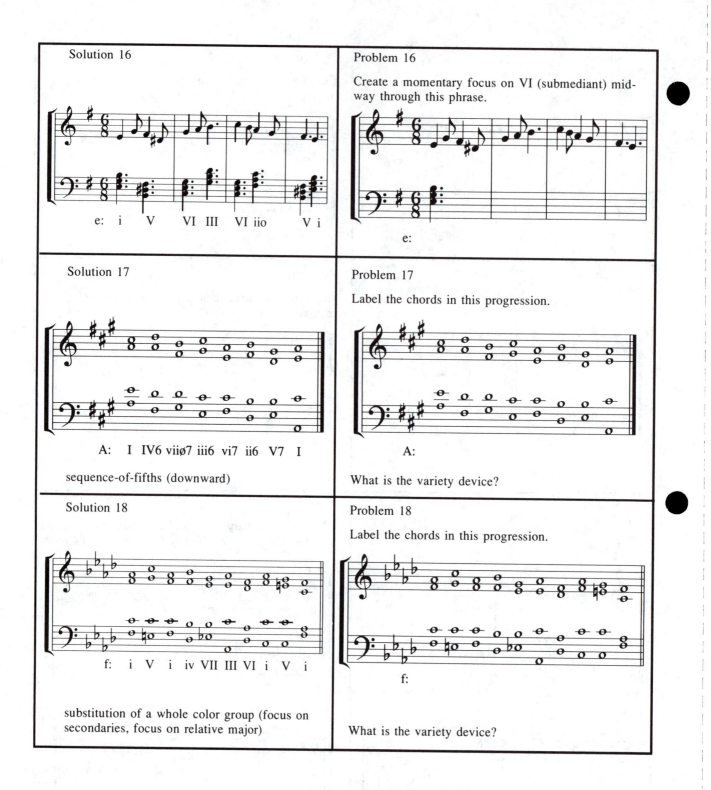

Solution 16

e: i V VI III VI iio V i

Problem 16

Create a momentary focus on VI (submediant) mid-way through this phrase.

e:

Solution 17

A: I IV6 viiø7 iii6 vi7 ii6 V7 I

sequence-of-fifths (downward)

Problem 17

Label the chords in this progression.

A:

What is the variety device?

Solution 18

f: i V i iv VII III VI i V i

substitution of a whole color group (focus on secondaries, focus on relative major)

Problem 18

Label the chords in this progression.

f:

What is the variety device?

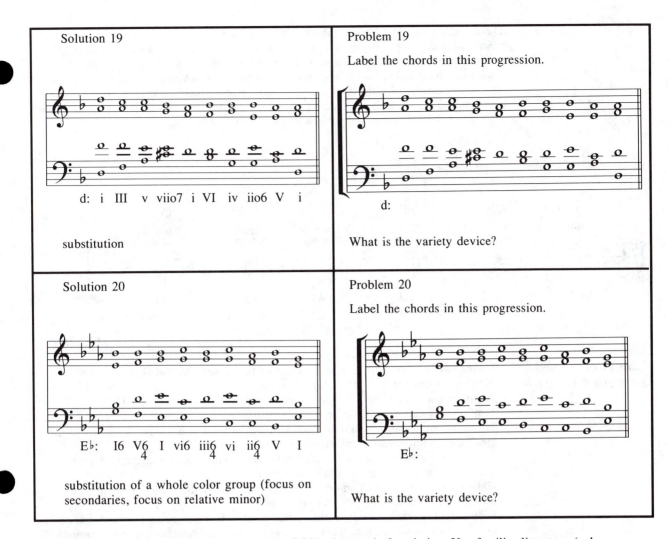

Solution 19

d: i III v viio7 i VI iv iio6 V i

substitution

Problem 19

Label the chords in this progression.

d:

What is the variety device?

Solution 20

E♭: I6 V6/4 I vi6 iii6/4 vi ii6/4 V I

substitution of a whole color group (focus on secondaries, focus on relative minor)

Problem 20

Label the chords in this progression.

E♭:

What is the variety device?

4. Find a melody that is based on a series-of-fifths harmonic foundation. Use familiar literature (solo or ensemble) or an anthology as sources. Folk songs, ''fake books,'' sheet music, or ''lead sheets'' are legitimate sources. Next, find examples of chord substitution, harmonic sequence, and focus on secondary chords.

Seventh Chords A **seventh chord** is a four-tone ''stack'' of thirds. These chords can be used to add interesting colors to the harmonization of a melody. Any triad can be changed to a seventh chord by adding a third above its fifth. The addition of sevenths to the four triad colors thirds results in seven different seventh chord colors.

Example 22. Seventh Chords

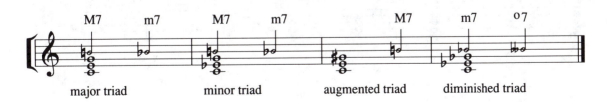

major triad   minor triad   augmented triad   diminished triad

293

The identification of most seventh chords can be written in several ways. Several methods for labeling seventh chords are presented in the next example. Only chords that appear normally in major or harmonic and melodic minor keys are included. Sevenths can be added to the four triad colors to create seven distinct seventh chord sounds. As indicated in the next example, only a major seventh can be added to the augmented triad because the distance between the fifth and the seventh is a diminished third, the enharmonic equivalent of a major second.

Example 23. Four Ways to Identify Seventh Chords

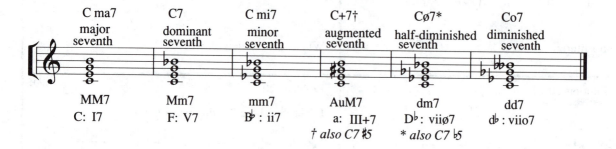

Commonly Used Seventh Chords

- **Major seventh** chord: A major triad with a major seventh added. **MM7** means major triad plus major seventh.
- **Dominant seventh** chord: A major triad with a minor seventh added. **Mm7** means major triad plus minor seventh.
- **Minor seventh** chord: A minor triad with a minor seventh added. **mm7** means minor triad plus minor seventh.
- **Augmented seventh** chord: An augmented triad with a major seventh added. **AuM7** means an augmented triad plus major seventh.
- **Half-diminished seventh** chord: A diminished triad with a minor seventh added. **dm7** means diminished triad plus minor seventh.
- **Diminished seventh** chord: A diminished triad with a diminished seventh added. **dd7** means diminished triad plus diminished seventh. This chord is made entirely of minor thirds.

If no alterations are used, four kinds of seventh chord are available in a major key. In major, the dominant seventh (V7) and leading tone seventh (viiø7) have unique sounds. They are the only seventh chords in major to contain a tritone, so they lack the stability of the minor seventh and major seventh chords.

Example 24. Seventh Chords Available in Major

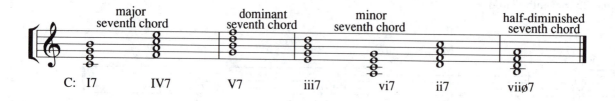

Accidentals in harmonic and melodic minor increase the number of available seventh chord colors. In harmonic minor, the raised leading tone (♯7) is used almost invariably in the dominant and leading tone seventh chords (V7 and viio7). The diminished seventh chord based on the raised $\hat{7}$ is unique to harmonic minor.

Example 25. Seventh Chords Available in Harmonic Minor

V7 (Mm7) and III+7 (AugM7) are available in harmonic and melodic minor because ♯7 is used in both minor variants. In addition, the use of ♯6 in melodic minor causes the IV7 to sound like a dominant seventh (Mm7). Notice that the leading tone seventh contains *both* ♯6 and ♯7.

Example 26. Additional Seventh Chords Available in Melodic Minor

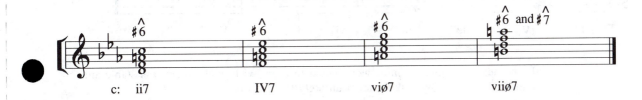

Seventh chords that occur in harmonic minor are the most commonly used, especially V7 and viio7. The use of the III+7 is quite rare, and more will be said about the III+7 in chapters on chromatic practices.

Seventh chords that occur in melodic minor are less frequently used. Some composers avoid the use of the altered IV7 to reserve the unique sound of the Mm7 for the dominant seventh chord (V7).

Seventh chords add interesting colors to a harmonization. If these colors are used extensively, however, the prevailing sound (sound norm) of seventh chords is established that neutralizes the variety of the added colors.

Seventh chords are less stable than major or minor triads. Seventh chords that contain tritones are even less stable. Most seventh chords make poor closing chords because their instability tends to offset the punctuating effect of the cadence. More will be said about the writing of seventh chords in chapters on the chorale and part-writing.

In the next example, the color of seventh chords was added to support a harmonic sequence pattern. Two settings of a phrase are given, and one utilizes every chord of the key.

Example 27. Seventh Chords in a Sequence

Version 1: a short sequence

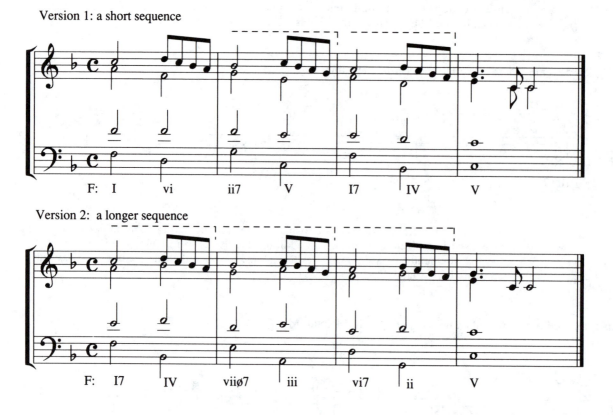

In the next example, sevenths were added to ii and vi to make them less stable and thus delay closure by making them unlikely tonic chords.

Example 28. Seventh Chords During Emphasis on Secondary Chords

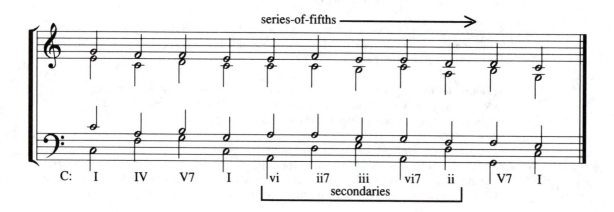

CHECKPOINT II (Seventh Chords)

1. Define these terms:

   seventh chord   major seventh chord

   minor seventh chord   augmented seventh chord

   diminished seventh chord   half-diminished seventh chord

   sound norm

2. Self-help Problems.

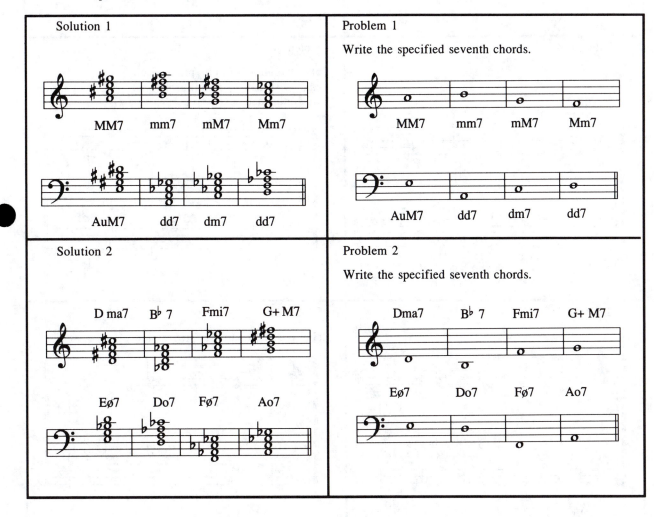

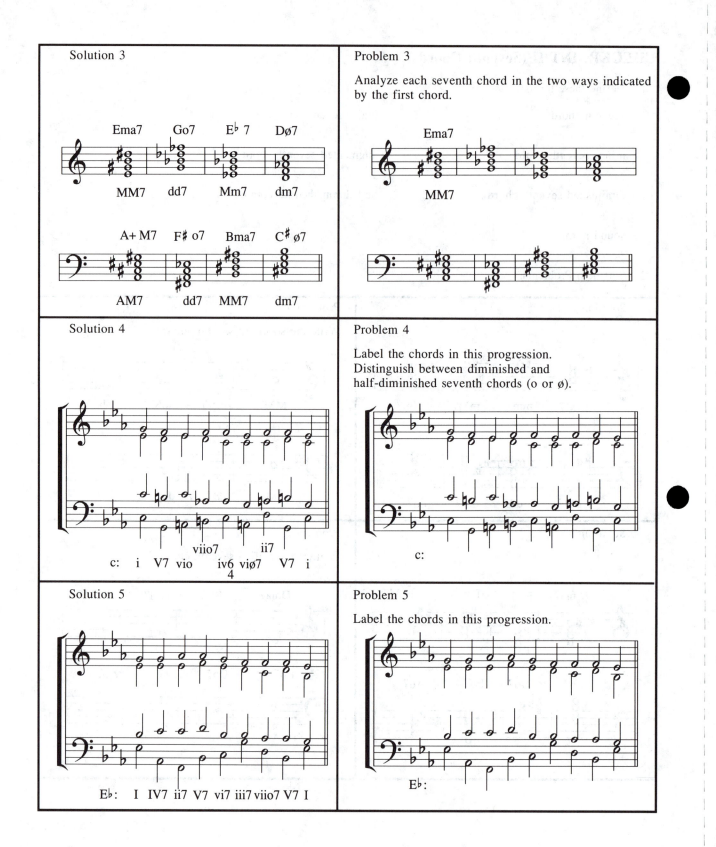

Solution 3

Ema7   Go7   E♭7   D∅7

MM7   dd7   Mm7   dm7

A+M7   F♯o7   Bma7   C♯∅7

AM7   dd7   MM7   dm7

Problem 3

Analyze each seventh chord in the two ways indicated by the first chord.

Ema7

MM7

Solution 4

c: i V7 vio iv6 vi∅7 V7 i
                viio7   ii7
                  4

Problem 4

Label the chords in this progression. Distinguish between diminished and half-diminished seventh chords (o or ∅).

c:

Solution 5

E♭: I IV7 ii7 V7 vi7 iii7 viio7 V7 I

Problem 5

Label the chords in this progression.

E♭:

SUMMARY

Many factors are involved in the creation of an interesting harmonization. Setting melodies is an art and craft that requires time to develop. Artistry grows out of excellent craftsmanship. You now understand the principles of harmonizing, but considerable repetition will be required to put these principles into practice. You can spend years discovering the myriad of ways composers have worked with these principles to create new, fresh settings. If you are interested in writing (composing, arranging), you will find that harmonization is a process that will provide you with years of exploring interesting and fresh ways to relate harmony with melody.

APPLICATIONS

Harmonize the following melodies with the harmonic variety devices that seem appropriate. Let your chord choices be governed by features you find in the pitch and rhythm foundation (skeleton) of the melodies. Keep the need for tonal focus in sight, especially at cadences. Label the chords in your harmonization. Be prepared to play your settings and discuss them intelligently. Apply the following Harmonizing Guidelines to these melodies. Later, find other versions of the melodies in scores, the library, or anthologies and compare your work to them. Find the original version of ''To a Wild Rose.''

HARMONIZING GUIDELINES

1. Planning
   - Examine the melody. Look for skeleton patterns that might suggest particular chord choices or a broad pattern like a background or ''macro'' progression. See if any variety procedures are built into the melody (i.e., series-of-fifths, harmonic sequence, substitution, non-tonic focus).
   - Isolate the phrase plan of a melody. See if contrasting phrases are part of this plan. This contrast should be reinforced by the harmonization.

2. Sketching
   - Rough in chords to reinforce tonal focus, especially at the beginning and end of the melody. This rough sketch will also establish a basic harmonic rhythm. Consider using variation devices in the middle of phrases or in the middle of the melody.
   - Look for opportunities to use variation devices, but do not forget the value of simplicity.
   - Remember that (a) fifth relations tonicize, (b) third relations provide color change and link fifth relations via successive substitutions, and (c) second relations provide melodic thrust, occasional color change, and are good harmonic satellites.

3. Testing
   - Play your sketch on some chording instrument on a trial-and-error basis. Judge the sound effects of your setting and be prepared to change your thinking until you achieve full support of the patterns in the melody. A good harmonization is seldom created in the first ''pass'' and must always be evaluated by its sound. Put yourself in the role of the listener.
   - Experiment with some alternative choices. You might discover something that prompts you to replace some of your first choices. Do not lose sight of the overall need for tonal focus. *Variation, like spice, can be overused, weakening both the effects of variety and the listener's sense of structure.*

MELODIES TO HARMONIZE

NAME _____ CLASS _____ DATE _____

1. To A Wild Rose (from Woodland Sketches)   MacDowell

2. The Ash Grove   Traditional

[See the setting of this melody by Benjamin Britten in <u>Folk Songs of the British Isle</u>, Boosey and Hawkes.]

3. Greensleeves   Traditional

[Numerous settings of this melody are under this title or as the Christmas song, *What Child is This?* Ralph Vaugh Williams wrote a fantasia on ''Greensleeves'' for strings and harp. Recordings and scores are available for additional study.]

4. Harmonize several folk songs. Attempt to apply most of the harmonic variety devices given in this chapter.

CHAPTER

14 HARMONY IN FOUR-PART VOCAL TEXTURE: PART WRITING

OVERVIEW

Melody, *Harmony*, and *Interval* paths merge to form the beginning of a series of four chapters on *Four Part Texture*. Information is presented on scoring, spacing, doubling, and basic part writing guidelines. These guidelines include information on motion factors, root relationships, setting soprano and bass lines, and detecting part writing errors.

Texture

Texture is the overall effect caused by the interaction of voices and components in a composition. **Chordal texture** is the effect caused by a flow of nonparallel chords. In its basic state, chordal texture is **monorhythmic** (all the voices share the same rhythms). Because of the rhythmic sameness among the voices, the listener pays attention to the overall effect of the flow of chords instead of the individual voices. The listener attends to the whole rather than to its parts.

About Example 1:

The next example is a chordal phrase typical of hymnody. As you listen to it, pay special attention to how you hear the texture. Are you aware of individual voices? If so, what ones? Describe this phrase's net effect.

The numbers and signs below this example describe the interval and motion relationships between the **outer voices**, the highest and lowest melodic streams in the texture. One is especially aware of these voices since they provide the perceptual "borders" of the texture. This two part **outer framework** is a very important component of chordal texture.

Example 1. Psalm 8 from The Book of Psalms, Ainsworth (1612)   Bourgeois

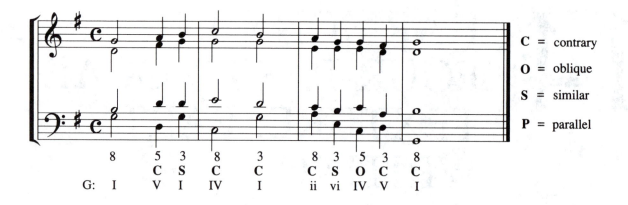

C = contrary

O = oblique

S = similar

P = parallel

8	5 3	8	3		8 3	5 3	8
C	S	C	C		C	S O	C	C
G: I	V I	IV	I		ii vi	IV V	I

Ideas can be superimposed on a chordal passage without obscuring the passage's basic monorhythmic movement. The next example is a variation on the first example. Non-chord tones are added to **embellish** the bass line. The resulting 2:1 rhythm adds melodic interest without detracting from the net chordal effect. Notes that occur simultaneously are aligned vertically.

Example 2. Psalm 8, Variation 1

G: I   V I   IV   I   ii vi   IV V   I

Dialogues

In the next example, non-chord tones were added to all the voices to shift interest from part to part. Notice the resulting conversation-like exchanges called **dialogues**. Can you still hear the basic monorhythmic movement in this variation? Note how the notes are aligned rhythmically in the score.

Example 3. Psalm 8, Variation 2

G: I   V I   IV   I   ii vi   IV V   I

Close Scoring

Chorales can be scored in four clefs, one clef for each voice. This is called **open scoring**. Chorales are also scored in two clefs with two voices per clef. The use of two clefs to score a four part chorale is called **close scoring** (see the previous examples). Notice how the high voices in each clef (i.e.,the soprano and tenor) are scored with stems up. The low voices in each clef are scored with stems down. Apply these **stemming rules** when writing settings in chordal texture.

Monorhythmic Texture

Part writing practices for chordal texture began to develop roughly half of a millennium ago. At one stage of development, an occasional passage in the ''familiar'' (chordal) style was used for contrast with the prevailing polyrhythmic texture of Renaissance vocal music. As you can see, the *familiar* style is monorhythmic chordal texture.

Example 4. ''Familiar'' Style. Tu pauperum refugium   Desprez

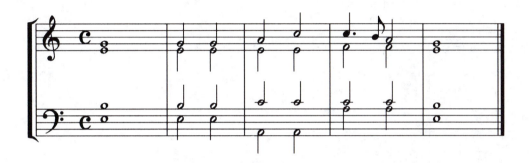

The chorale style continued to develop as a genre for congregational singing. It was based on tunes familiar to the members of the congregation and, in its simplest form, was written so persons with limited musical training could participate. Through history, most hymnals have been written to be accessible to members of church congregations.

Practical Vocal Ranges

The next example includes some practical and conservative limits for voice ranges. If necessary, these can be extended a step or so to complete a melodic pattern in a particular voice. A voice should not be required to linger in the extremely high or low part of its range. Notice that the tenor lies an octave below the soprano. The bass lies a ninth below the alto.

Example 5. Practical Voice Ranges

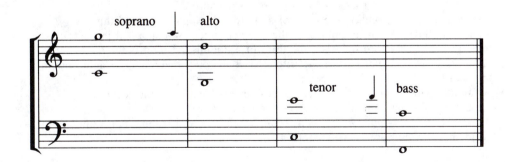

Spacing

Homogeneous spacings among the three **upper voices** (i.e., soprano, alto, tenor) produce a uniform, cohesive chord sound. Spacings that do not exceed an octave between adjacent upper voices, or a twelfth between the tenor and bass also produce a uniform, cohesive chord sound. These spacings roughly parallel the interval pattern in the harmonic series. In wider spacings, chord tones may stand out as individual sounds instead of contributing to the chordal whole.

Some examples of homogeneous spacing patterns follow. Each chord contains one or more notes that lie at the limit of practical vocal range. Examine each voice and determine the notes that can not be moved any higher or lower without going out of range.

Example 6. Practical Spacing Limits

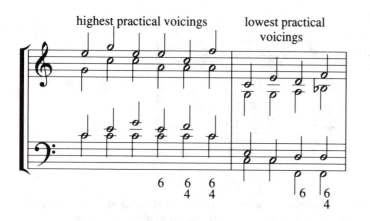

Doubling

Simple arithmetic dictates that one note of a triad must be doubled in four part texture. If one uses the harmonic series as a model, the root of a triad is the best tone to double, the fifth the next best, and the third the least desirable. [In the first six harmonics, the root appears three times, the fifth twice, and the third only once.] Doubling is easy to do when dealing with one chord at a time, but can be difficult when connecting the voices in a series of chords. This connection of voices is called *part writing* or *voice leading*. Generally, part writing problems can be minimized by following the doubling guidelines below.

Doubling Guidelines

(bold numbers refer to chords in the next example)

• Double the bass of root position and second inversion chords (see chords **1** and **2**).
• Double the soprano of first inversion chords (see chord **3**).
• Be cautious about doubling the third of a chord. Although a doubled third is avoided ordinarily, it is acceptable if the doubled notes are contained in contrary moving lines (see chord **4**). Also, the third of a diminished triad is the best tone to double because it is not part of the tritone so is the only melodically stable tone in the chord.*
• As an alternative, double scale steps one, four, and five since the recurrence of these tones will help maintain focus on the keynote.
• *Avoid doubling any melodically active tone* (members of a tritone, notes altered by accidentals, leading tones) (see chord **4**).

As suggested here, any of these guidelines can be overridden by strong linear patterns.

Example 7. Doubling Guidelines illustrated

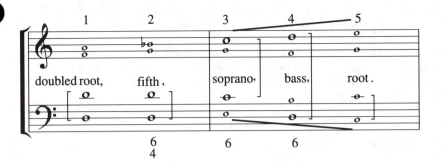

The spacing and doubling profile of the harmonic series can be used as a general model when writing a chorale or scoring an arrangement or original composition.

Voice Continuity

Each voice should be regarded as a vocal line in monorhythmic chordal texture. Each line should be easy to sing, usually accomplished by writing each line mainly in steps with occasional small skips. *Augmented or diminished melodic intervals* tend to invite more rehearsal errors than other intervals and should be used *only* with special care. Put yourself in the place of the persons who will attempt to sing the parts you write. Perform the parts yourself to test their singability. As will be seen later, difficult intervals are effective under certain circumstance.

Relative Motion

The interplay of motion factors is an important factor in the chorale texture. These factors include parallel, contrary, similar, and oblique motion. If all the parts move continually in the same direction (parallel and/or similar motion), the net result is "thickened" melody (parallelism). This **parallel sweep** may be an effective chorale arranging device but does not contribute to the independence of voices.

In the first measure of example 8, notice how the bass moves opposite the three upper voices, an effective contrast in motion . In the second measure, the voices are **paired** two against two in contrasting motion. This can be heard as two thickened melody lines moving in opposition to each other, essentially two part texture.

Example 8. Voice Groupings Defined by Motion Factors

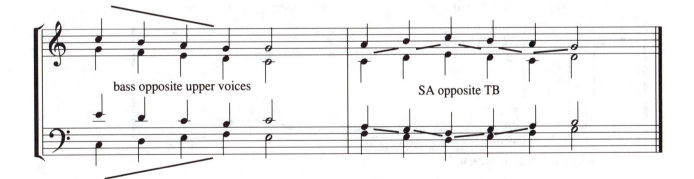

The direction certain intervals are approached from is important to the preservation of chordal texture. Perfect unisons, fifths, and octaves detract from the independence of voices if approached in similar or parallel motion. This is most noticeable if both the notes of these intervals are in the outer voices, the soprano and bass. **Direct fifths and octaves** (i.e., the intervals are approached in similar motion) will not disturb this effect if one note of the interval is concealed in an **inner voice** (i.e., the alto or tenor). Parallel octaves, fifths, and unisons stand out in the flow of voices and *are avoided no matter where they are located. Every* progression in the next example has flawed voice leading.

Example 9. Direct and Parallel Perfect Consonance

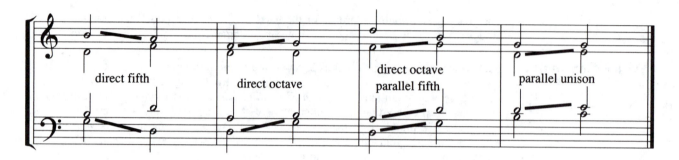

Thirds, fourths, and sixths can be approached freely in similar or parallel motion.

Voice Crossing and Overlapping

In the vocal medium, normal score order is soprano above alto, alto above tenor, and tenor above bass. A **voice crossing** occurs if this order is changed, for example, by placing the tenor above the alto in a chord. **Voice overlapping** is a special case of voice crossing that occurs in adjacent chords if one voice moves into the range previously occupied by another voice. The repetition of a common tone by another voice does not constitute voice crossing.

Example 10. Voice Crossing and Overlapping

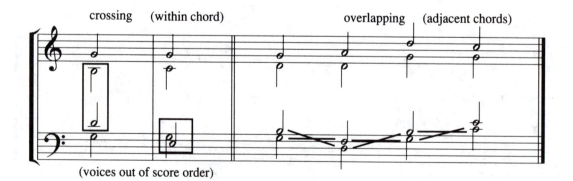

One way we identify a particular voice is by its position in a stack of voices. Voice crossing and overlapping may cause us to confuse one voice with another. Any voice crossing or overlapping that contributes to this kind of confusion is not acceptable. As a general rule, avoid this in your own work. Voice overlapping *is* acceptable when

- Voices move to other chord tones within the same harmony; or
- A particular voice is completing a strong melodic pattern (such examples abound in Bach's music).

The next example shows an acceptable overlap from the movement of voices to other pitches within the same chord. Large melodic skips are acceptable because they are easy to hear in unchanging harmony. This is also true when moving to other positions of the same chord.

Example 11. Overlap in Unchanging Harmony

The next example is a remarkable case of voice overlapping (isolated in boxes). The tenor line passes above the alto and forms a unison with the soprano (second box)! What musical effect is created by this dramatic overlap? Are there other cases of crossing or overlapping in this phrase?

Example 12. Ein feste Burg (No. 273)   J. S. Bach

Root Relationships

The melodic intervals formed by the roots of adjacent chords are significant. This is called a **root relationship**. Each root relationship has unique effects and voice leading features. These features are easy to remember if you think of them in one of the three basic root relationship categories.

PART WRITING GUIDELINES

For Root Position Progressions

- Second Relations (roots a second apart, no common tones): Move the upper voices to the nearest available notes contrary to the bass motion.
- Third Relations (roots a third apart) and fifth relations (roots a fifth or fourth apart): Retain the common tone(s) in the same voice(s). Move the remaining voice(s) to the nearest available note contrary to the bass. If common tones cannot be held in the same voice, then move all voices the shortest distance to new chord tones, giving special attention to how perfect fifths and octaves are approached.

Example 13. Basic Part Writing Patterns (root position)

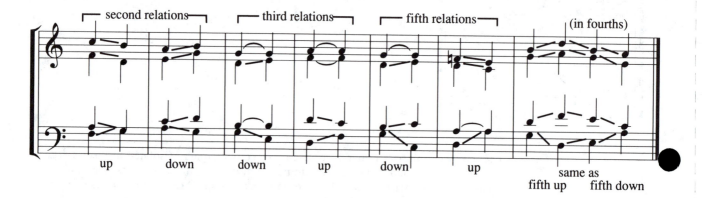

> **PERSON TO PERSON:** The use of these guidelines will result in a flow of uniformly sonorous chords brought by consistency in doubling and spacing and singable voice connections. Under these guidelines, the lines may be undistinguished and repetitive, a tradeoff between a satisfactory overall chordal effect and interesting lines. Regard the guidelines as prescriptions for "safe" choral scoring.

310

CHECKPOINT I (Basic SATB (Soprano, Alto, Tenor, Bass) writing, root position)

Self-help Problems.

Solution 1

Problem 1

Write a SATB setting of each two-chord progression. Closely follow the part writing guidelines above. Label the chords. The root of each chord is in the bass.

C: iii   ii   V   vi   vi   V

C:

Solution 2

Problem 2

Write a SATB setting of each two-chord progression. Closely follow the part writing guidelines above. Label the chords. The root of each chord is in the bass.

C: iii   I   ii   IV   vi   IV

C:

Solution 3

Problem 3

Write a SATB setting of each two-chord progression. Closely follow the part writing guidelines above. Label the chords. The root of each chord is in the bass.

C: vi   ii   vi   iii   vi   ii   opt.

C:

Inversions and Voice Leading

The addition of inversions to a flow of chords tends to make the bass more conjunct, more melodic. Inversions also add enough variables to make a "write by rule" approach unwieldy. The best approach is to apply the following principle for part writing and treat each progression as an individual case.

Part Writing Principle

a. Move voices the shortest distance to new chord tones.
b. Keep common tones in the same voice.
c. Approach perfect harmonic intervals and dissonance with caution.
  • Avoid direct motion in outer voices to harmonic P8, P5, unison, seconds, sevenths (no restriction on direct motion to thirds, sixths, T, and P4).
  • Avoid parallel harmonic unison, P8, P5, seconds, sevenths, and T no matter where located (no restriction on parallel thirds, sixths, and P4).

Details on writing second inversion triads will be given in a later chapter.

Example 14. Basic Part Writing Patterns (with inversions)

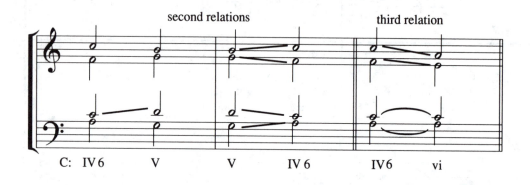

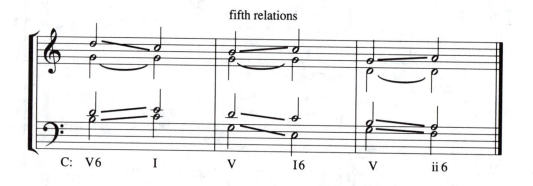

CHECKPOINT II (Basic SATB part writing, first inversion)

● Self-help Problems.

Solution 1

C: IV6 V   iii ii6 iii6 IV6 opt.

5ths

Problem 1

Write a SATB setting of each two-chord progression. Closely follow the part writing principles on the previous page. Label the chords.

C: 6   6   6

Solution 2

C: V iii6 vi6 I iii6 I6

Problem 2

Write a SATB setting of each two-chord progression. Closely follow the part writing principles on the previous page. Label the chords.

C: 6   6   6   6

Solution 3

C: V ii6 V6 I IV6 viio6

Problem 3

Write a SATB setting of each two-chord progression. Closely follow the part writing principles on the previous page. Label the chords.

C: 6   6   6   6

Phrases and Voice Leading

A cadence provides punctuation and interrupts the flow of voices. Part writing guidelines can be suspended between a cadence and the next phrase, but remember that singers may use the cadence chord as a cue for their pitches in the next phrase. Put yourself in the singers' place and give them a logical cue.

Example 15. Voice Continuity at Cadences

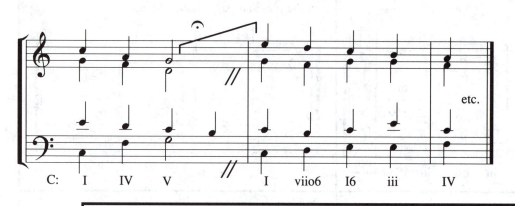

C: I   IV   V   I   viio6   I6   iii   IV   etc.

PERSON TO PERSON: The basic voice leading procedures in this unit are guidelines for writing a satisfactory chordal texture. The guidelines cannot always be followed strictly when connecting a series of chords. They are not a recipe for success but rather a set of observations about how to create an acceptable and easily rehearsed four part choral arrangement.

Musical effect can be overlooked as one struggles with the complexities of voice leading. For this reason, avoid the temptation to complete the part writing exercises as paper puzzles. Keep in touch with the reality of sound by playing your work at the keyboard, or have a group of singers in your class perform your work while you listen to it critically. This puts you in close touch with the effects of the vocal medium and makes you more aware of the patterns that produce singable instead of awkward passages.

The following factors detract from a smooth SATB setting:

• disjunct lines except in the bass
• direct fifths and octaves in the outer voices
• parallel P5, octaves, unison, or dissonance
• doubled thirds (except in diminished triads or in strong linear patterns)
• voice crossing that blurs the identity of a voice

Think about the following when connecting the voices of chords:

• move each voice the shortest distance to new chord tones
• strong melodic pattern can override otherwise undesirable factors
• the inner voices (i.e., alto and tenor) are less noticeable so some otherwise undesirable movements can be concealed in the inner voices

CHECKPOINT III (Basic SATB part writing, summary)

● 1. Explain these terms:

texture	chordal texture
outer voices	monorhythmic texture
embellished line	outer framework
dialogue	open scoring
upper voices	close scoring
SATB	stemming rule (close scoring)
doubling rule	parallel sweep
paired voices	inner voices
direct fifth	direct octave
voice cross	voice overlap

● 2. Explain voice leading guidelines related to each root relationship class.

3. Write a short paragraph discussing the following topics:

- affect of inversion on lines and part writing

- part writing continuity following a cadence

- differences in the treatment of outer and inner voices

- thinking of your work as a simple choral arrangement to be performed by singers

- harmonic series as a model for spacing and doubling

●

4. Self-help Problems.

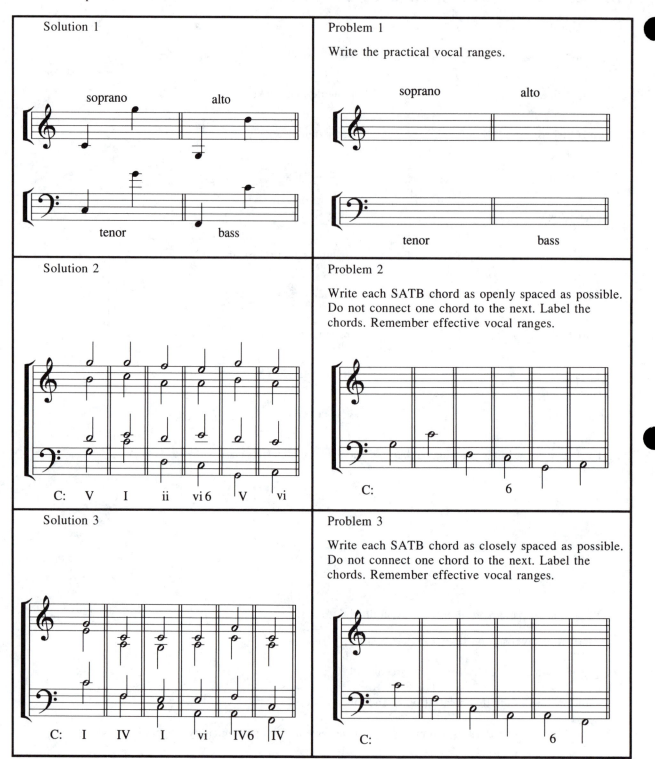

Solution 1

soprano   alto

tenor   bass

Problem 1

Write the practical vocal ranges.

soprano   alto

tenor   bass

Solution 2

C: V   I   ii   vi 6   V   vi

Problem 2

Write each SATB chord as openly spaced as possible. Do not connect one chord to the next. Label the chords. Remember effective vocal ranges.

C: 6

Solution 3

C: I   IV   I   vi   IV6   IV

Problem 3

Write each SATB chord as closely spaced as possible. Do not connect one chord to the next. Label the chords. Remember effective vocal ranges.

C: 6

Solution 4

Problem 4

Complete the following motion examples in two part texture.

contrary   oblique

similar   parallel

Solution 5

Problem 5

Complete an SATB setting of each two-chord progression. Apply the part writing guidelines strictly. Label the chords.

C: ii vi   ii V   V I   IV I

C:

Solution 6

Problem 6

Complete a strict SATB setting of each two-chord progression. Label the chords.

C: IV ii   iii V   IV V   ii I

C:

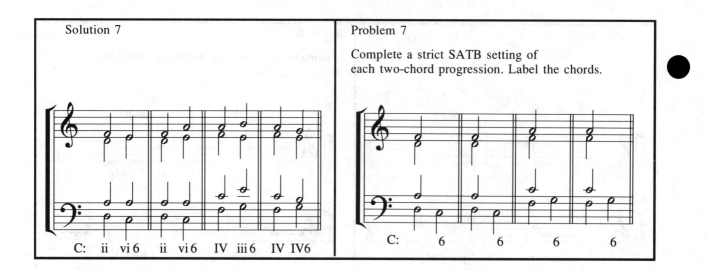

Solution 7

Problem 7

Complete a strict SATB setting of each two-chord progression. Label the chords.

C: ii vi6 ii vi6 IV iii6 IV IV6

C: 6 6 6 6

5. **Error Detection.** Several phrases below contain part writing problems. Use the signs given to make editorial marks on the copy to show that you can locate and identify the problems. This exercise can help you better isolate problems in your own work.

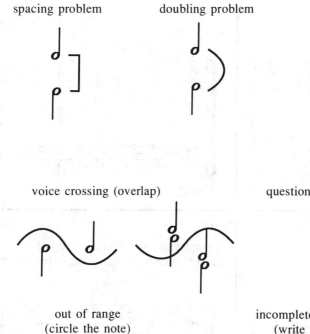

spacing problem

doubling problem

questionable melodic interval

voice crossing (overlap)

questionable direct or parallel motion

out of range
(circle the note)

incomplete chord
(write inc)

NAME _____ CLASS _____ DATE _____

● Problem 1:

g:

● Problem 2:

F:

●

Problem 3:

C:

> **PERSON TO PERSON:** Harmonizing melodies and bass lines is an art and craft that can take years to develop fully. The ideas presented to you in these pages are just a start. Perhaps this beginning will help you better appreciate and understand the thinking of composers and arrangers. It may also encourage you to work at understanding and developing your own latent creativity.

APPLICATIONS IN SATB WRITING

Bass Lines

1. Set the following bass lines in four voices (SATB). First, label the chords (write Roman numerals below the notes). Add tenor, alto, and soprano voices above the bass lines. Apply the voice leading guidelines given in this unit strictly. Think of voice leading patterns in one of three categories, second, third, and fifth relations. Do not alter the bass notes.

The hints below may help you overcome common bass line setting problems.

Hint 1: If a spacing problem develops and continues between adjacent voices, the problem can usually be solved by switching the notes between the two parts (i.e., moving the tenor notes to the alto and the alto notes to the tenor). One of the voices may have to be transposed an octave in this switch.

Hint 2: Sometimes, one can solve a problem by working backwards from where the part writing was successful.

Bass Line 1:

F: 6

Bass Line 2:

C: 6   6   6

Bass Line 3:

G: 6   6

        6   6

Bass Line 4:

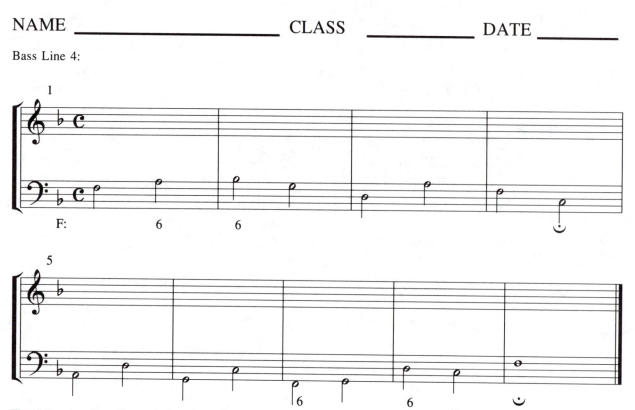

The following bass lines are in minor. The ''#7'' above the music is a reminder to use the leading tone (the raised seventh step) in dominant and leading tone chords (V, viio). The movement from a predominant chord (iio or iv) to V or viio when using harmonic minor may result in a melodic augmented second unless a raised sixth is used or the natural sixth is returned to the fifth step. Label the chords and make certain the labels indicate the chord color.

Bass Line 5:

Bass Line 6:

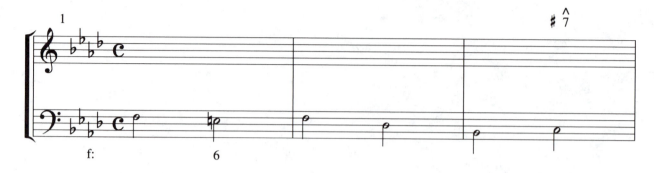

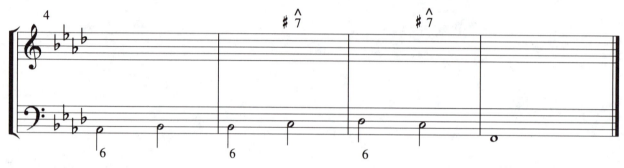

Bass Line 7:

Melodies

Harmonize the following melodies and set them in SATB texture. Label the chords. Apply the voice leading guidelines given in this chapter. Use the harmonizing guidelines presented in earlier chapters. Remember that bass lines can be more disjunct than other lines yet can be made more conjunct by using inversions. Chords should be selected to support the pitch and rhythmic skeleton of the melody. Use standard cadence progressions. Remember that chord rhythms move more slowly than melodic rhythms.

Melody 1: All Through The Night   Traditional

Melody 2: Psalm 8   Bourgeois

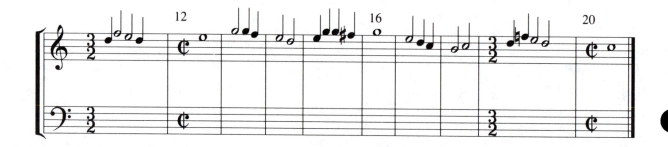

Melody 3: Wir Christenleut'   J. S. Bach

g:

B♭:   g:

Melody 4: Jesu Meine Freude   J. S. Bach

e:

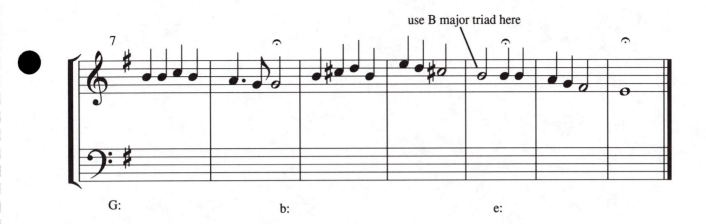

G: b: e:

331

CHAPTER

15 HARMONY IN FOUR-PART VOCAL TEXTURE: ELABORATION WITH NONCHORD TONES

OVERVIEW

The *Four-Part Texture Path* continues with instruction on nonchord tones. This includes ideas about the use of nonchord tones to create melodic overlays, particularly dialogues and couplings among voices. Special voice leading problems that arise from the use of embellished melodic movement are addressed. An analysis style is proposed that accounts for differences between monorhythmic background and melodic overlay. This style allows alternate ways to interpret and describe certain situations.

Nonchord Tones

Nonchord tones are harmonic satellites used to embellish melodies and textures. A nonchord tone is not a member of the chord it embellishes. Embellishments can add one or more layers of rhythmic activity to the underlying monorhythmic harmonic flow.

In the **monorhythmic chorale,** harmony and voice movement coincide with strong rhythmic points (beats, meter accents, major accent points). Nonchord tones move at more rapid **rhythm layers** than chord rhythms. Note values in these nonchord tone layers are usually adjacent to the note values of the basic harmonic rhythm. In the next example, compare the original phrase with its reduction. How does this **reduction** (skeleton) relate to the original phrase? What is the rhythmic relationship between the notes in the reduction and the removed notes?

Example 1. Nun freut euch (no. 183)   J. S. Bach

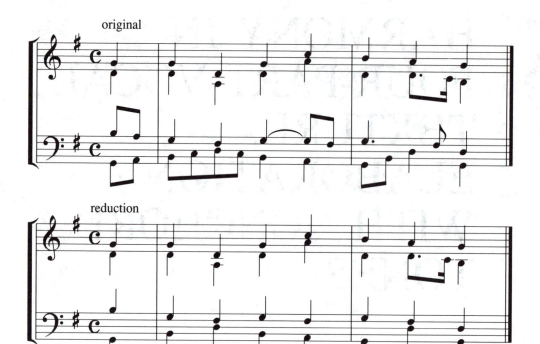

The next example has three levels of rhythmic activity. Rhythmic layers of quarter and eighth note values are superimposed on the basic chorale rhythm of half notes. An isolated pair of sixteenth notes embellishes the eighth note layer.

Example 2. Heilig, heilig (No. 235)   J. S. Bach

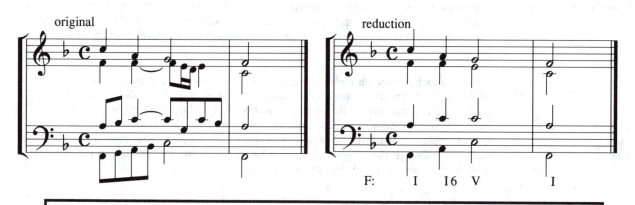

Additional Thoughts on Example 2: Multiple layers of rhythmic activity influence how we analyze and perform a passage. More than one acceptable reduction is possible where numerous layers are involved. In example 2, the elimination of eighth and sixteenth notes produces an informative layer of half and quarter notes. The harmony does not change at the second beat and this quarter note could be removed to create a layer of half notes. Do you think a reduction to whole notes would be meaningful? Why or why not? When performing or conducting this passage, you can choose how to bring out certain rhythmic levels. For example, the chorale could be conducted in two half note beats per bar to emphasize its smoothly flowing lines, its **monorhythmic basis,** and to de-emphasize beat-to-beat accents. It could be conducted in four quarter note beats per bar to emphasize the nonchord tone pattern in the alto part (see beats 3–4).

The next example exhibits a more complex rhythmic overlay than the previous example. The overlay obscures the monorhythmic basis of the chorale. A reduction is more difficult to derive. The identity of the tenor and bass parts is somewhat vague because of the way they intertwine. As you study and perform this example, are you aware of its several rhythmic layers? How would you approach this passage as a conductor/interpreter? Can you see more than one possible reduction? Do you see how alternate reduction solutions could influence your interpretation of this passage?

Example 3. Nun lieget alles unter dir (No. 343)   J. S. Bach

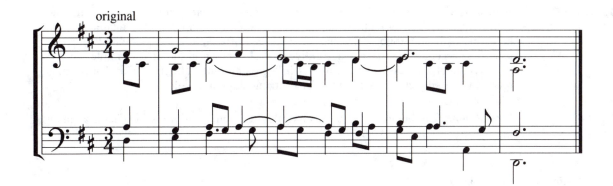

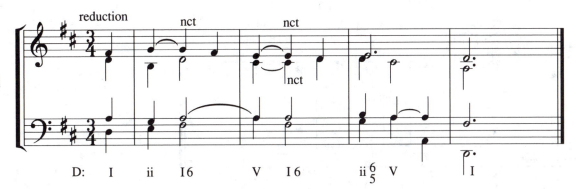

D: I   ii   I6   V   I6   ii$\frac{6}{5}$ V   I

Nonchord Tone Categories

Most nonchord tones can be placed in one of the melodic pattern categories below.

1. Approached <u>and</u> left by step, rhythmically accented* or unaccented.
2. Approached <u>or</u> left by skip, accented* or unaccented.
3. Premature or delayed voice movement of one or more chord tones, accented* or unaccented.
4. Notes held through chord changes.

   *note: accented nonchord tones seem more dissonant, more "pungent" than unaccented nonchord tones.

The nonchord tones will be presented in these four broad categories during the remainder of this chapter.

I. STEP/STEP PATTERNS

Passing Tone
A **passing tone** is the middle note in a three-note scale pattern and is approached and left by step. Occasionally, one passing tone directly follows another in a four-note scale pattern. Accented passing tones seem more dissonant than unaccented passing tones.

Coupled Passing Tones
Passing tones can occur simultaneously in two or more voices. **Coupled** passing tones move in parallel thirds, sixths, and sometimes fourths, and also move in contrary motion.

Passing Chord
A **passing chord** occurs if most or all of the voices appear to move in a passing tone pattern. It is heard as a melodic connection between two chords rather than a harmonic entity (a group of passing tones instead of a chord). Passing chords are usually unaccented and have a decorative role. As shown in the next example, not every voice of the passing chord moves in a passing tone pattern. Notice that passing tones and passing chords are useful for bridging skips in a voice.

Passing Tone Dialogues
Passing tones can be arranged to create **dialogues**, conversation-like exchanges among the voices.

Example 4. Passing Tones and Chords

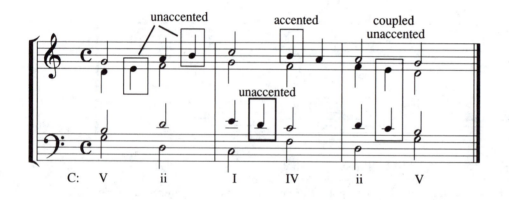

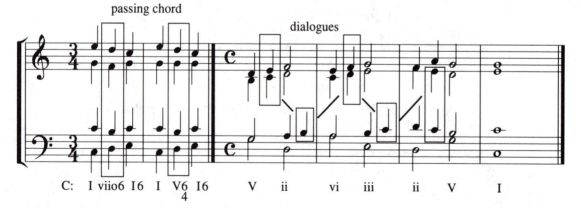

Neighbor Tones
A **neighbor tone** is approached and left by step in a returning note pattern. Neighbor tones are usually unaccented but accented neighbor tones occur occasionally. Neighbor tones can occur simultaneously in two or more voices. When this happens, they are usually coupled in parallel thirds, sixths, and sometimes fourths. Coupled neighbor tones move in contrary pattern.

Neighbor Chord

A **neighbor chord** occurs if voices in a neighbor tone pattern move simultaneously. Neighbor tone patterns can be arranged so conversation-like exchanges (dialogues) occur among the voices. In the next example, notice how neighbor tones and chords are used to decorate otherwise common tones in a voice. They are useful for adding rhythmic interest to slow moving or static voices.

Neighbor Group

A **neighbor group** occurs if a chord tone is preceded by both its **upper** and **lower** neighbors. One of the nonchord tones in a neighbor group does not resolve by step.

Example 5. Neighbor Tones and Neighbor Chord

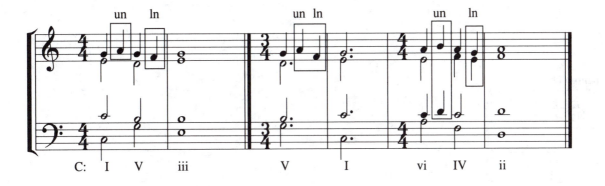

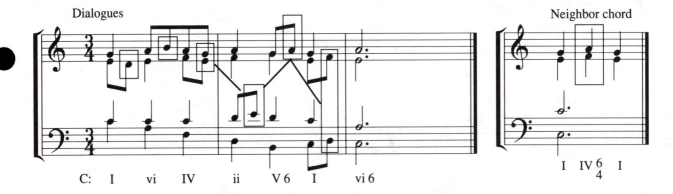

II. STEP/SKIP or SKIP/STEP PATTERNS

Appoggiatura

The **appoggiatura** is approached by skip and left by step (usually in the direction opposite the skip). It is accented and is sometimes called a **leaning tone**. Some authorities call any accented nonchord tone that resolves by step an appoggiatura. Some pianists use the term this way, too. We will use the *skip/step* definition to ensure the distinction between the appoggiatura and the accented passing tone.

Appoggiaturas can occur simultaneously in two or more voices. Coupled appoggiaturas usually move in parallel thirds or sixths and can be included in dialogues among the voices. A **leaning chord** occurs if some of the voices move in an appoggiatura pattern. In the example that follows, notice which tone remains fixed (and doubled). Appoggiaturas can decorate both steps and skips in the basic voice leading.

337

Example 6. Appoggiaturas

coupled

C: I   V   I   V

leaning chord

6   5
4   3

dialogue

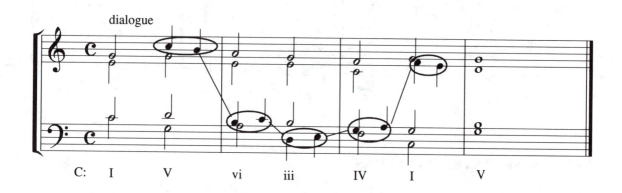

C: I   V   vi   iii   IV   I   V

Cambiata

The **cambiata** is the unaccented version of the appoggiatura. It is approached by skip and left by step, usually with a change of direction following the skip. Cambiatas can occur simultaneously in two or more voices, usually coupled in parallel thirds or sixths. Dialogue patterns can be established through using cambiatas. The **neighbor group** was the pattern used for the cambiata by Renaissance composers like Palestrina.

338

Example 7. Cambiatas

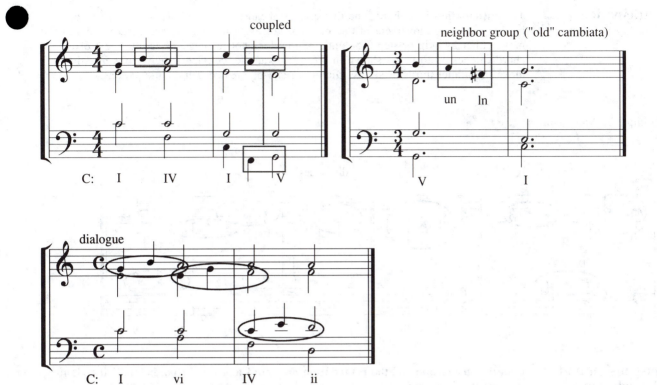

Escape Tone

The **escape tone** (Fr. *Échappée*) has a step-skip melodic pattern, the reverse of the skip-step pattern of the appoggiatura and cambiata. Usually, a change in direction follows the first note. The escape tone, like the cambiata, is unaccented.

Escape tones can occur simultaneously in two or more voices. When this happens, they usually move in parallel thirds or sixths. Escape tones can be used to form dialogues between voices. Although not shown in the example, simultaneous escape tones can move in contrary motion, too.

Example 8. Escape Tones

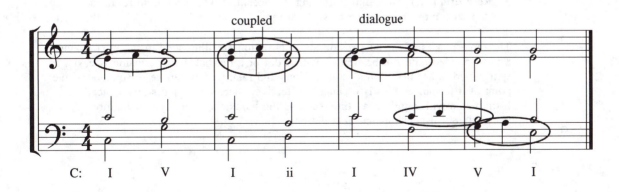

III. DELAYED OR PREMATURE VOICE MOVEMENT

Anticipation

The **anticipation** is a chord tone that arrives ahead of its chord. This tone is caused by the premature movement of one or more voices. Anticipations are unaccented and move either by skip or step. The anticipation does not resolve; instead, the rest of the chord catches up to it. As shown in the next example, coupled anticipations usually move in parallel thirds or sixths. Dialogues can be created using anticipations.

Example 9. Anticipations

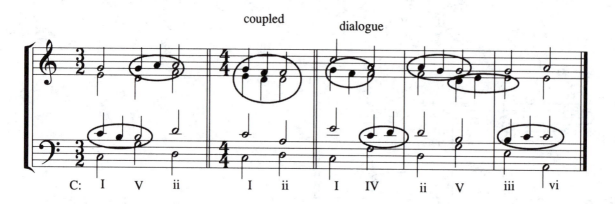

Suspension and Retardation

Both the **suspension** and the **retardation** are chord tones that "lag behind" the chord movement. Their names imply the suspending or retarding of time. Their pattern is delayed step motion. The only difference between the two patterns is in the direction each resolves. The *retardation moves UP*—and the *suspension moves DOWN* (both BY STEP). Both become nonchord tones during a chord change then **resolve** (i.e., move to new chord tones) after the other voices of the chord have completed their movement. The chord changes on an accent, or creates the impression of an accent. The resolution movement follows the accent.

Both the suspension and the retardation have three phases.

1. **Preparation** (P). The unaccented point at which the note is a chord tone in the first chord.
2. **Suspension** (S) or Retardation (Ret). The accented point at which the chord changes and the note remains behind as a nonchord tone.
3. **Resolution** (R). The point following the accent at which the note resumes step-wise movement to the new chord tone.

The three phases of the suspension and retardation are illustrated in the next example. The suspended note can be written with a dot or a tie, but the suspension is easier to spot if tied rather than dotted. Suspensions and retardations can be re-sounded at the point of dissonance. This is especially effective where additional stress is needed. Instruments with rapid decay time such as the harpsichord or a guitar require rearticulated suspensions and retardations.

Example 10. Suspensions and Retardations

Decorated Resolution

The resolution of a suspension or a retardation can be embellished by other nonchord tone patterns or chord tones that look like nonchord tone patterns (quasi nonchord tones). This embellishment can stress the importance of the resolution, especially at critical points like climaxes or cadences at ends of sections.

Typically, decorations are inserted between the dissonance and the resolution note. In the next example, the resolution note remains unaccented. Some of the notes are quasi nonchord tones. Why aren't they true nonchord tones?

Example 11. Decorated Resolutions

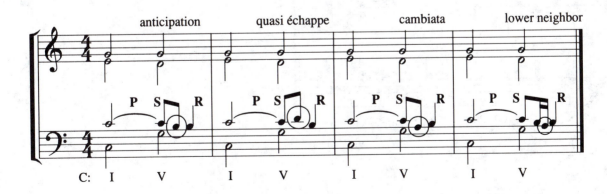

The resolution of suspensions and retardations is sometimes accompanied by a **change of bass,** a change of harmony, or movement in another voice. The resolution note is always a chord tone, regardless of changes.

Example 12. Change of Bass or Chord

C: I   V   V⁶₄   I   V   iii 6   ii 6

IV. PEDAL AND OSTINATO

Pedal Tone

A **pedal** tone is a **drone** tone, an unchanging pitch often heard on bag pipes or the hurdy gurdy ("crank organ"). This drone is sustained through chord changes, sometimes part of the harmony and sometimes not. A pedal tone **alternates** between consonance and dissonance as the harmonies change. Tonic and dominant notes are common choices for pedal tones because they help reinforce focus on the tonic pitch. Typically, **tonic** and **dominant** pedals are used prior to or during cadences that mark the close of major sections of a piece.

In the next example, two analyses of the harmony are provided. The harmonic rhythm of the first version is in half notes. This requires that more tones be regarded as nonchord tones. The harmonic rhythm of the second version moves in quarter notes so every tone can be included in one of the chords.

Example 13. Pedal Tones

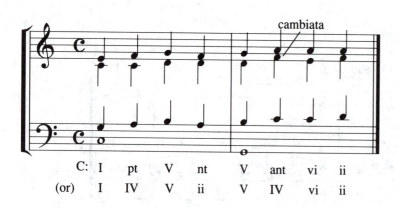

C: I   pt   V   nt   V   ant   vi   ii
(or) I   IV   V   ii   V   IV   vi   ii

Primitive Pedal

In some music, the notes in the tonic fifth sound simultaneously as a pedal interval. This is called a **primitive** or **pastoral** pedal. The notes in the pedal interval can be sustained, repeated, or alternated during the course of the pedal.

Example 14. Primitive Pedal

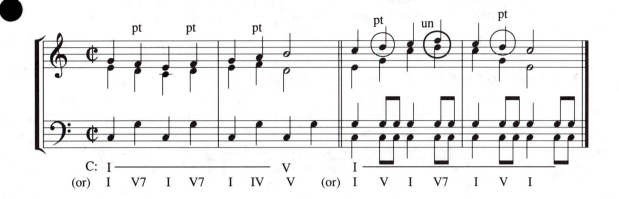

C: I ———————————— V   I ——
(or) I V7 I V7 I IV V   (or) I V I V7 I V I

Ostinato

The **ostinato** is closely related to the pedal tone. It is a short repeating pattern that persists "obstinately" in the background. Most ostinatos can be reduced easily to one focal pitch that recurs like a repeating pedal tone, so an ostinato can be seen as an embellished pedal tone.

Example 15. Ostinato

C: I   V   ii   vi   iii   ii   V

SUMMARY

Uses of Nonchord Tones

Nonchord tones add interest to a chordal setting by creating

- Additional rhythmic layers
- Additional melodic figures
- Intensified interplay among voices

Embellished voices attract the listener's attention momentarily. This is most effective where nonchord tones are used like motives to create thematic exchanges among voices.

Embellished voices add new dimensions to the music and create new voice leading problems. The risk of writing exposed direct or parallel perfect and dissonant intervals increases with greater activity and complexity in the voices.

343

The next example explores cases where independent motion exposes intervals that would have been concealed within inner voices. Each measure is a variation on the basic progression given at the beginning of each line. Which of these measures is acceptable to your ear? Which are not? Can you explain why you rejected certain patterns?

Example 16. Voice Leading Problems Caused by Nonchord Tone Figures

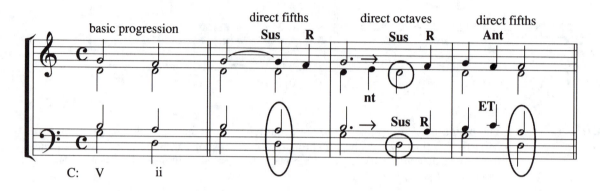

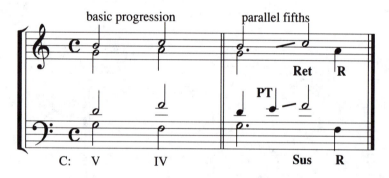

Many variables are involved in an embellished texture, so a write-by-rule approach is somewhat unwieldy. Remember that independent movement is heard as figure and thus requires special treatment. Your ear is the best tool available for testing the results of your work. It will detect any incongruous sounds from voice leading flaws. Be sure to play your work to evaluate its sound.

Analysis Alternatives

The use of nonchord tones adds variables to the texture. Sometimes, this makes it possible to analyze a given harmony in more than one way. Alternatives can be equally correct if they are based on a logical interpretation of the data and if consistency is maintained with other similar alternatives in the analysis. The next example contains chords that can be analyzed more than one way.

344

Example 17. Analysis Alternatives

An Wasserflussen Babylon (No. 5)   J. S. Bach

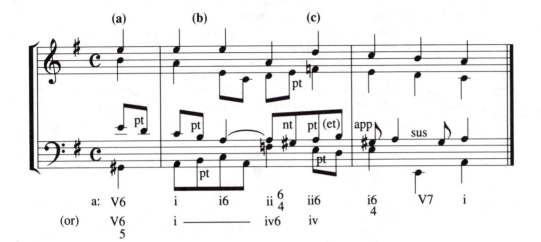

The letters above the example match the items below.

a. The passing tone D can be seen as the seventh of the chord or as an unaccented passing tone, a very common treatment of sevenths of chords.
b. The first two beats can be heard as a root position chord followed by the first inversion of the same chord. Thus, there is no change of harmony in the first two beats of this measure. The root of the chord is the focal pitch of the group of four eighth notes in the bass.
c. The fourth beat (bar 1) poses a typical problem of interpretation. One must decide which part of the beat to regard as harmony and which to regard as non-harmony. If one decides on the iv chord solution, the E in the bass is an accented passing tone and the B in the tenor is an escape tone. If one decides on the ii6 chord solution, both the tenor A and the bass E are accented passing tones.

PERSON TO PERSON: Alternative ways to analyze a passage may be puzzling, especially to the individual who hopes for "right-or-wrong" solutions. Music abounds with situations where two or more valid solutions are possible. Music simply cannot be analyzed by rule; it is an exercise in critical thinking. Your goal in analysis is to arrive at an understanding about details of a composition, how these details relate to the whole, and how you will interpret them as a practicing musician.

You must learn to isolate what is significant in a work so you can summarize and apply your findings. An account of every detail in a composition seldom helps to communicate one's ideas about the gist of a work. It is important to learn to structure your thinking, develop musical logic, and share your findings effectively with others. Solid analytical technique is essential to every aspect of musical activity. This technique develops throughout the professional life of the musician.

Do not expect to learn how to analyze music in only one course. Analysis is a critical-technical view of music that is developed and applied in a series of music courses and activities, not just form and analysis. Analysis is a conceptual approach to music that grows and matures as the musician learns more and more about music.

345

Sample Nonchord Tone Contexts

Examples 18 through 22 are a theme and variations on a chorale phrase. These examples demonstrate a few ways nonchord tones can be used to add interest to a basic chordal setting. Compare each variation to the theme.

Take special notice of the following when studying the next five examples.
• voice pattern decorated by nonchord tone pattern
• new contexts from the addition of voice couplings and dialogues
• new rhythmic ideas from nonchord tones
• use and timing of tension and repose patterns

Perform the theme and variations with expression. Experiment with different interpretations. Will differences in the variations help you set up some contrast between each example?

Example 18. A Theme for Variations

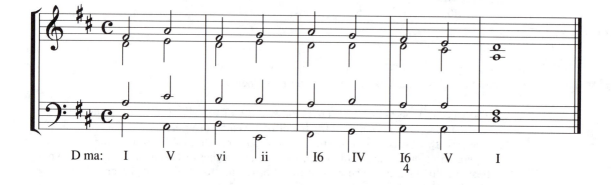

The voice leading in the previous example is strict, a literal application of voice guidelines. Movement of individual voices is kept to a minimum. The alto voice is repetitious. The overall chordal effect took precedence over interest in the individual parts.

In Variation I, passing tones bridge skips in the upper voices. A few neighbor tones decorate repeating notes.

Example 19. Variation I

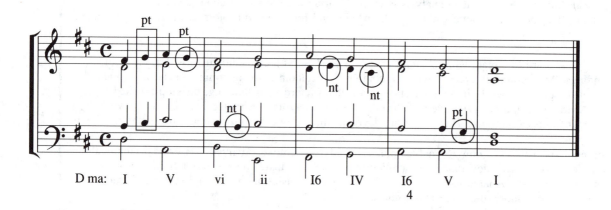

Variation II includes anticipations, suspensions, and retardations. All embellish step-wise movement in the basic voice leading.

Example 20. Variation II

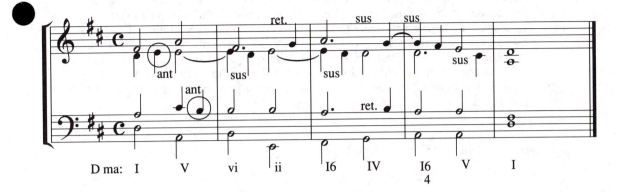

D ma: I   V   vi   ii   I6   IV   I6   V   I
                                     4

Variation III shows how appoggiaturas, cambiatas, and escape tones can decorate both steps and skips in the original voice leading.

Example 21. Variation III

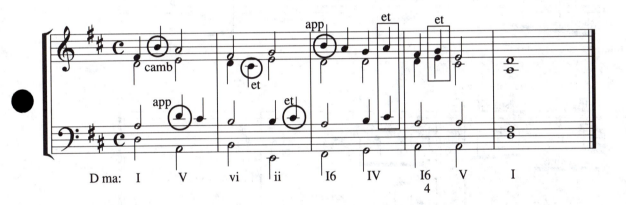

D ma: I   V   vi   ii   I6   IV   I6   V   I
                                     4

Variation IV, the final variation, is a composite of several nonchord tones. Nonchord tones create and add melodic dimensions. Do you think these nonchord tones interact with each other to create additional layers of meaning?

Example 22. Variation IV, ''Finale''

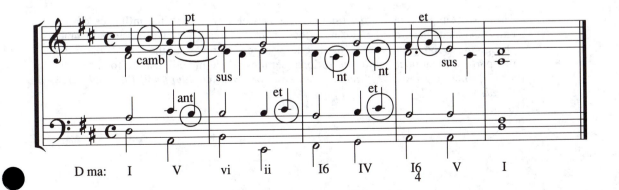

D ma: I   V   vi   ii   I6   IV   I6   V   I
                                     4

347

Sample Analyses The next example illustrates one of Bach's nonchord tone strategies. Notice the strong directional flow caused by the nonchord tone melodies in each voice and the voice interaction set up by this. What voice seems most prominent? Can you explain this? How does it compare and relate to the other voices? Take special note of the passing chords. Only one analysis is given but others exist, especially for chords that contain nonchord tones. The second phrase seems more complex than the first. What musical effect is created by this change in complexity? Perform this example several times, then explain how the change in complexity affected your musical interpretation of the passage.

Example 23. Herr ich habe missgehandelt (33)   J. S. Bach

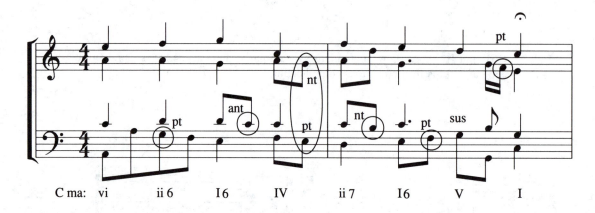

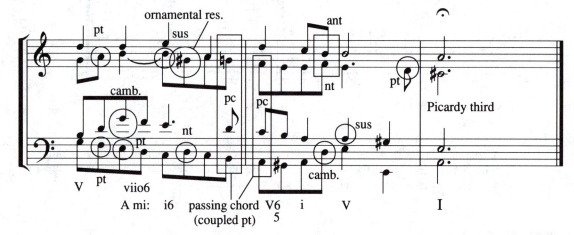

The next example contains the final two phrases of a chorale. What influence do the embellishments have on the closing effect of the final cadence? Do the embellishments change the mood at the end? [This is one of several chorales in the "371" based on this particular chorale melody. Additional settings of the melody can be found in the "371" under the title, *Oh, sacred head, now wounded (O Haupt voll Blut und Wunden).]*

348

Example 24. Befiehl du deine Wege (286)   J. S. Bach

A ma: V6   I   IV6   I   ii6   V   I
        5   D ma: I

IV6   I   V6 ——————————— B mi: V7   i   V

The next example illustrates how a suspension pattern used as a motive can help reinforce a sequence. A suspension is used as a closing figure in both the original and the sequence pattern. Each suspension extends into the next idea and helps create an interlocking chain of ideas. One chord is labeled "V7/ii," signifying that the chord is a secondary dominant. This genre of chords will be discussed in later chapters on chromaticism. [Notice the rhythmic alignment of the voices, their note heads, and stems. Be sure to duplicate this format when completing voice leading assignments.]

Example 25. Meinen Jesum lass ich nicht (152)   J. S. Bach

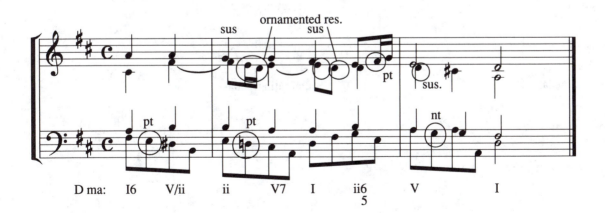

D ma: I6   V/ii   ii   V7   I   ii6   V   I
                                                5

CHECKPOINT

1. Explain these terms:

nonchord tone

monorhythmic chorale

reduction

passing tone

dialogue

neighbor chord

upper neighbor

pedal tone

drone tone

ostinato

leaning tone

cambiata

échappée

retardation

resolution

change of bass

dominant pedal

passing chord

monorhythmic basis

rhythm layer

elaboration rhythm

neighbor tone

coupling

neighbor group

lower neighbor

primitive pedal

pastoral pedal

appoggiatura

leaning chord

escape tone

anticipation

suspension

preparation

tonic pedal

alternating pedal

2. Self-help Problems. Solutions are on the following page.

Problem 1

Label the chords and fill in the missing quarter notes with passing tones. Use the passing tones to fill in skips.

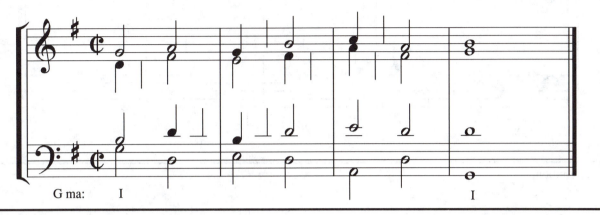

Problem 2

Label the chords and fill in the missing quarter notes with neighbor tones. Decorate common tones with neighbor tones.

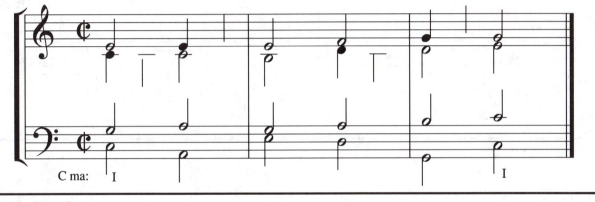

Problem 3

Label the chords and fill in the quarter note appoggiaturas.

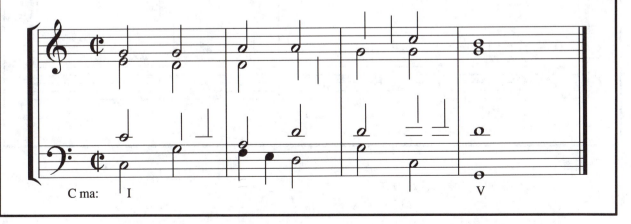

Solution 1

G ma: I   V (7)   vi   iii6   ii   V   I

Solution 2

C ma: I   vi   iii   ii (7)   V   I

Solution 3

C ma: I   V   ii6   ii   V   I   V

Problem 4

Label the chords and fill in the blanks with quarter note cambiatas.

C ma: I   6   6   I

Problem 5

Label the chords and fill in the blanks with quarter note escape tones.

C ma: I   I

Problem 6

Label the chords and fill in the blanks with quarter note anticipations.

D ma: I   I

Solution 4

C ma: I IV vi V6 ii6 V I
(7ths as cambiatas)

Solution 5

C ma: I V ii vi6 ii V I

Solution 6

D ma: I V iii vi IV V I

Problem 7

Label the chords and fill in the blanks with quarter note suspensions.

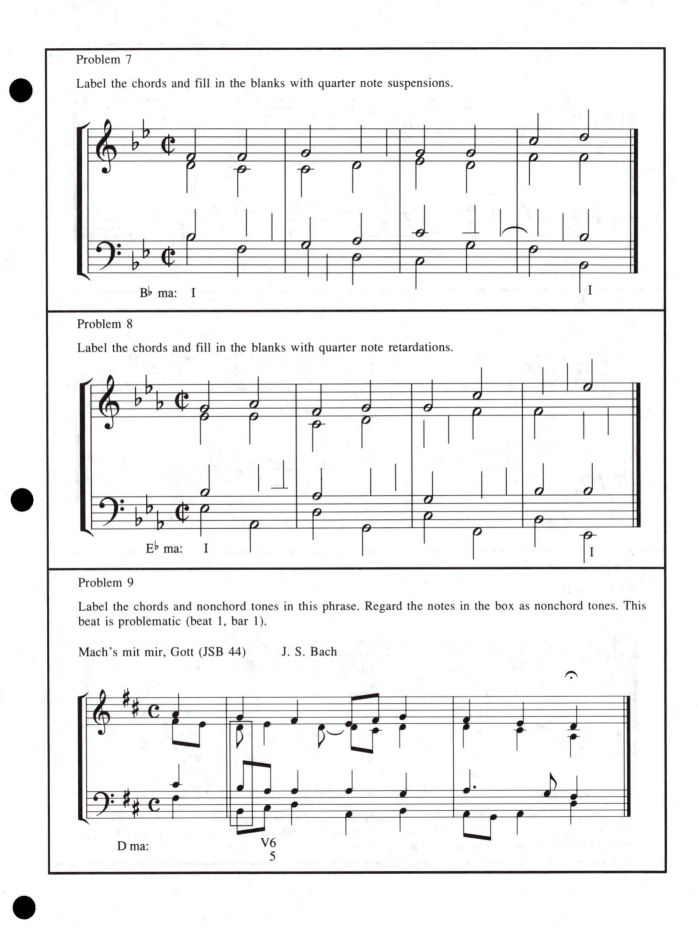

B♭ ma: I   I

Problem 8

Label the chords and fill in the blanks with quarter note retardations.

E♭ ma: I   I

Problem 9

Label the chords and nonchord tones in this phrase. Regard the notes in the box as nonchord tones. This beat is problematic (beat 1, bar 1).

Mach's mit mir, Gott (JSB 44)   J. S. Bach

D ma: V6
                                5

355

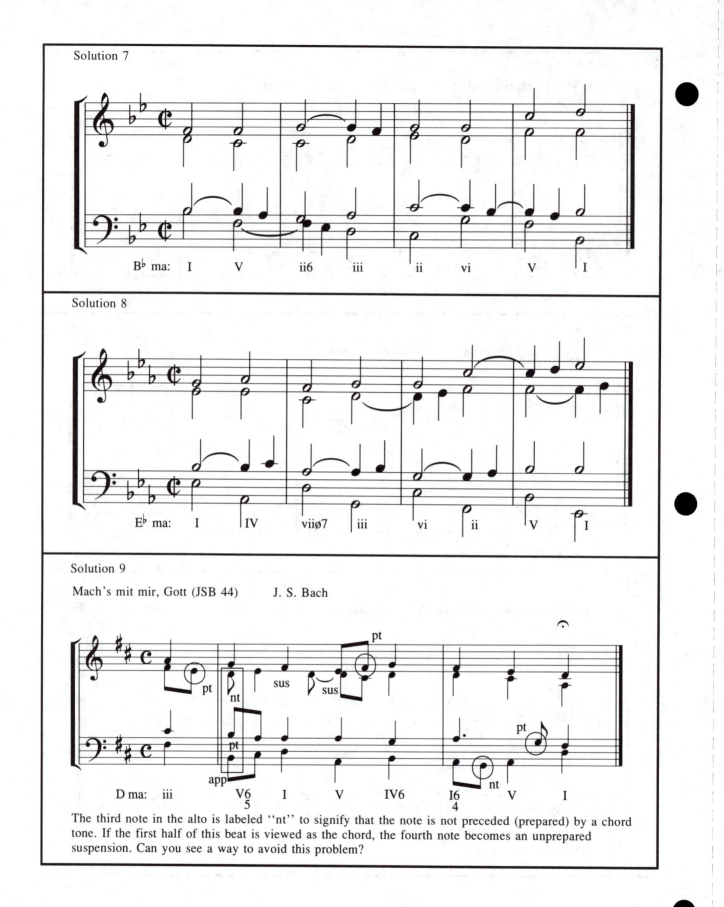

Solution 7

B♭ ma: I   V   ii6   iii   ii   vi   V   I

Solution 8

E♭ ma: I   IV   viiø7 iii   vi   ii   V   I

Solution 9

Mach's mit mir, Gott (JSB 44)   J. S. Bach

D ma: iii   V6   I   V   IV6   I6   V   I
             5   4

The third note in the alto is labeled "nt" to signify that the note is not preceded (prepared) by a chord tone. If the first half of this beat is viewed as the chord, the fourth note becomes an unprepared suspension. Can you see a way to avoid this problem?

Problem 10

Label the chords and nonchord tones.

F ma:

Problem 11

Label the chords and nonchord tones.

O welt, sieh hier dein Leben (366)   J. S. Bach

A ma: I6
                                          4

Problem 12

Label the chords and nonchord tones.

G ma:

357

Solution 10

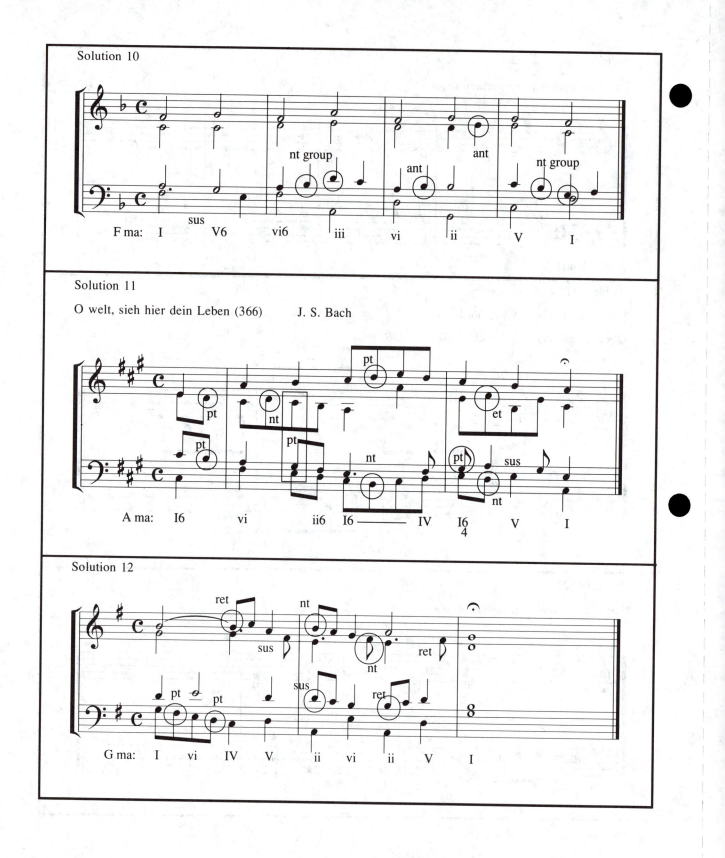

Solution 11

O welt, sieh hier dein Leben (366)   J. S. Bach

Solution 12

Problem 13 [solution is on the next page]

Label the chords and nonchord tones.

Jesu, meine Freude (96)   J. S. Bach

D mi:

3. **Error Detection.** Use these signs to mark the voice leading errors problems.

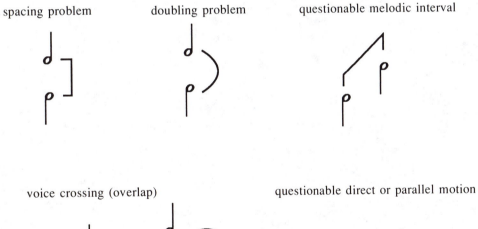

spacing problem   doubling problem   questionable melodic interval

voice crossing (overlap)   questionable direct or parallel motion

out of range   incomplete chord
(circle the note)   (write inc)

Solution 13

Jesu, meine Freude (JSB 96)   J. S. Bach

D mi: i   i6 viio4   i6   V   i   i   IV7 viio6 i6   iv6   V
                   3   4

Voicing Problem 1

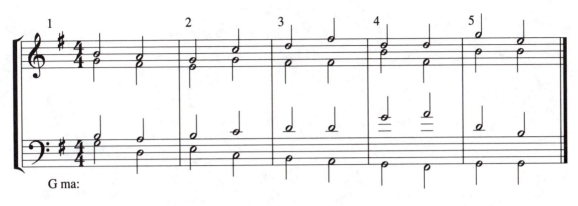

G ma:

Voicing Problem 2

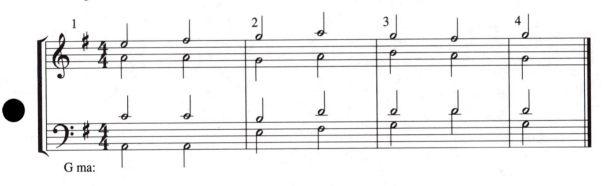

G ma:

APPLICATIONS

NAME _____ CLASS _____ DATE _____

Analysis

1. Label the chords and nonchord tones in this chorale. Changes of key are indicated below the music. Make the labels relate to each new key. Some progressions are labeled for you. As a choir director, how would you interrelate the moving voices? Do the nonchord tones make particular voices stand out? How would you perform the lines created by the nonchord tones?

O Wie selig JSB 28   J. S. Bach

● **Bass Lines**

2. Label the chords, then complete a four-part setting of this bass line. <u>Always</u> use the raised seventh of harmonic minor. Use the raised sixth of melodic minor to avoid +2 melodic intervals. Add nonchord tone patterns, but avoid undesirable direct or parallel motion that results from the independent voice motion. Add nonchord tones to create couplings and dialogues. Use nonchord tones to avoid "dead" spots in the rhythm continuity. Any voice, including the bass, can be decorated. Avoid augmented or diminished melodic intervals.

B mi:

3. Label the chords, then complete a four-part setting of this bass line. Add nonchord tones to create conversation-like exchanges among the voices. Avoid undesirable direct or parallel motion that results from this independent motion. Any voice, including the bass, can be decorated.

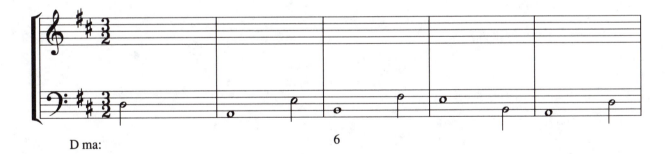

D ma: 6

4. Label the chords, then complete a four-part setting of this bass line. Add nonchord tones to make the parts and relationship between parts interesting.

B♭ ma: 6

5. Label the chords, then complete a four-part setting of this bass line. Use the raised seventh of harmonic minor. Avoid augmented or diminished melodic intervals.

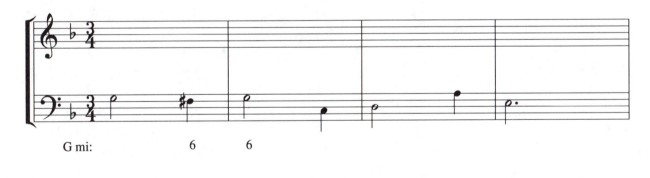

G mi: 6   6

6

6. Select one of your harmonizations from an earlier chapter and add nonchord tones to it. If you prefer, write a theme with variations to experiment with the different effects of nonchord tone couplings and dialogues.

CHAPTER

16 HARMONY IN FOUR-PART VOCAL TEXTURE: UNSTABLE CHORDS

OVERVIEW

The *Four-Part Texture Path* continues with information on connecting the voices of second inversion triads and seventh chords. Special attention is given to chords that contain tritones and other active tones. The chapter concludes with a commentary on the effective uses of unstable chords in musical composition.

Unstable Chords

Major and minor triads are useful phrase closing chords because of their inherent stability. Augmented, diminished, and inverted triads (especially second inversion) are less satisfactory as terminal chords because they contain unstable elements that make them less reposeful.

Unstable chords can be used to write expressive or dramatic music. Part of the impact of music is from the interaction between **tension and repose.** Conflict can be added through unstable chords. This conflict can be resolved by the use of **stable,** more reposeful chords.

Some chords are unstable because they contain melodically active notes. An **active tone** is a leading tone or a note in dissonant interval like a tritone or seventh. Also, active tones are created by accidentals used in harmonic or melodic forms of minor. These active notes require special handling in chordal texture.

Part-writing techniques addressed in this chapter are
• Treatment of active tones
• Treatment of unstable chords in chordal texture
• How to use unstable chords strategically

371

SECOND INVERSION TRIADS

The voice leading of second inversion triads derives from treating the perfect fourth as a dissonance in two-part texture. In its classic resolution pattern, the top note of the fourth moves down a step while the bottom note remains stationary. Harmonically, the top note of the fourth is treated as an unstable pitch. The interval might seem "top heavy" because its root is on the top. The voice leading pattern for second inversion triads based on this treatment of the fourth are the **leaning** and **neighbor chords.**

Leaning Chords

The **leaning chord** resolves to a root position triad. Its function is to embellish the resolution chord in the fashion of a **nonchord tone cluster.** The voices of the leaning chord are written below.

- bass is doubled
- root and third of the chord resolve down by step
- fifth of the leaning chord is the common tone in the progression

The first measure of the next example illustrates how the 6 and 4 move down a step to the 5 and 3 of a root position triad. In the second measure, the (8) indicates a doubled bass that moves to a seventh (7) in the next chord. The last measure includes a leaning $^6_4$. The doubled bass of the $^6_4$ chord becomes the doubled $^6_4$ root of the resolution chord. The remaining voices move down a step to the notes of a root position triad.

Example 1. Leaning Chord

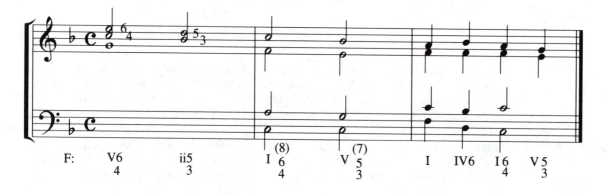

The leaning chord decorates a root position triad and provides a momentary delay of an expected root position chord. Leaning chords embellish cadences, so leaning chords are sometimes called **cadential $^6_4$ chords** or **embellishing $^6_4$ chords.** The delayed resolution caused by the cadential $^6_4$ helps place special focus on the cadence of the following chorale excerpt.

Example 2. Cadential $^6_4$

Valet will ich dir geben, No. 108 (286)   J. S. Bach

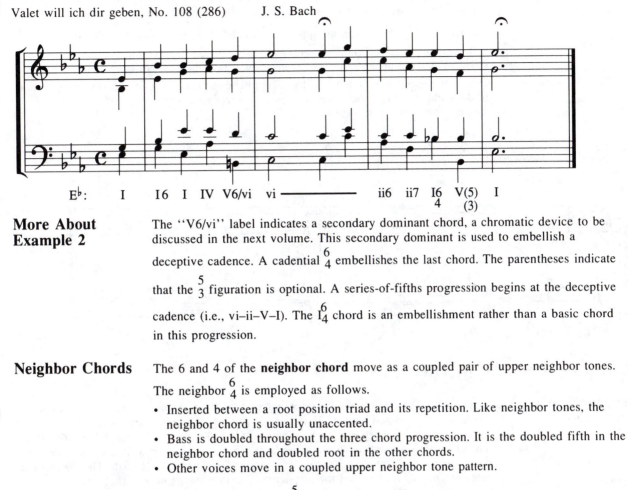

E♭:   I   I6 I   IV   V6/vi vi ——————————— ii6 ii7 I6   V(5) I
                                                          4   (3)

More About Example 2

The "V6/vi" label indicates a secondary dominant chord, a chromatic device to be discussed in the next volume. This secondary dominant is used to embellish a deceptive cadence. A cadential $^6_4$ embellishes the last chord. The parentheses indicate that the $^5_3$ figuration is optional. A series-of-fifths progression begins at the deceptive cadence (i.e., vi–ii–V–I). The I$^6_4$ chord is an embellishment rather than a basic chord in this progression.

Neighbor Chords

The 6 and 4 of the **neighbor chord** move as a coupled pair of upper neighbor tones. The neighbor $^6_4$ is employed as follows.

- Inserted between a root position triad and its repetition. Like neighbor tones, the neighbor chord is usually unaccented.
- Bass is doubled throughout the three chord progression. It is the doubled fifth in the neighbor chord and doubled root in the other chords.
- Other voices move in a coupled upper neighbor tone pattern.

In the next example, the $^5_3$ figure is optional for the first chord in each measure.

Example 3. Neighbor Chord.

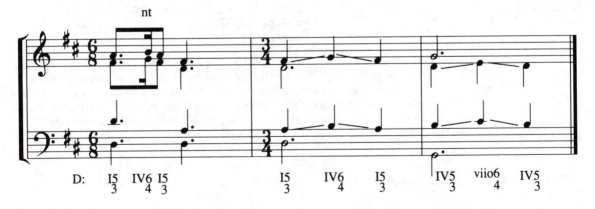

D: I5   IV6 I5   I5   IV6   I5 | IV5   viio6   IV5
      3   4   3   3   4   3 | 3   4   3

Passing Chords

The **passing chord** provides a linear connection between a root position chord and its first inversion. Its voice leading pattern is different than the leaning and neighbor chords, especially the treatment of the sixth and fourth. The passing O(4,^{6}) chord is employed as follows.

- Inserted between a chord and its first inversion and has a function similar to an unaccented passing tone.
- Bass is doubled. The doubled note is contained in two contrary moving passing tone lines, one of which is the bass. These are called **mirror** lines.
- Root of the $_4^6$ chord is in an upper voice and functions as a common tone throughout the three chord progression.
- The remaining upper voice moves in a lower neighbor pattern.

About Example 4   One of the upper voices contains the bass pitches in reverse order. In each progression of three chords, one upper voice moves in a lower neighbor pattern while the other remains stationary as a common tone.

Example 4. Passing Chord

C: I6   V$_4^6$ I   ii   vi6$_4$ ii6

CHORDS CONTAINING TRITONES

Tritone Resolution   Voice leading of the harmonic tritone is based on the way the tritone is treated as a dissonance in two-part texture. In its classic resolution pattern, both notes of the tritone move in contrary motion by diatonic step to the notes of a resolving interval. If the notes move towards each other (inward) the resolving interval is a third. If they move away from each other (outward) the resolving interval is a sixth. The *diminished fifth contracts to a third* and the *augmented fourth expands to a sixth*.

Example 5. Tritone Resolution

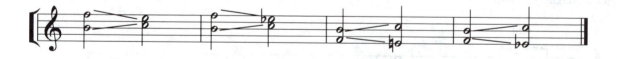

In major and natural minor keys, the diminished triad is the only triad that contains a tritone. In major, the diminished triad is the vii° chord. Its tritone bridges steps 7–4 (4–7 if inverted). In natural minor, the diminished triad is the ii° chord. Its tritone bridges steps 2–6 (6–2 if inverted). Most often, the triad and its tritone are inverted (see the brackets).

Example 6. Tritones in Diatonic Major and Minor

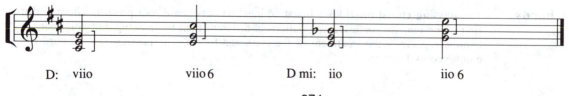

D: viio   viio 6   D mi: iio   iio 6

The two diminished triads in harmonic minor are ii° and vii° (the latter caused by #$\hat{7}$).
The two diminished triads in melodic minor are vi° and vii° (caused by #$\hat{6}$ and #$\hat{7}$
respectively). These chords are shown in the next example.

Example 7. Tritones in Natural, Melodic, and Harmonic Minor Scales

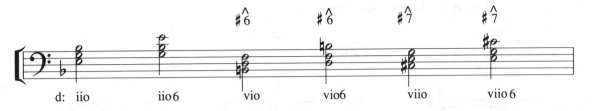

Voice Leading of Active Tones

Active tones are (1) both notes in a tritone, (2) one of the notes in a dissonance, (3) the top note of a perfect fourth, (4) leading tones, or (5) any chromatically altered note. *An active tone is a poor choice for doubling* because of its instability and demand for resolution. Often, *altered tones move in the direction of their alteration.* If a note is raised, it resolves upward. If the note is lowered, it resolves downward. Leading tones resolve upward. *Strong lines can override any of these tendencies.*

> **PERSON TO PERSON:** The ideas presented so far in this unit are general guidelines rather than inviolate laws. You will find it difficult to strictly resolve ALL active tones ALL of the time. Sometimes, strict voice leading is inappropriate. Your best course of action is to be aware that notes that attract the listener's attention require the most careful treatment. Active tones in the outer voices of a texture are especially noticeable. These should be handled with the greatest care. If active tones are in the inner voices, they are apt to escape the listener's attention and can be handled more freely. The continuation of a strong melodic pattern is more important than the strict resolution of active tones contained within it. Part of your development is to learn to decide how to handle each individual case. A good question to ask yourself is, "Do I write the unstable chord strictly—or emphasize some other factor?"

Voice Leading of Diminished Triads

Two of the notes in a diminished triad are active tones. The third note is the only melodically inactive note in the chord because it is the only tone not included in the tritone. Although the third is doubled only under special conditions in other chord colors, it is the best note to double in the diminished triad. *vii°* is a substitute for *V* or *V7* and is often followed by *I* or *vi*. If vii°'s third is doubled and the notes of the tritone resolved strictly, the result is a tonic chord that lacks a fifth.

Example 8. Diminished Triad, Strict Voice Leading

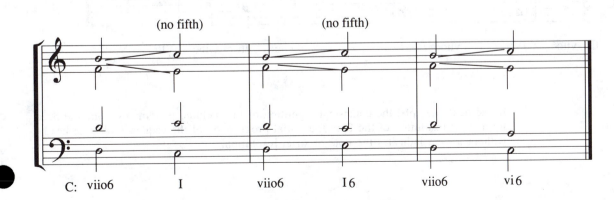

If both tones of the tritone are in the outer voices, they are very evident to the listener. Under these conditions, both tones should be resolved strictly. If one tone is concealed in an inner voice, it can be moved freely. The use of a first inversion diminished triad automatically puts one of the active tones in an inner voice. The next example is a variation on the previous example. As indicated by the lines, the active tone in the inner voice is not resolved strictly but moved in a way to ensure that the resolving chord has no omissions. The "cue" notes indicate the notes that should have been used in a strict resolution.

Example 9. Less Restricted Treatment of the Tritone

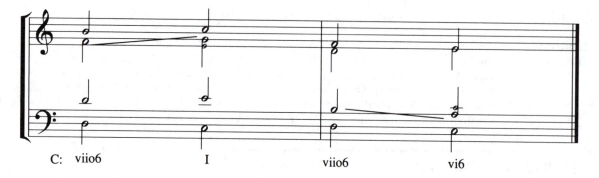

C: viio6   I   viio6   vi6

About Example 10   A melodic pattern can take precedence over the need for strict resolution of the tritone. In the first and second measures, the resolution of F is **delayed** and does not resolve in the voice where it originally appears (see the first two dotted lines).

The dotted lines show how the repeated F helps transfer the resolution to another voice. In the last two bars, the circled notes outline the essential notes of an embellished movement from F to E. In the last bar, the tenor B and the bass F resolve opposite normal tendencies. The converging lines focus the listener's attention on the melodic pattern instead of the notes in the tritone.

Example 10. Non-strict Tritone Resolutions

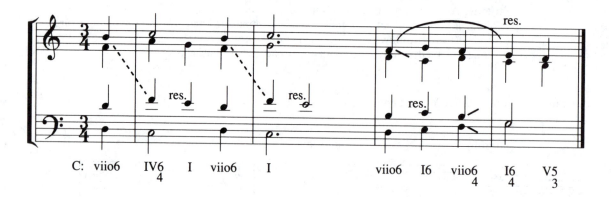

C: viio6   IV6   I   viio6   I   viio6   I6   viio6   I6   V5
            4   4   4   3

In the next example, the consistent repetition of the melodic patterns override the need for a strict resolution of the B in the initial progression of the sequence. A note head without a stem indicates the note of strict resolution.

Example 11. Tritone in Harmonic Sequence

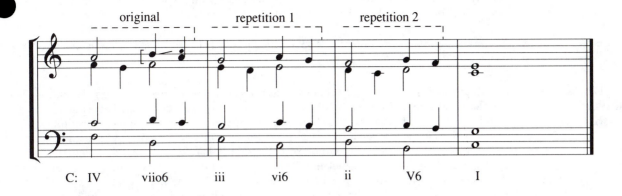

C: IV   viio6   iii   vi6   ii   V6   I

TRITONES IN ROOT POSITION SEVENTH CHORDS

**Dominant
Sevenths**

The interval between the third and seventh of the dominant seventh chord is a tritone. In a root position progression, the strict resolution of this tritone results in the omission of the fifth in one of the chords in the progression. If the V7 is resolved deceptively (to the vi chord), the resolution chord will have a doubled third or fifth.

Example 12. Tritone in V7

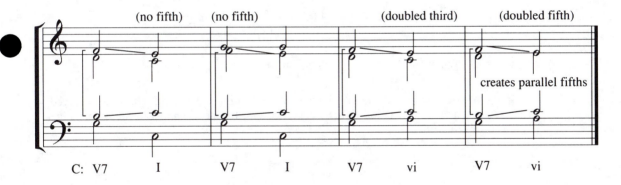

C: V7   I   V7   I   V7   vi   V7   vi

In the next example, one note in each tritone is resolved irregularly to avoid omission of chord tones. Because the notes that resolve irregularly are buried in the inner voices, this movement will escape the attention of the listener. The cue notes indicate the notes of strict resolution.

Example 13. Resolutions With No Omissions

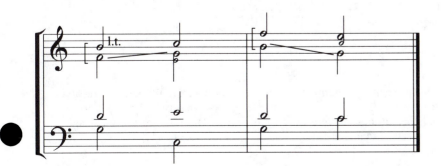

The "371 Chorales," contain many examples of chords with omitted fifths caused by the strict resolution of the tritone. Exceptions to this to ensure complete chords are equally common. Apparently, Bach used context as a guide when deciding whether to omit a part of the chord or to resolve a tritone irregularly.

Voice leading of inverted dominant seventh chords will be discussed in the next chapter.

Voice Leading of Diminished Seventh Chords

The diminished seventh chord contains two tritones. These lie between the root and fifth and the third and seventh of the chord respectively. The diminished seventh chord is the leading tone seventh chord in harmonic minor. As a dominant substitute chord, it resolves to the tonic, or deceptively to the submediant chord. As shown in the next example, the strict resolution of both tritones may cause weak doublings in the resolving chord (see the brackets). This can be avoided by allowing the notes of the upper tritone to move in direct fifths (see measure 3). The movement of o5 to P5 is direct, not parallel. A complete resolving chord with solid doublings results if the fifth is omitted from the diminished seventh chord (see measure 4).

Example 14. Diminished Seventh Resolutions

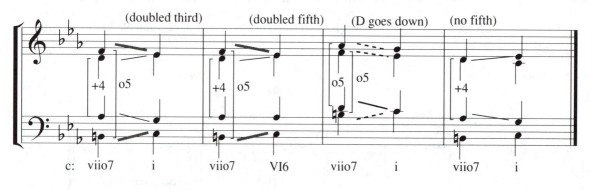

In the next example, resolutions of notes in the diminished seventh chord are delayed by suspension or retardation figures. Nevertheless, tritone members in the outer voices are resolved strictly.

Example 15. Delayed Resolutions

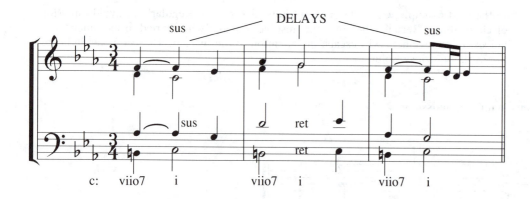

Recurring melodic patterns in a harmonic sequence can override the need to resolve the notes in a tritone strictly. In the next example, the original two-chord pattern is sequenced twice. The tritones are indicated by brackets. The roots of the viio7 and viø7 move by skip rather than step.

Example 16. Irregular Resolutions in a Harmonic Sequence

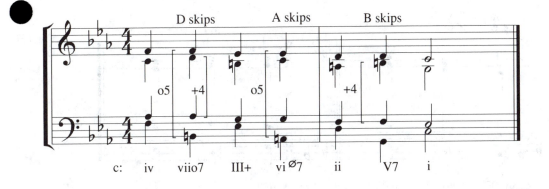

c: iv   viio7   III+   vi ø7   ii   V7   i

The diminished seventh chord is made of equal-size intervals, all minor thirds. Both fifths contained in the chord are diminished (e.g., mi 3 + mi 3 = o5). The two tritones give the chord strong melodic tendencies.

As shown in the next example, the chromatic scale can be divided into three diminished seventh chords. All diminished seventh chords are inversions or enharmonic spellings of these three chords. Any part of this chord can be heard as the root of the chord. Because of this ambiguity, the role of a diminished seventh is easily redefined by a composer or arranger. This makes the diminished seventh chord especially useful in chromatic harmonies (discussed in the next volume).

Example 17. Diminished Sevenths in the Chromatic Scale

The voice leading of inverted diminished seventh chords will be discussed in the next chapter.

Half-diminished Seventh

The half-diminished seventh contains only one tritone. This chord appears as
• viiø7 in major and melodic minor
• viø7 in melodic minor
• iiø7 in natural minor

Example 18. Half-diminished Sevenths

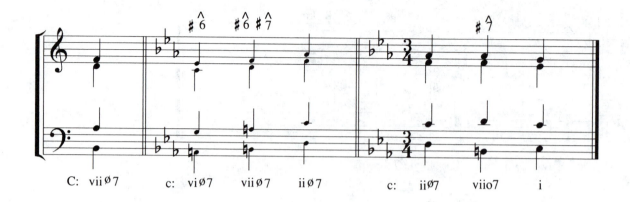

C: viiØ7   c: viØ7   viiØ7   iiØ7   c: iiØ7   viio7   i

The voices of half-diminished seventh chord can be moved as in the diminished seventh. These chords are frequently employed in second relation progressions.

Example 19. Strict Resolutions of Tritones

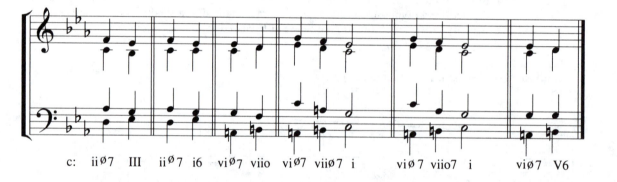

c: iiØ7   III   iiØ7   i6   viØ7   viio   viØ7   viiØ7   i   viØ7   viio7   i   viØ7   V6

The iiØ7 and vi°7 can be used as substitute chords. Each contains all the tones of the chord it replaces.

Example 20. Half-diminished Substitute Chords

c: iv   iiØ7   i   viØ7

The next example shows the voice leading of half-diminished seventh chords in a harmonic sequence. This version utilizes raised sixth and seventh steps frequently.

Example 21. Seventh Chords in Harmonic Sequence (version 1)

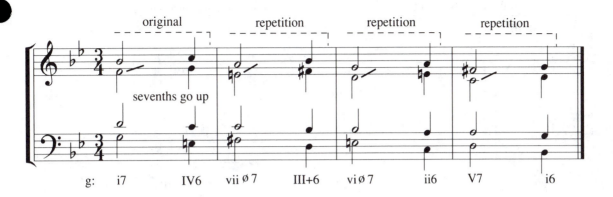

g: i7   IV6   vii ⌀7   III+6   vi ⌀7   ii6   V7   i6

The next example is a version of the previous phrase that remains mainly in natural minor. The raised seventh is used only at the cadence.

Example 22. Voice Leading Seventh Chords in Harmonic Sequence (version 2)

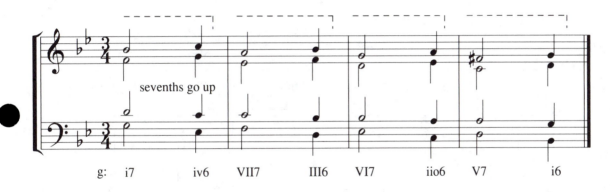

g: i7   iv6   VII7   III6   VI7   iio6   V7   i6

Voice leading of inverted half-diminished seventh chords will be discussed in the next chapter.

SEVENTH CHORDS WITHOUT TRITONES

The Minor Seventh Chord

The minor seventh chord (mm7) contains no tritones and occurs as the ii7, iii7, and vi7 in major. In natural minor, the minor seventh chord occurs as i7, iv7, or v7. The iv7 is used most often. The unaltered iv7 and ii⌀7 are the preferred pre-dominant seventh chords, but the V7 of harmonic minor is almost always used instead of the v7 of natural minor. The i chord is preferred over the i7 because the seventh reduces the stability of the tonic chord.

The melodic tendencies of the minor seventh chord are less pronounced than those of chords containing tritones. The seventh chord lacks tones with pronounced ''tendency'' like the leading tone or notes in a tritone. Even so, the seventh of the minor seventh chord can be resolved downward to be consistent with the treatment of melodically active chords.

In major keys, the ii7, a pre-dominant chord, is an effective substitute for IV because it contains all the notes of IV. It also stands in a fifth relation to V, creating a short series-of-fifth progression homing on I. Lines indicate irregular voice leadings. A fifth was omitted where strict voice leading is used.

381

Example 23. Minor Seventh in Fifth Relations

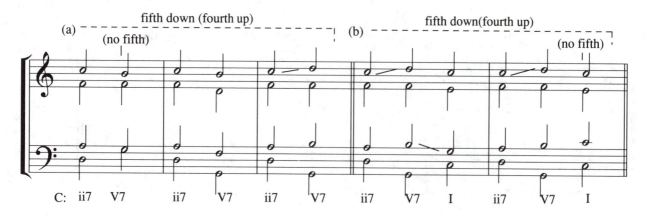

The next example contains three versions of the same series-of-fifths progression to illustrate the effects of strict and non-strict voice leading options. Lines indicate non-strict voice movement. Strict voice leading (seventh down, third up) results in the omission of the fifth in either the seventh chord or the resolution chord. Compare the three measures. Should the seventh be resolved downward as in the V7? If not, why was upward movement acceptable?

Example 24. Minor Seventh in a Series-of-fifths Progression

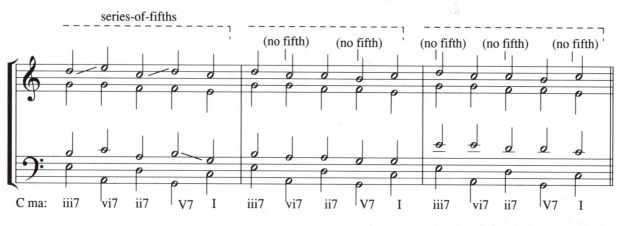

About Example 25

Three common tones are present in the IV–ii7 progression. Two common tones are present in the ii7–vi progression. The increased likelihood of common tones in progressions that contain seventh chords enhances "nearest tone" voice leading. Common tones are marked with slurs, irregular voice leading with lines.

Example 25. Minor Seventh in Various Progressions

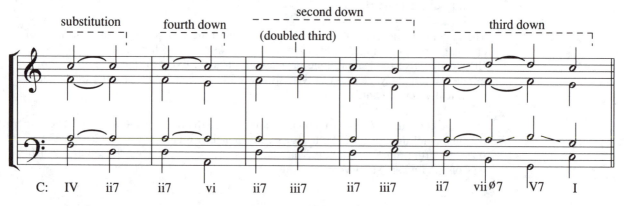

382

The Major Seventh Chord

Bach used the major seventh chord (MM7) only occasionally, but the major seventh chord is used frequently in modern music. The major seventh chord has "bite" in its sound but is melodically quite stable. It occurs in major as I7 and IV7. The seventh can resolve as easily upward as downward (because the seventh of the I7 is the leading tone).

In the next example, lines indicate the movement of sevenths. Slurs indicate sevenths that remain stationary as common tones in a progression. Does the voice leading of the sevenths seem inappropriate? Compare the I7 to the IV7. Do the sevenths of these chords have tendencies to move differently than shown?

Example 26. Voice Leading of Major Seventh Chords

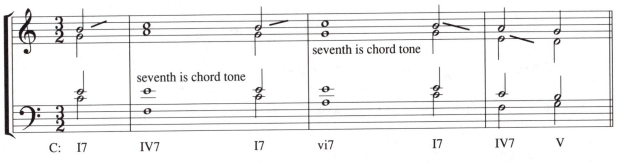

Bach's use of the MM7 in "Herr Jesu Christ" provides a point of tension just before a change of key. He allowed a "hanging" seventh in the voice movement (i.e., not resolved in any way). How do you account for this?

Example 27. Herr Jesu Christ, du höchstes Gut (No. 73), last phrase

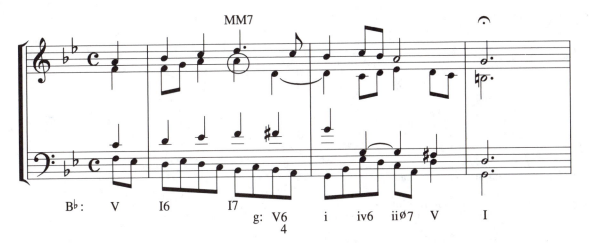

SUMMARY: Melodically active tones can be moved strictly or freely depending on context. Strict treatment of an active tone is necessary if it is in an outer voice of a chord, but the strict resolution of the tritone can result in resolution chords with omitted tones or weak doublings. If an active tone is concealed in an inner voice, it tends to escape notice, and can be handled to avoid a compromise of sound quality. A strong melodic pattern tends to override the need to resolve an active tone strictly, so if an active tone is part of a strong line, its treatment should be governed by the demands of the pattern. One can easily illustrate any voice leading situation with a "laboratory" example, yet, this illustration may not consider significant factors that stem from longer contexts. Part of your development in part writing skills lies in your ability to make decisions about these variables on an individual basis, to judge a unique context as it unfolds.

CHECKPOINT

1. Define these terms:

    stable chord   unstable chord

    active tone   leaning chord

    delayed resolution   tension and repose

    cadential $^6_4$ nonchord tone cluster

    neighbor chord   neighbor tone cluster

    passing chord   mirror lines

    inert tone   decorated resolution

    embellishing $^6_4$

2. Define these chords and explain how each of their voices is usually moved.

    minor seventh chord

    major seventh chord

    dominant seventh chord

    half-diminished seventh chord

    diminished seventh chord

3. Write a short paragraph discussing each topic.

    influence of melodic context on resolution

    influence of harmonic sequence on resolution

    delayed, transferred, and decorated resolutions

4. Self-help Problems.

Solution 1	Problem 1
active dissonant altered harmonic melodic	Unstable chords contain melodically _____ notes. These notes are active because they are parts of _____ intervals or have been _____ chromatically. Accidentals used in _____ and _____ minor always create active tones.
Solution 2 step seconds, sevenths, tritone P4 Both step	Problem 2 In two-part texture, one tone of a dissonant interval resolves by _____. Dissonant intervals include _____, ____, and the _____. Although a perfect consonance, the _____ is treated as a dissonant interval in certain chords. _____ notes of the tritone resolve by _____
Solution 3 P4 down (fixed, held) third down, third down, step	Problem 3 The voice movement of some second inversion triads follows the treatment of the _____ as a dissonant interval in two-part texture. The top note of this interval resolves _____ a step while the other note remains _____. This interval resolves to a _____. In most $^6_4$ chords, the fourth above the bass resolves _____ a step to a ____. The sixth above the bass moves _____ a _____ to a fifth.
Solution 4 leaning (cadential), neighbor, passing	Problem 4 The three classic voice movements of the second inversion triad are called the _____, _____, and _____ $^6_4$ chords.
Solution 5 two embellish cadence cadential, embellishing accented common double step root	Problem 5 The leaning $^6_4$ chord is part of a ___- chord pattern. It is used to _____ or decorate a root position triad, very often the dominant chord at a _____. For these reasons, the leaning $^6_4$ is also called the _____ or _____ $^6_4$. The leaning $^6_4$ is usually _____ rhythmically. The fifth of the chord is the _____ tone in the pattern and is the best tone to _____. The 6 and 4 move down by _____ to the notes of a _____ position triad.

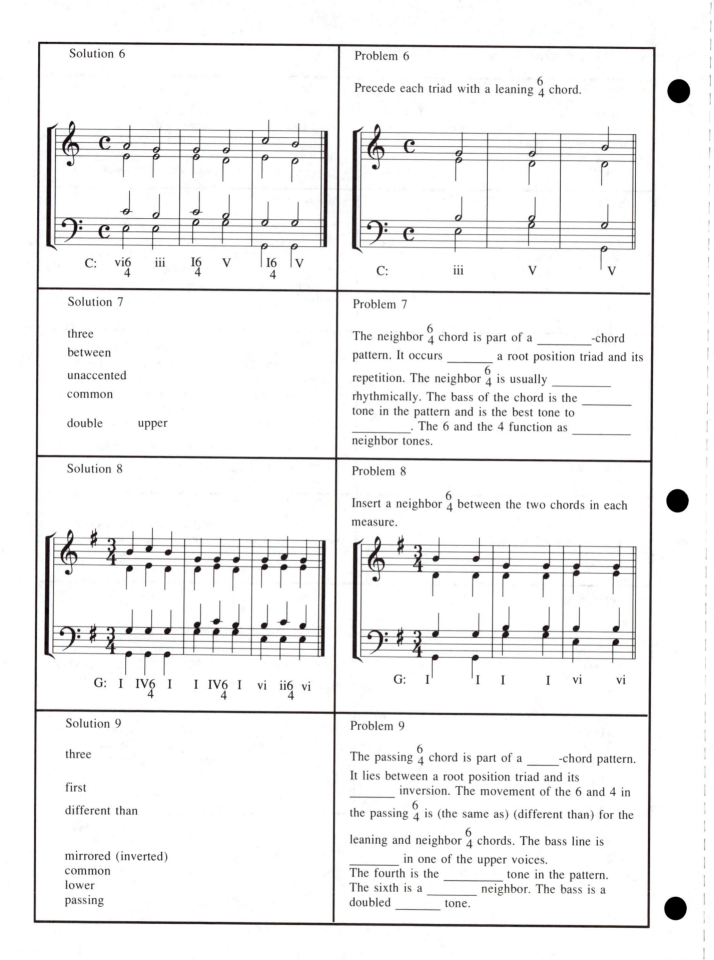

Solution 6

C: vi6/4   iii   I6/4   V   I6/4   V

Problem 6

Precede each triad with a leaning $\frac{6}{4}$ chord.

C: iii   V   V

Solution 7

three

between

unaccented

common

double   upper

Problem 7

The neighbor $\frac{6}{4}$ chord is part of a _____ -chord pattern. It occurs _____ a root position triad and its repetition. The neighbor $\frac{6}{4}$ is usually _____ rhythmically. The bass of the chord is the _____ tone in the pattern and is the best tone to _____. The 6 and the 4 function as _____ neighbor tones.

Solution 8

G: I IV6/4 I   I IV6/4 I   vi ii6/4 vi

Problem 8

Insert a neighbor $\frac{6}{4}$ between the two chords in each measure.

G: I   I   I   I   vi   vi

Solution 9

three

first

different than

mirrored (inverted)
common
lower
passing

Problem 9

The passing $\frac{6}{4}$ chord is part of a _____-chord pattern. It lies between a root position triad and its _____ inversion. The movement of the 6 and 4 in the passing $\frac{6}{4}$ is (the same as) (different than) for the leaning and neighbor $\frac{6}{4}$ chords. The bass line is _____ in one of the upper voices.
The fourth is the _____ tone in the pattern.
The sixth is a _____ neighbor. The bass is a doubled _____ tone.

386

Solution 10

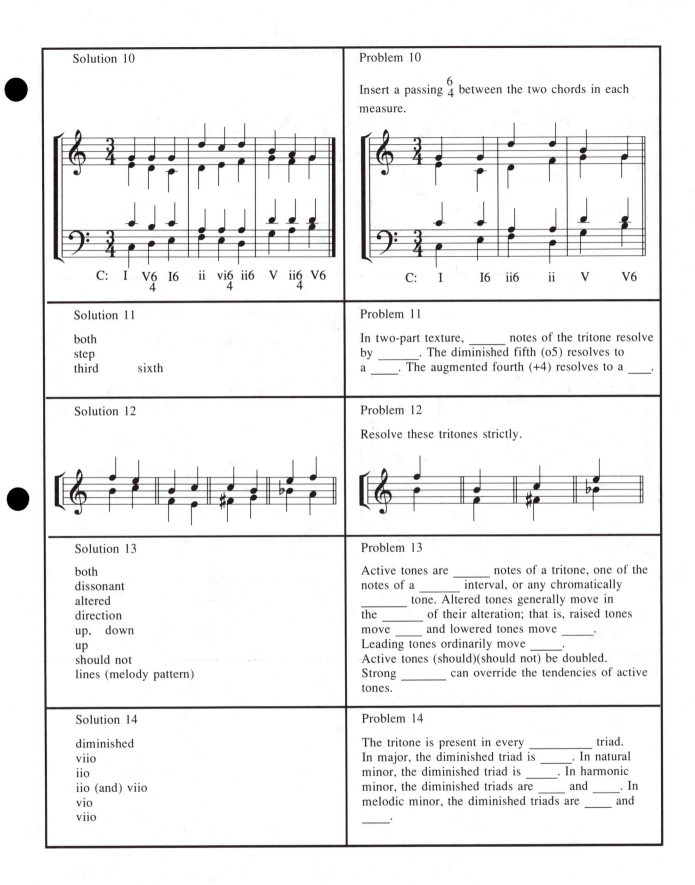

C: I V6/4 I6 ii vi6/4 ii6 V ii6/4 V6

Problem 10

Insert a passing $^6_4$ between the two chords in each measure.

C: I I6 ii6 ii V V6

Solution 11

both
step
third   sixth

Problem 11

In two-part texture, _____ notes of the tritone resolve by _____. The diminished fifth (o5) resolves to a ____. The augmented fourth (+4) resolves to a ___.

Solution 12

Problem 12

Resolve these tritones strictly.

Solution 13

both
dissonant
altered
direction
up,   down
up
should not
lines (melody pattern)

Problem 13

Active tones are _____ notes of a tritone, one of the notes of a _____ interval, or any chromatically _____ tone. Altered tones generally move in the _____ of their alteration; that is, raised tones move ____ and lowered tones move ____.
Leading tones ordinarily move _____.
Active tones (should)(should not) be doubled.
Strong _____ can override the tendencies of active tones.

Solution 14

diminished
viio
iio
iio (and) viio
vio
viio

Problem 14

The tritone is present in every _____ triad. In major, the diminished triad is ____. In natural minor, the diminished triad is ____. In harmonic minor, the diminished triads are ____ and ____. In melodic minor, the diminished triads are ____ and ____.

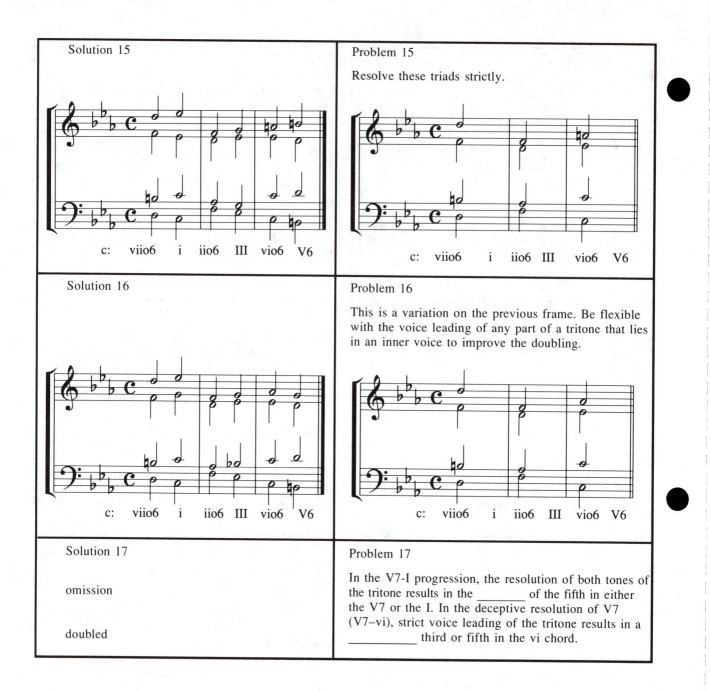

Solution 15

c: viio6 i iio6 III vio6 V6

Problem 15

Resolve these triads strictly.

c: viio6 i iio6 III vio6 V6

Solution 16

c: viio6 i iio6 III vio6 V6

Problem 16

This is a variation on the previous frame. Be flexible with the voice leading of any part of a tritone that lies in an inner voice to improve the doubling.

c: viio6 i iio6 III vio6 V6

Solution 17

omission

doubled

Problem 17

In the V7-I progression, the resolution of both tones of the tritone results in the _____ of the fifth in either the V7 or the I. In the deceptive resolution of V7 (V7–vi), strict voice leading of the tritone results in a _____ third or fifth in the vi chord.

Solution 18

(no fifth) (no fifth)

G: V7 I V7 I V7 I

Problem 18

Resolve the tritones to attain the effect specified.

(no fifth) (no fifth)   complete

g: V7 I V7 I V7 I

Solution 19

G: V7 I V7 I V7 I

Problem 19

Resolve the tritones to avoid omitted chord tones. Active tones that lie in inner voices need not be resolved according to their tendencies.

g: V7 I V I V7 I

Solution 20

(no fifth)

c: viio7 i viio7 VI6 viio7 V7 i

Problem 20

Resolve both tones of the tritones when possible.

(no fifth)

c: viio7 i viio7 VI6 viio7 V7 i

389

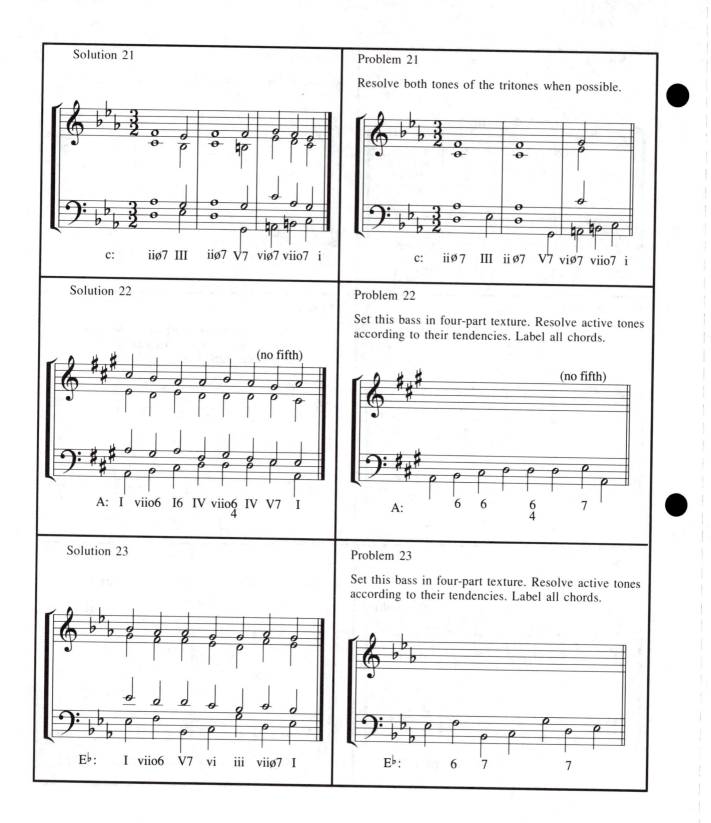

Solution 21

c: ii∅7 III   ii∅7 V7 vi∅7 viio7 i

Problem 21

Resolve both tones of the tritones when possible.

c: ii∅7   III   ii∅7   V7   vi∅7   viio7   i

Solution 22

A: I   viio6   I6   IV   viio6/4   IV   V7   I

Problem 22

Set this bass in four-part texture. Resolve active tones according to their tendencies. Label all chords.

(no fifth)

A: 6   6   6/4   7

Solution 23

E♭:   I   viio6   V7   vi   iii   viio∅7   I

Problem 23

Set this bass in four-part texture. Resolve active tones according to their tendencies. Label all chords.

E♭:   6   7   7

390

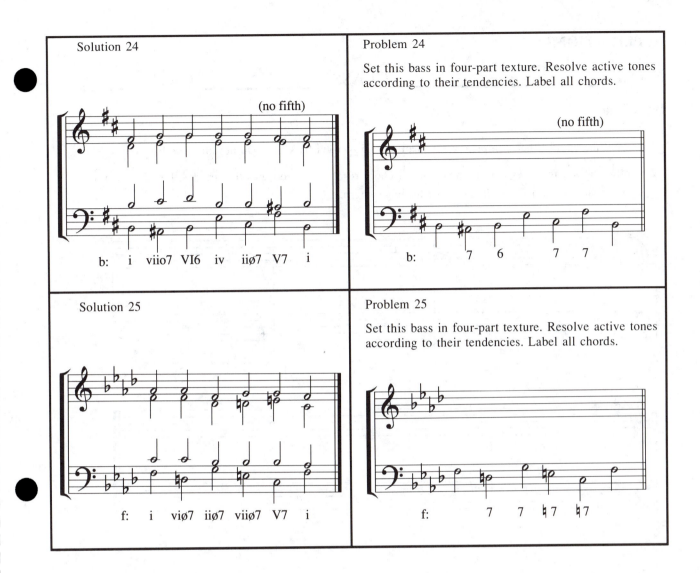

Solution 24

(no fifth)

b: i viio7 VI6 iv iiø7 V7 i

Problem 24

Set this bass in four-part texture. Resolve active tones according to their tendencies. Label all chords.

(no fifth)

b: 7   6   7   7

Solution 25

f: i viø7 iiø7 viiø7 V7 i

Problem 25

Set this bass in four-part texture. Resolve active tones according to their tendencies. Label all chords.

f: 7   7   ♮7   ♮7

NAME _____ CLASS _____ DATE _____

Bass Lines

1. Label the chords, then complete a four-part setting of each bass line. Do not alter the bass notes. The $\frac{5}{3}$ following a $\frac{6}{4}$ indicates that the notes of a $\frac{6}{4}$ chord resolve to a root position triad $\frac{5}{3}$. Identify each $\frac{6}{4}$ pattern and write it in its classic voice-leading pattern.

2. Label the chords, then complete a four-part setting of each bass line. Do not alter the bass notes. Both of these lines are in minor keys. A #$\hat{7}$ above a chord indicates that the raised seventh step should be included in the chord. Remember to avoid any augmented or diminished melodic intervals these accidentals might create. Know what chord colors result from the use of accidentals. Watch for any tritone bearing chords because these require special handling. DO NOT double active tones (i.e., accidentals, parts of tritones, dissonance).

a.

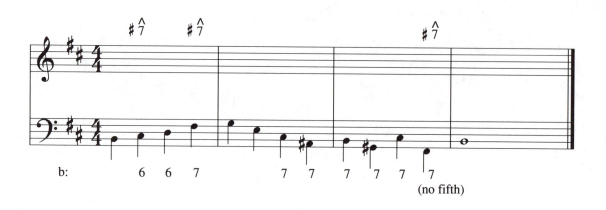

b.

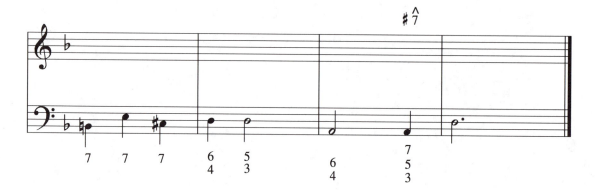

3. Label the chords, then complete a four-part setting of each bass line. Do not alter the bass notes.

a.

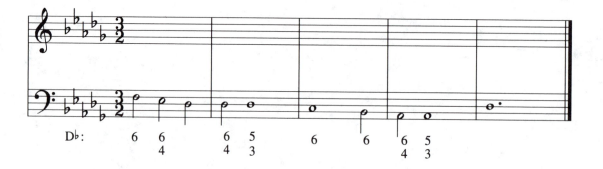

b.

Melodies

4. Harmonize one or both of these chorale melodies and label the chords you use. Use mainly quarter and/or half note chord rhythms. Review the harmonizing guidelines presented in earlier chapters. Use this exercise to review harmonizing in general. Look for opportunities to use unstable chords ($^6_4$, diminished, V7, viio7, iiø7, etc.). Some basic key changes are indicated. Mentally change key signatures at these points and label the chords in the context of the new keys. Always perform and listen to the results of your work. Make listening a significant part of your education.

   a. Herzliebster Jesu, was hast du (No. 59, *371 Four-Part Chorales*, J. S. Bach)

b:

D:

b:

b. Nun danket alle Gott (No. 32, *371 Four-Part Chorales,* J. S. Bach)

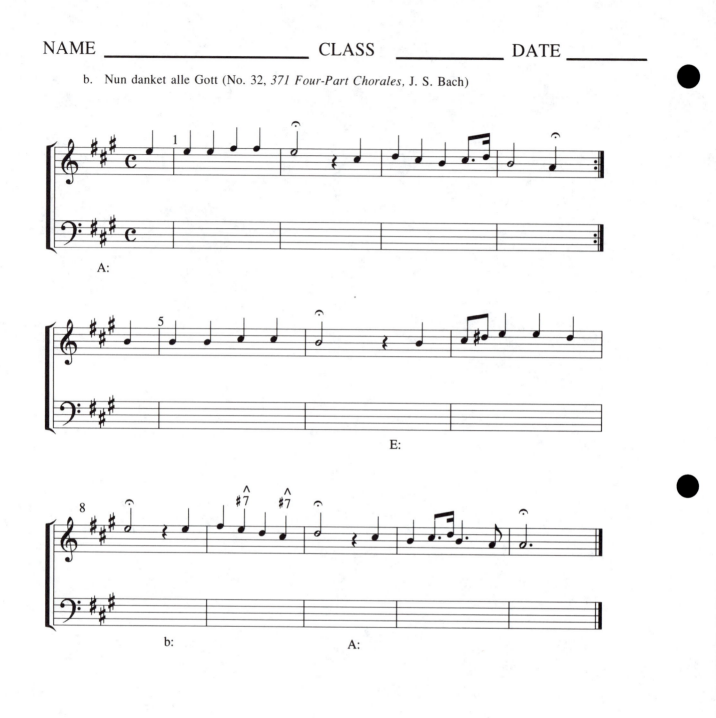

17 HARMONY IN FOUR-PART VOCAL TEXTURE: FIGURED BASS

OVERVIEW

The *Four-Part Texture Path* concludes with instruction on bass figures in harmonic analysis. This includes criteria for interpreting bass figures, realizing figured bass, and using figures to indicate accidentals, nonchord tone patterns, and seventh chords.

FIGURED BASS

In previous chapters, numbers were written under bass notes to represent the intervals contained in the harmony. This is derived from **figured bass**, a kind of shorthand scoring that was used extensively during the seventeenth and eighteenth centuries. Originally, a figured bass was a bass line that had Arabic numerals and other signs added to it. It was used in keyboard accompaniment parts as a form of harmonic abbreviation. These accompaniment parts were called **continuo** in most kinds of ensemble music and were often doubled by low string instruments.

Realization

Figured bass as a basis for improvisation is no longer a widespread performance practice, yet knowledge of figured bass helps to better understand, read, and perform **Baroque** music. Modern publications of Baroque music usually include a **realized bass.** This **realization** is an editor's interpretation of the figured bass, written out for the convenience of the performer. Some editors include the original figured bass notation with their realization so the user can check the source. Performers who understand realization techniques can modify these versions or make up their own.

Harmonic Analysis Notation

Today, a system derived from figured bass notation is used for labeling chords. It is well suited for describing harmony in music written since about 1600, but this system must be modified or combined with other approaches if applied to certain kinds of chromatic passages or twentieth century music.

Figured bass signs are usually abbreviated. In the next example, the common abbreviations are written beneath the chords. Use of the numbers enclosed in the parentheses is optional. Complete figures are used only under certain conditions, to be discussed later in this chapter. Ordinarily, a root position triad requires no figures and a first inversion triad is indicated by a "6."

Example 1. Figuration of Triads

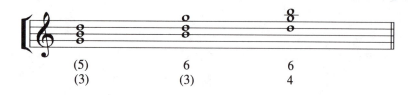

Abbreviated figuration is also used to label seventh chords. In the next example, optional figures are enclosed in parentheses. Notice that all but the root position seventh chord contain two numbers in their abbreviated figures. Since the bass note carries information about the chord, only the number "7" is needed to indicate a root position seventh chord. The numbers $\frac{6}{5}$ and $\frac{4}{3}$ point to the root and seventh lie of the chord (the larger number always refers to the root). A "2" is the minimum figuration needed to indicate **third inversion** since the seventh is in bass. Most often, third inversion is indicated by $\frac{4}{2}$.

Example 2. Figuration of Seventh Chords

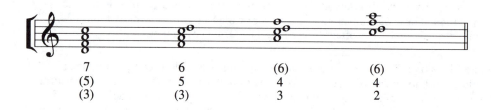

Figuration of Accidentals

Figured bass also provides a way to indicate the presence of accidentals in the harmony. These accidentals are used as follows:
a. An **accidental beside a number** (either side) shows how a particular interval is to be changed in relationship to the key signature. A sharp sign by a number means to raise the indicated note, a flat by the number means to lower the indicated note. A natural sign can indicate either a raised flat or a lowered sharp.
b. A **line through a number,** usually a diagonal, means to raise the note specified by that number. Sometimes, a small vertical line is placed through the end of the horizontal line on the "4." These lines have the same meaning as a sharp, a double sharp, or a naturalized flat.
c. An **accidental by itself** can be used instead of the numeral "3." For example, a free-standing flat sign below a bass note means that the third above the bass is to be lowered.

Examples of chromatic alterations follow. Since the bass note carries information about the harmony, no special signs are needed if the bass note is altered with an accidental. Use of complete figures may be required if accidentals are involved (i.e., $\frac{6}{3}$ instead of 6). Sometimes, more than one way to label a chord is available.

Example 3. Notation of Chromatic Alteration

A stand-alone accidental shows how the note a third above the bass is to be altered. If no other numbers are present in the figuration, one can assume that only the third of a root position triad is to be modified.

Example 4. Stand-alone Accidentals

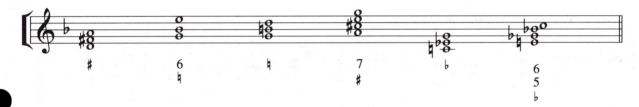

Figuration of Melodic Patterns

Bass figures can provide information about nonchord tones in the voice motion. A series of consecutive numbers like "4 3," "2 3," or "7 6" indicates step movement in one of the upper voices. As shown in the next example, these numbers are placed in the approximate rhythmic position of the moving notes. Although a number may indicate a nonchord tone, it does not show how it was approached. Thus, the kind of nonchord tone to be included is not specified by figured bass. In the next example, the same numbers are used to indicate three different kinds of nonchord tone movement.

Example 5. Melodic Pattern Figuration

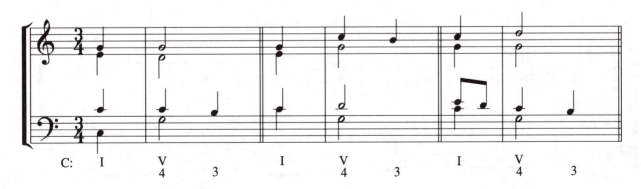

In the next example, the number "8" indicates a **doubled octave** needed to prepare or resolve a nonchord tone pattern. The numbers "7-8" indicate a step movement in one of the upper voices, but is not specific about the type of nonchord tone involved.

403

Example 6. Figuration of Octave Doublings

In the next example, the figuration of chord and melody tones are mixed together.

Distinguish harmonic figuration from melodic figuration. Stacked figures like $\frac{6}{4}$ and $\frac{4}{3}$ are familiar ways to indicate chord inversions. Figures in a row like "4 3" refer to melodic motion. A "dash" mark indicates that a number is to be carried over into the next figure. Notice the "6" followed by a **dash** (-) over a "5." This indicates that the "6" in the first chord is to be doubled in the first chord. One of these notes is to be carried over to the next chord while the other moves down a step to "5." In harmonic analysis, one need not indicate every movement of nonchord tones with figured bass.

Example 7. Combined Harmonic and Melodic Figuration

Accidentals can be included with mixtures of harmonic and melodic figuration. This may complicate the task of distinguishing between harmonic and melodic figuration. When studying the next example, remember that a stand alone accidental can be used as a replacement for the number "3."

Example 8. Chromatic, Harmonic, and Melodic Figuration Combined

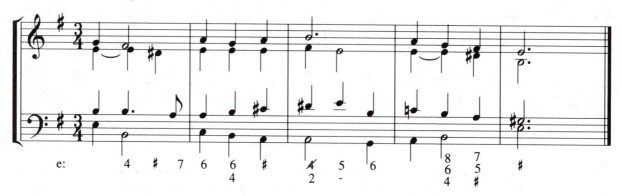

404

Voice Leading of Inverted Seventh Chords

The third and seventh are moved the same way in root position or inverted seventh chords (i.e., the third goes up and the seventh goes down). Fewer voice leading problems occur when writing inverted seventh chords because the bass can move by step rather than by leap (skip). In the next example, all voices, including the bass, move minimum distances. In third relations, three of the four voices can carry over as common tones. The remaining voice can move by step.

Example 9. Voice Movement of Inverted Seventh Chords

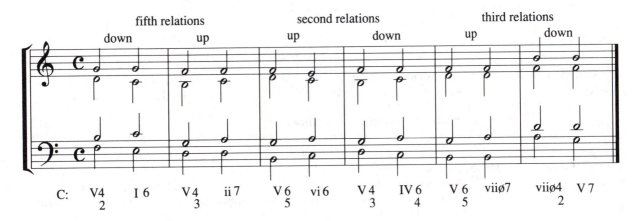

Minor Seventh Chords

Minor seventh chords (mm7) contain no tritones and their voices can be moved with less caution. Yet, the voice leading of the minor seventh chord is often modeled after the strict treatment required for less stable chords (i.e., third goes up, seventh goes down). In example 10, the lines indicate how the sevenths move.

Example 10. Voice movement of Minor Seventh Chords

Major Seventh Chords

Major seventh chords (MM7) contain no tritones. Like the minor seventh, the major seventh chord can be voiced with few restrictions or it can follow the voice leading patterns of less stable chords, depending on context. In the next example, the lines indicate how the sevenths move.

Example 11. Voice Movement of Major Seventh Chords

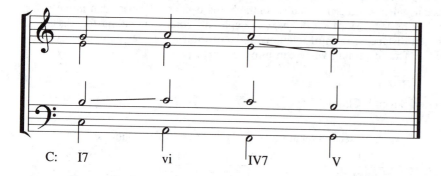

C: I7   vi   IV7   V

Series of Seventh Chords

Nonstandard movements of the third and seventh may be required when you set a series of several seventh chords. These are acceptable to the listener if the notes are
• Concealed in inner voices
• Incorporated in strong melodic lines
• Incorporated in recurring patterns like harmonic sequences

Seventh Chords in Major

In the next four examples, ascending and descending scales are harmonized with seventh chords. Find the third and seventh in each chord and observe how each is moved. Lines show atypical voice leadings of sevenths. Slurs indicate that a seventh remains motionless as a common tone in the next chord. Listen carefully to the examples, taking special note of the various treatments of the active tones in the chords. Some of the chords function like passing chords (i.e., a chord used as a quasi-passing tone bridge between a chord and its inversion).

Example 12. A Descending Major Scale

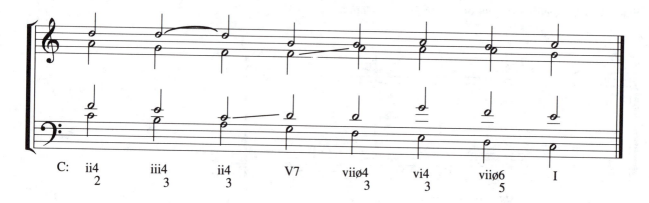

C: ii4   iii4   ii4   V7   viiø4   vi4   viiø6   I
       2   3   3   3   3   5

In the next example, the soprano of the sixth chord moves by skip instead of resolving downward. This should help avoid other problems caused by a different voice movement in the last three chords. Try moving the c differently to see if any problems develop.

406

Example 13. An Ascending Major Scale

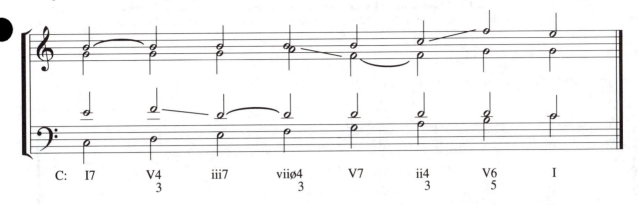

C: I7   V4   iii7   viiø4   V7   ii4   V6   I
          3   3   3   5

Seventh Chords in Minor

In the next example, natural minor is used until the next to last chord. The leading tone is included in the dominant chord in the cadence of the phrase (harmonic minor). Does the use of this accidental help confirm that c is the tonic pitch? Try the passage without any accidentals.

Example 14. A Descending Minor Scale (natural)

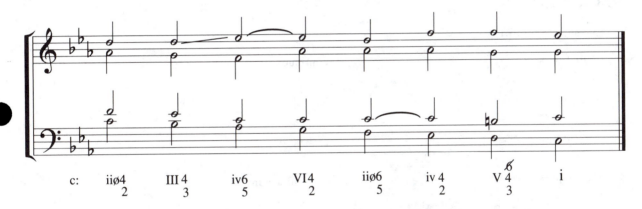

c: iiø4   III 4   iv6   VI4   iiø6   iv 4   V 4⁶   i
    2   3   5   2   5   2   3

In the next example, the raised sixth step is rarely used in the upper voices even though the bass outlines a melodic minor scale. Was the natural sixth step always resolved according to its tendency (i.e., down to the dominant note)? The dashed line indicates that F is transferred to another voice as a common tone, further delaying an eventual normal resolution of a seventh. Could the bass of chord 6 be resolved differently?

Example 15. An Ascending Minor Scale (melodic)

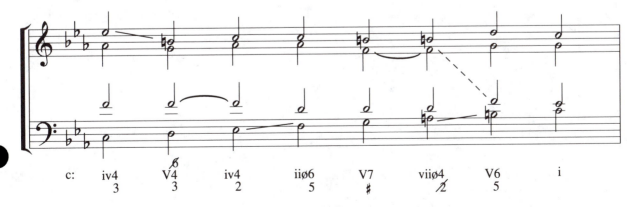
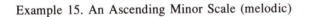

c: iv4   V4⁶   iv4   iiø6   V7   viiø4   V6   i
    3   3   2   5   ♯   2   5

A raised sixth step is used to avoid a melodic augmented fourth between the second and third bass notes of example 16; otherwise, only raised sevenths are used. The tenor moves in a descending chromatic pattern, softening the downward movement of the leading tone (notes 3 and 4).

Example 16. A Phrase in Minor Rich in Seventh Chords

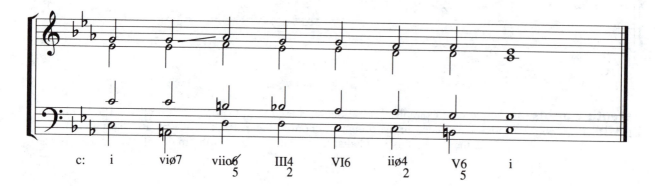

CHECKPOINT

1. Explain the following:

    figured bass   continuo

    Baroque   lead sheet

    realized bass   realization

    triad figures   dash after number

    third inversion   accidental next to number

    line through number   seventh chord figures

    indication of octave doubling   stand alone accidentals

    figuration of nonchord tones   voicing of inverted seventh chords

2. Self-help Problems.

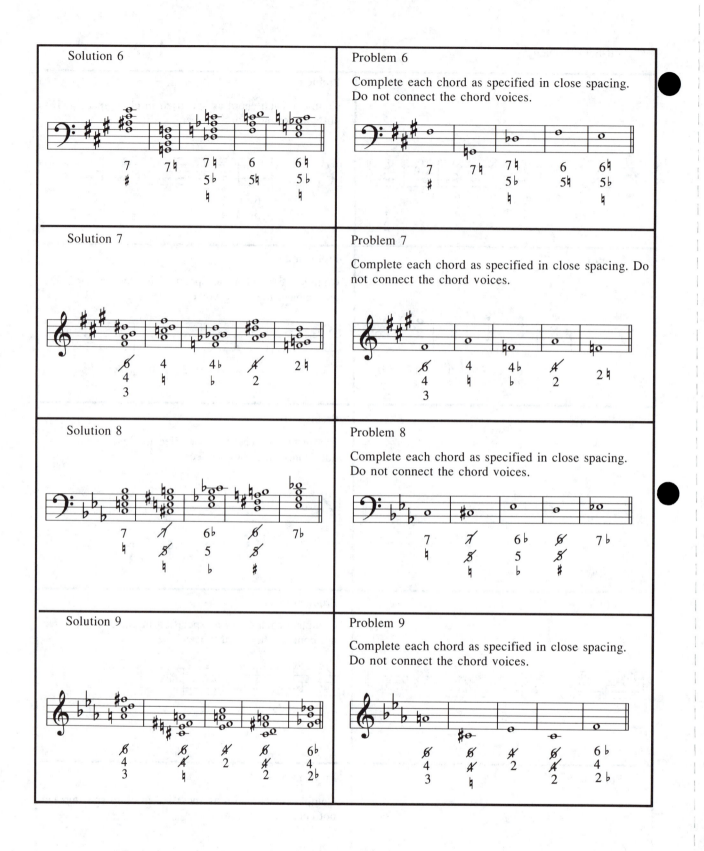

Solution 6

Problem 6

Complete each chord as specified in close spacing. Do not connect the chord voices.

7   7♮   7♮   6   6♮
♯   5♭   5♮   5♭
                   ♮   ♮

Solution 7

Problem 7

Complete each chord as specified in close spacing. Do not connect the chord voices.

6̸   4   4♭   4̸   2♮
4   ♮   ♭   2
3

Solution 8

Problem 8

Complete each chord as specified in close spacing. Do not connect the chord voices.

7   7̸   6♭   6̸   7♭
♮   8̸   5   8̸
          4♭   ♭   ♯

Solution 9

Problem 9

Complete each chord as specified in close spacing. Do not connect the chord voices.

6̸   6̸   4̸   6̸   6♭
4   4̸   2   4̸   4
3   ♮   2   2♭

Solution 10

Problem 10

Realize the figured bass. Connect the voices of each two-chord progression. Use "nearest tone" voice movement. Complete all parts of chords.

$$\begin{matrix}6\\5\end{matrix} \qquad \begin{matrix}4\\3\end{matrix} \qquad \begin{matrix}6\\5\end{matrix}\ 7 \qquad 2\ \begin{matrix}6\\5\end{matrix}$$

Solution 11

Problem 11

Label the chords, then connect the voices of the chords in each measure. Use complete chords and "nearest tone" voice movement.

C: V$\begin{smallmatrix}6\\5\end{smallmatrix}$ vi V$\begin{smallmatrix}4\\3\end{smallmatrix}$ vi6 V$\begin{smallmatrix}4\\2\end{smallmatrix}$ vi6 vii$\emptyset$6 I6

Solution 12

Problem 12

Label the chords, then connect the voices of the chords in each measure. Use complete chords and minimum voice movement.

C: vii$\emptyset\begin{smallmatrix}4\\3\end{smallmatrix}$ I$\begin{smallmatrix}6\\4\end{smallmatrix}$ vii$\emptyset\begin{smallmatrix}4\\3\end{smallmatrix}$ I6 vii$\emptyset\begin{smallmatrix}4\\2\end{smallmatrix}$ I$\begin{smallmatrix}6\\4\end{smallmatrix}$ V$\begin{smallmatrix}6\\5\end{smallmatrix}$ IV$\begin{smallmatrix}6\\4\end{smallmatrix}$

Solution 13

Problem 13

Label the chords, then connect the voices of the chords in each measure. Use complete chords and minimum voice movement.

C: viiø6 vi6 viiø6 vi6 viiø4 vi6 viiø4 vi
5   5   4   4   3

C: 6 6   6 6   4 6   4
   5   5 4   3 4   2

Solution 14

Problem 14

Label the chords, then connect the voices of the chords in each measure. Use complete chords and minimum voice movement.

C: V6 IV6 V4 viiø6 viio6 V4 viio4 V4
   5 4   3 5   5♭   3   ♭   2

C: 6 6   4 6   6   4   4   4
   5 4   3 5   5♭ 3   ♭   2

Solution 15

Problem 15

Label the chords, then fill in the missing parts in quarter note rhythms.

E♭: I V - vi IV IV V   I
       4 3   8 7 6 - 8 7 8 7
               3 2   4 3

E♭:
       4 3   8 7 6 - 8 7 8 7
               3 2   4 3

412

Solution 16

Problem 16

Label the chords, then fill in the missing parts in quarter note rhythms.

D: I IV I   ii vi ii V I V   I
    6 5 -   6 6 4 5 6 6 -
    4 - 3   4   2 2 3 4 -
                           3

D:
            6 5 -   6 6 4 5 6 6 -
            4 - 3   4   2 2 3 4 -
                                   3

Solution 17

Problem 17

Label the chords, then fill in the missing parts in quarter note rhythms.

a: i V - iv - V   i V - i
    4 #   2 3 7 6   4 3 6 5
           4 -   4 #
           3 -

a:
         4 #   2 3 7 6 4 3 6 5
                4 -   4 #
                3 -

Solution 18

Problem 18

Label the chords, then part write each measure separately using "nearest tone" voice movement.

G: V 6   I   V 4   I   V 4   I 6
       5   3   2

G: 6   4   4   6
       5   3   2

413

Solution 19

F: V6/5 ii 6 V4/3 ii V4/2 ii 6

Problem 19

Analyze the harmony, then part write each measure separately using "nearest tone" voice movement.

F: 6/5 6 4/3 4/2 6

Solution 20

A: V6/5 vi V4/3 vi 6 viiø6 I6 viiø4/2 I6/4

Problem 20

Analyze the harmony, then part write each measure separately. Make each voice move in step motion.

A: 6/5 4/3 6 6/5 6 4/2 6/4

Solution 21

E♭: viiø4/2 vi V4/2 IV V6/5 IV6 viiø4/3 vi6/4

Problem 21

Analyze the harmony, then part write each measure separately.

E♭: 4/2 4/2 6/5 6 4/3 6/4

Solution 22

D: V   viiø7 V viiø viiø V7 viiø V
    6   4   6   4   6   4
    5   3   5   2   5   3

Problem 22

Analyze the harmony. Part write each measure separately using "nearest tone" voice movement.

D:
    6   7   4   6   4   7   6   4
    5   3   5   2   5   3

Solution 23

d: i viio i VI   V   i   V
    6   6   6   4   6   ♯
                       2

Problem 23

Analyze the harmony. Part write the whole phrase using "nearest tone" voice movement.

d:
    6   6♯   6   4♯ 6   ♯
                     2

Solution 24

B♭: I V   vi V7 vi viiø V7 I
        6   6   4
        5   2

Problem 24

Analyze the harmony. Part write the whole phrase using "nearest tone" voice movement.

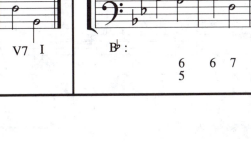

B♭:
    6   6   7   4   7
    5   2

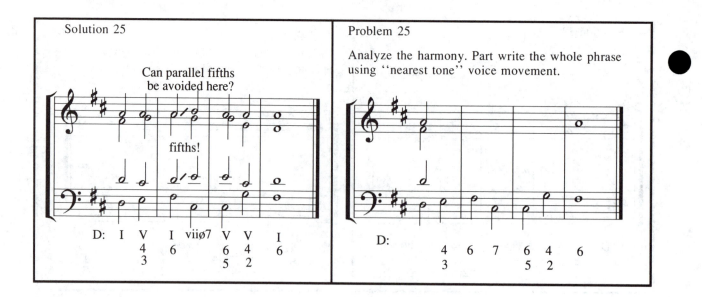

Solution 25

Can parallel fifths be avoided here?

fifths!

D: I V⁴₃ I⁶ viiø7 V⁶₅ V⁴₂ I⁶

Problem 25

Analyze the harmony. Part write the whole phrase using "nearest tone" voice movement.

D: 4 6 7 6 4 6
   3   5 2

APPLICATIONS: Bass Line Realization and Analysis

NAME _____ CLASS _____ DATE _____

1. Label the chords indicated by these figured bass lines, then realize the lines in SATB texture. Do not change the bass. Suggestions for harmonic rhythm are written below some of the bass notes. Always perform and listen to the results of your work. Make listening a significant part of your education.

(a)

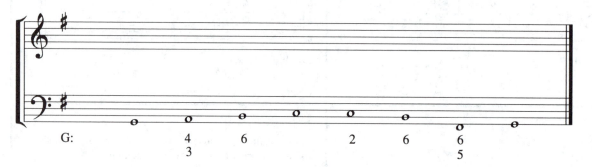

G: 4   6   2   6   6
              3   5

(b)

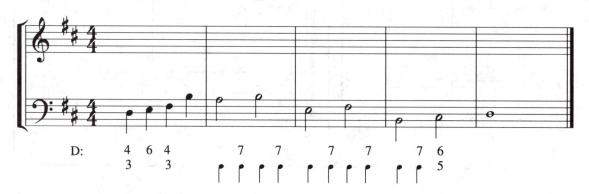

D: 4 6 4   7   7   7   7   7 6
     3   3   5

416

2. Label the chords indicated by these figured bass lines, then realize the lines in SATB texture. Do not change the bass. Harmonic rhythms are sometimes suggested below the bass.

(a)

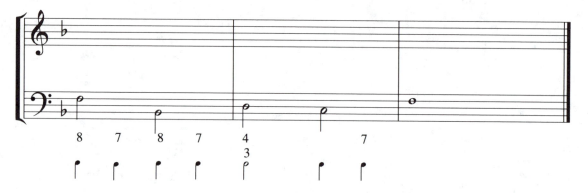

(b)

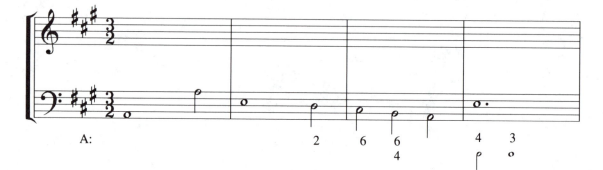

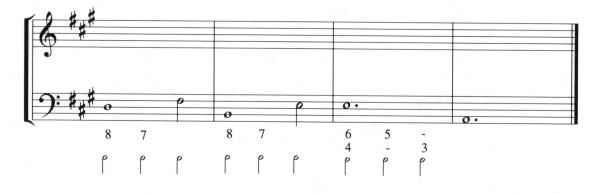

3. Label the chords indicated by these figured bass lines, then realize them in SATB texture. Do not change the bass. Give special attention to the indications of chromatic alteration that occur in minor keys. Avoid augmented melodic intervals in the voicing. The figures below the bass contain indications of alterations in the three upper voices. No indication is needed if the accidental is already visible in the bass.

(a)

(b)

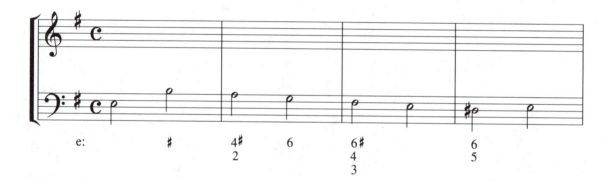

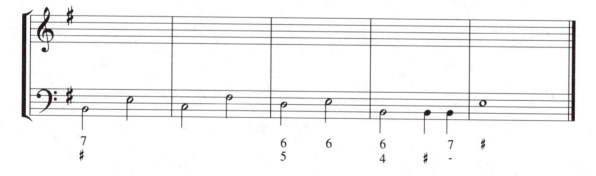

(c)

4. Analysis: label the chords in this phrase. Circle and identify each nonchord tone. Use two analysis options for measures one and three.

Ach was soll ich Sunder machen (No. 39)   J. S. Bach

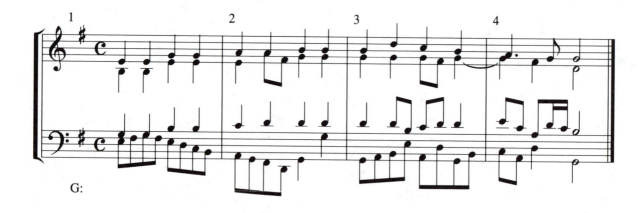

G:

5. Analysis: label the chords in this phrase. Circle and identify each nonchord tone. Label chromatic alterations in the three upper voices.

Christus, der uns selig macht (No. 198)   J. S. Bach

a:

6. Analysis/Realization: analyze the harmonies implied by this figured bass, then realize them in four voice texture. Do not change the bass. Add a continuity of nonchord tone patterns to carry and shift attention through the voices.

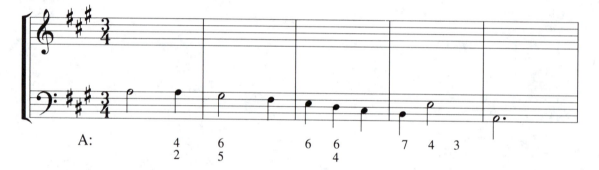

7. Realization: identify the chords indicated by this figured bass using root/chord quality signs (i.e., the first chord is "A♭ Ma"). Indicate chord positions with the abbreviations R, 1, 2, or 3 (i.e., the first chord is "A♭ Ma, R").

Recit: Thy Rebuke hath Broken His Heart   Messiah   Handel

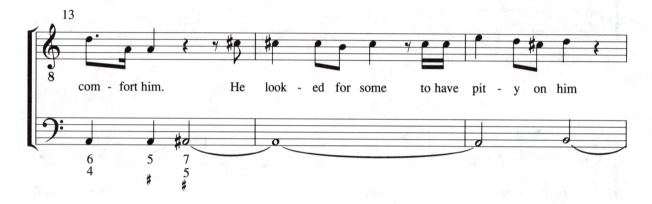

8. Place the chord labels of your analysis of "Thy Rebuke Hath Broken His Heart" in this grid. The numbers in the boxes correspond to measure numbers.

1	2	3	4	5	6
7	8	9	10	11	12
13	14	15	16	17	18

9. Analyze the harmonies implied by this figured bass, then realize them in four-voice texture. Watch for melodic augmented intervals and tritones. Do not change the bass. Add a continuity of nonchord tone patterns to carry and shift the listener's attention among the voices.

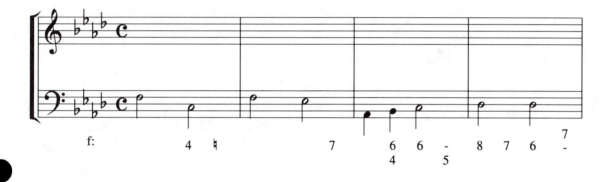

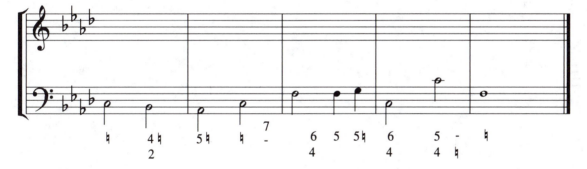

18 HARMONIC TEXTURE: ACCOMPANIED MELODY

OVERVIEW

This chapter includes a presentation of texture as the synthesis of elements of composition, a composite of rhythm, melody, and harmony. All topic paths come together in this chapter. This chapter links experiences with the four-part vocal score to other types of homophonic patterns as another step in the improvement of score reading, analysis, interpreting, and writing techniques.

Texture

The term *texture* is an adaptation of a term used to describe the construction, looks, and feel of fabrics. The structure and the weave of textiles has its loose analogy in music. In music, **texture** is an overall pattern in a composition that results from the interaction of melody, harmony, and rhythm.

One can think of a musician as a sonic weaver who manipulates the ''warp'' and ''weft'' of the fabric of sound. This fabric can be tightly or loosely woven, smooth or coarse, and can be made of many fine threads or just a few heavy strands. Musical texture is a sonic environment where musical ideas are woven and intertwined.

The pattern of musical texture can be changed in the course of a composition. These changes help define the shape of a composition, especially if they coincide with changes in thematic material, key, or mode.

Monophonic and Homophonic Textures

The simplest musical texture is **monophonic** because it is made of only one element, a melody. **Homophonic** texture consists of a principal melody and an accompaniment. The chorale is a type of homophonic texture because it is a hymn or psalm tune accompanied by the other voices in the ensemble.

Polyphonic Texture

Polyphonic means multiple or many voices. This texture consists of two or more important melodies. The most important effect of polyphony is the interaction of independent melodies. Polyphony also refers to a category of contrapuntal compositions including canzoni, canons, fugues, and inventions. A round is a simple form of polyphony.

Mixture of Texture Features

Homophonic and polyphonic features are often mixed together in compositions so pure examples of either type of texture are difficult to isolate. For example, most of Bach's chorale settings, although essentially homophonic, include polyphonic features that result from conversation-like exchanges among the voices.

Two versions of a chorale phrase follow. The first version includes ornamentation. The ornamented voices stand out from the rest of the texture. A particular voice may momentarily attract the listener's attention because of its special movement. Voices may interact with each other in a conversation-like exchange, or may join forces through couplings.

The second version of the phrase is simplified, the result of removing the ornamentation. The texture is reduced to its basic, monorhythmic, chordal pattern—the harmonic core of the texture. In the simplified version, the soprano voice stands out as the principal melody. The other voices provide support for this melody. The flow of harmonic sounds is now more evident. Compare the two versions of this phrase. Are you aware of the monorhythmic chorale as a foundation for the elaborated voices? Do you hear both the homophonic and polyphonic aspects of this phrase? After comparing the versions, locate and identify the nonchord tones in the original phrase.

Example 1. Wir Christenleut (No. 360)   J. S. Bach

original

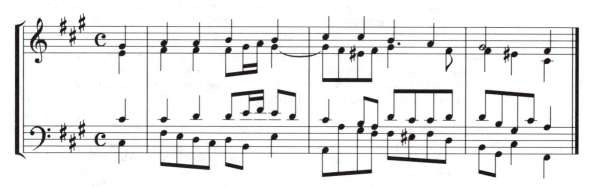

reduction: notice the series-of-third relations at the beginning.

430

Another setting of this chorale melody follows. Additional movement created by use of nonchord tones highlights the tenor voice and helps set up a dialog between the alto and tenor. How do differences in texture and harmonization create differences in mood between the two settings of the chorale melody? Locate and identify the nonchord tones in the original setting of the phrase.

The slash mark in the chord label in the last measure indicates a secondary dominant. Secondary chords will occur in other examples in this chapter, but a detailed explanation of this technique is reserved for a later course. Briefly, any chord can be preceded (and tonicized) by its own dominant chord.

Example 2. Wir Christenleut (JSB 321)   J. S. Bach

original

reduction: notice the chromatic bass.

Although a chorale should be performed with emphasis on the overall chordal effect, added melodic fragments and their conversation-like interaction can be brought out through expressive performance practices. Each coupling and dialogue can be set off with a contrasting dynamic wave. This enhances the added polyphonic dimensions of the setting and strengthens the impression of these melodic overlays as figures against a monorhythmic harmonic background.

ACCOMPANIED MELODY

Accompanied melody is a form of homophony. The monorhythmic chorale is homophony because its tune is heard as the principal melody and the remaining voices are heard as its accompaniment. The block chord harmonization of a melody is a similar form of homophony. In the discussion that follows, notice the various kinds of accompaniment patterns that can be superimposed on a block chord harmonization.

431

Harmony and Accompaniment

Although accompaniments vary in pattern and complexity, most can be easily reduced to a simple harmonic core (monorhythmic chordal background). This reduction reveals the harmonic/rhythmic foundation of a composition.

Example 3. Ich Grolle Nicht   Schumann

<u>Afterthoughts on example 3</u>: The texture of *Ich Grolle Nicht* contains three components, the melody, a bass line, and a stream of reiterating chords. This pattern is maintained throughout the composition (a complete version can be found in any of several anthologies of music). Only a few changes were required to reveal the harmonic core of this composition. The reduction of this passage was created primarily by omitting the reiterations of chords and the octave doubling of the bass. Details about the contribution of the accompaniment are extremely important to both the vocalist and the accompanist. The accompaniment helps establish and support the moods in the composition. The accompanist's principal task is to support the vocalist, but independent features in the harmony and bass can be brought out by the pianist. Movement in the piano part should be brought to the fore whenever the melody is static, as at non-terminal cadences. If the accompaniment is entirely subservient to the melody, its influence on mood will be greatly reduced. The flow of accents and dynamics is regulated by the monorhythmic foundation of the accompaniment.

Accompaniment Patterns

Accompaniments are created by superimposing patterns (figure) on a harmonic foundation (ground). Figure is added to this ground in rhythmic streams, motives, melodic links, embellishing chords, ostinatos, and full-blown but subordinate melodies such as obbligatos or counter melodies.

Reiteration

A basic progression can be "motorized" with repeating rhythms. This kind of **reiteration** is used by most arrangers and composers to add figure and motion to an accompaniment.

Example 4. Repetition in Accompaniments

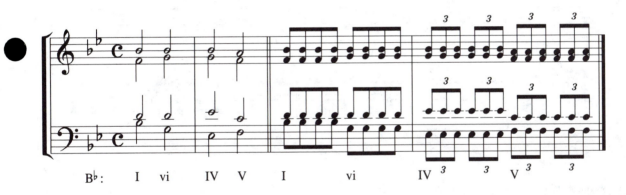

Reiteration can be an important component in the fabric of a composition. Notice the three texture components in the following excerpt: the melody, the reiterating rhythm, and the bass line motive.

Example 5. Who is Sylvia   Schubert

Moderato

434

Composers and arrangers control the interaction between accompaniment and melody over a wide range of gradations. The listener's attention can be directed to or away from accompaniment figures through this control. By controlling the interaction, composers create an interplay between a melody and its environment.

Think about the interplay between melody and accompaniment as you study the next example. Simplify the accompaniment to block chords (reiteration removed) and play it. Now play it as written. What does the superimposed rhythm figure add to this example? Identify and describe the textural components. How many are there?

Example 6. Piano Sonata No. 1, Op. 2, No. 1 (first movement)   Beethoven

Allegro

The next example consists of a melody and a **rhythmically figured harmonic** background. Compared to previous examples, this figure gives more thematic significance to the accompaniment. Is there a tighter relationship between this melody and its environment?

435

Example 7. Das verlassen Magdlein   Wolf

Langsam

pp

Früh,   wann die   Häh - ne krähn,

pp

a:

eh' die Stern lein schwind - den,   muss ich am Her - de stehn,   muss Feu - er zün - den.

Arpeggiation

An arpeggio is the melodic presentation of a chord. **Arpeggiation** adds rhythmic figure and a contour element to the harmonic background.

Example 8. Arpeggio Figures

Bb :   I   vi   IV   V   I   vi   IV   V

Rhythmic figure and contour can create a sense of underlying movement at more than one rhythmic level. The arpeggio pattern in the *Nocturne* is in sixteenth notes. The contour pattern of an arch cycles every dotted quarter note, creating a second rhythmic level. Notice the slowness of the harmonic rhythm. The first chord is sustained for four measures. The rhythms of the arpeggio and the recycling arch provided a sense of motion. The pattern subsides into the background as soon as the melody enters.

Example 9. Nocturne in D-flat Ma, Op. 27, No. 2   Chopin

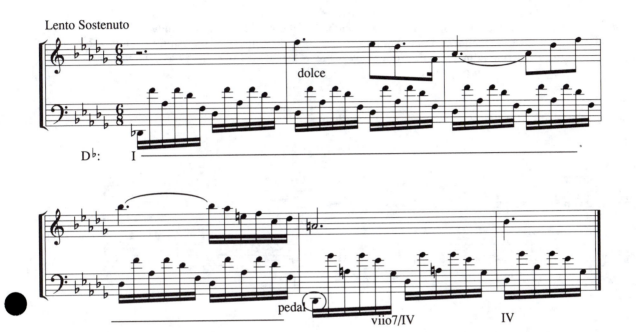

Alternating Chord Elements

Figure can be added to a basic progression by **alternating** the bass and other voices on different parts of the chord. Two versions of this pattern are given in the next example suggesting that several patterns can be derived from a given progression of chords.

Example 10. Alternating Chord Elements

PERSON TO PERSON: Composers place great significance on background material. Originality in accompaniment patterns adds a great deal to the character of a composition and can make the difference between ordinary and captivating material. You will become more aware of the contributions made by accompaniment patterns if you perform and listen to texture components separately (a standard rehearsal technique). When studying an example, rehearsing a composition, or writing your own composition or arrangement, consider each component by itself momentarily. This technique helps one better understand how the various elements work together in a particular composition. This can be very productive in rehearsals when working on intonation, balance, and expression.

Two texture components are contained in the next excerpt, a melody and an accompaniment based on alternating chord elements. The alternating pattern also adds rhythmic motivation. Notice how Chopin heightened interest by avoiding literal repetition of pattern.

Example 11. Mazurka 5 in B-flat Ma, Op. 7, No. 1   Chopin

Alternation of chord elements can be combined with arpeggiation.

Example 12. Alternation with Arpeggiation

Passing tones can be added to make conjunct links between arpeggiated chord tones, as in the third measure of the next example. This provides a momentary break in the arpeggio pattern that sets up the closure in the next measure.

Example 13. Piano Sonata No. 8, Op. 13 (third movement)   Beethoven

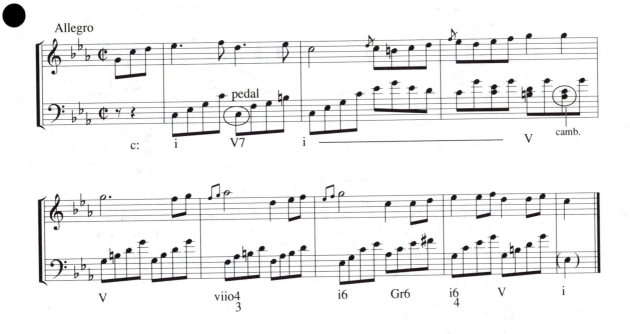

The texture of the next example is made of several closely woven components, a melody, arpeggiated chords, sustained chords, and alternating chord elements. These elements are so highly integrated that one may find it difficult to separate one component from the other. Can you find each separate component? What affect might this blurring of components have on a performer's rendition of the phrase?

Example 14. Intermezzo in A Ma, Op. 118, No. 2   Brahms

The next excerpt combines a melody, a bass line, and alternating chord elements. The alternation is set in a reiterating rhythm.

439

Example 15. Prelude 9 in E Ma   Chopin

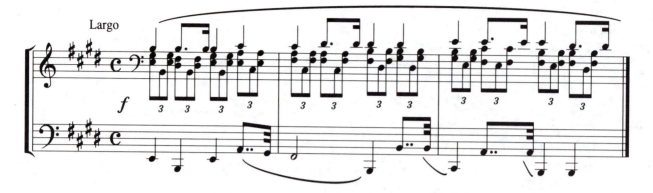

Pedal Tones

A **pedal tone** is a pitch sustained through changing harmonies. In its simplest form, it is a **drone** tone, a sustained pitch held while chords change. It can provide a continuing pitch reference that helps stabilize the harmony. The **tonic** and **dominant** pitches are the most common pedal tones because they help place focus on the tonal center of a composition.

In the next example, a reiterating dominant pedal tone appears first in the bass (bars 1 and 2) and later in the soprano (bars 3 and 4). This indicates that a pedal tone can be written in any voice.

Example 16. Pedal Tones in Texture

The next example illustrates a **reiterating** primitive (pastoral) pedal. Note the position of the melody in relationship to the other parts in the texture. The continuing use of the tonic fifth creates a solid tonal center.

Example 17. Mazurka 3 in E Ma, Op. 6, No. 3   Chopin

The next example contains both a dominant and a tonic pedal. Each tone is decorated by neighbor tones in a recurring pattern. The pedal tones form a background V-I progression that promotes a particularly strong closure and focus on the keynote.

Example 18. Sonata No. 3, C Ma   Beethoven

Scherzo, allegro

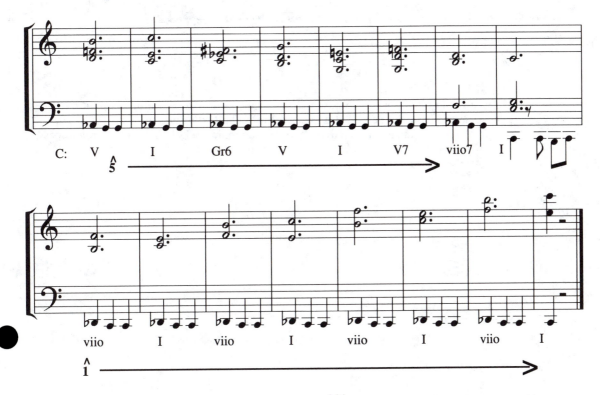

A reiterating pedal is used in an inner voice in the next example (the note G). There are two components in the texture—a coupling of the melody and bass in parallel tenths and a dominant pedal enclosed within these two parts.

Example 19. Humming Song   Schumann

Nicht schnell

C:

Ostinato

An **ostinato** is a reiterating pattern that serves as an ornamented pedal. The recurring focal pitch of an ostinato is heard as the pedal tone, while all other notes in the pattern are heard as satellites. A simple ostinato is shown in the next example. Which note do you hear as the focal pitch in the recurring pattern?

Example 20. Ostinato

B♭:   I   vi   IV   V   I   vi   IV   V

If an ostinato is written in the bass part it is called a **basso ostinato**. A repeating phrase in the bass can be called a **ground bass**. The texture in the next example is made of three elements; a melody, a chordal harmonic background, and a ground bass. The bass outlines the movement between G and D.

442

Example 21. Dido's Lament (from Dido and Aeneas) Purcell

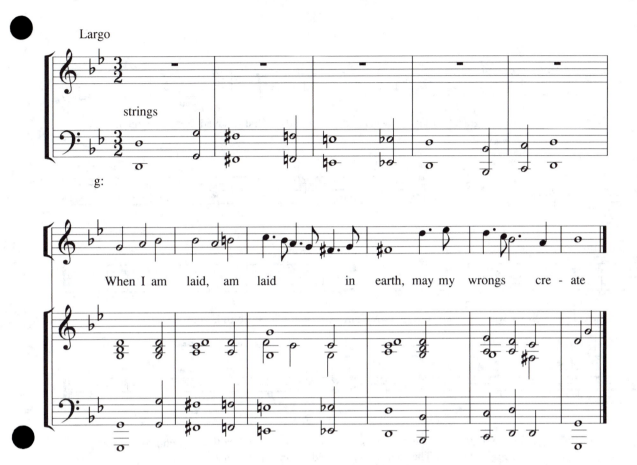

When I am laid, am laid in earth, may my wrongs cre - ate

Melody in Soprano

In homophonic texture, the melody in the soprano is favored most by composers and arrangers. In this arrangement, the melody and the bass line lie in the outer voices of the texture (the most easily heard). These two voices establish the high and low limits of the texture and are the poles accompaniment patterns operate between. With few exceptions, most of the examples of homophony given in this book feature the melody in the soprano. This represents a cross section of homophonic literature. All of the tunes of Bach's 371 Four-Part Chorales are located in the soprano voice.

Melody in Mid-Texture

Sometimes, a **secondary melody,** an **obbligato** or a **counter melody,** may be placed above the melody. The piccolo line in the trio of Sousa's "Stars and Stripes Forever" march is a classic example of an obbligato placed above the principal melody. The trombone line adds a second counter melody below the melody.

One setting of "Amazing Grace" has the melody placed in the tenor, an inner voice. This seems to be the preferred location of the melody in this genre of American Folk Hymnody. Some notes are harmonized with perfect fifths, giving the setting a certain stark charm. The soprano functions loosely as an obbligato.

Example 22. from Southern Harmony   William Walker

Amazing Grace

The texture of the next excerpt consists of a melody, reiterating chords, and an arpeggio pattern. The melody is located in an inner voice.

Example 23. Intermezzo, Op. 119, No. 3   Brahms

Melody in Bass   In example 24, accompaniment and melodic figures alternate cyclically. The melody lies in the bass and is doubled at the octave. How do you account for the agitated effect of this excerpt? How would you render this passage as a performer?

444

Example 24. Prelude 22   Chopin

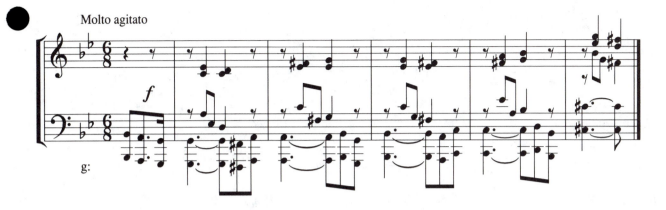

Molto agitato

The melody is also located in the bass in the next example. An arpeggiated melody covers a relatively wide range in each of its successive waves. The accompaniment is made of two rhythmic levels of reiteration. This pattern changes near the end of the excerpt. How would you describe the mood and impact of this example? Compare it to the previous example. How do you account for the differences in impact between the two? How would you render the music as a performer?

Example 25. Prelude 6   Chopin

Lento assai

soto voce

445

CHECKPOINT

1. Briefly define these terms:

texture	monophonic
homophonic	polyphonic
reiteration	rhythmically figured harmony
arpeggiation	alternating elements
pedal tone	drone
tonic pedal	dominant pedal
reiterating pedal	ground bass
ostinato	basso ostinato
secondary melody	obbligato
counter melody	

2. Self-help Problems.

Solution 1	Problem 1
monophonic homophonic accompanied homophonic monorhythmic have	The context made of a single melody is _____ texture. The context made of a principal melody and an accompaniment is _____ texture. Both _____ melody and the chorale are considered types of _____ texture. Most chorales, especially those with elaborated voices, can be reduced to a harmonic core called the _____ rhythmic chorale. This means that all the voices (have) (do not have) the same rhythms.
Solution 2	**Problem 2**
polyphonic do not have polyrhythmic at different times	The context that is made of independent and interacting melodies is _____ texture. All the voices (have) (do not have) the same rhythms in this texture. Because of this, the texture is _____ rhythmic. The independence of the voices can be enhanced as the peaks and valleys of their contours occur (simultaneously) (at different times).

Solution 3 polyphony are not increasing conversation layers	**Problem 3** If the voices of the monorhythmic chorale are embellished, an element of _____ has been added to the texture. Thus, most compositions (are) (are not) pure examples of homophonic or polyphonic textures. The addition of nonchord tones to the monorhythmic chorale adds interest by _____ rhythm pace, setting up _____-like exchanges among the voices, and establishing _____ of rhythmic activity.
Solution 4 accompanied background (core) harmonizing reiterating (repeating) rhythm arpeggios alternated Nonchord motives	**Problem 4** Another form of homophony is called _____ melody. Accompaniments can be reduced to a monorhythmic harmonic _____. Some individuals start with this pattern when _____ a melody, then "texturize" it with one of several typical accompaniment patterns. The pattern most directly related to a block chord harmonization is _____ chords. This adds a new layer of _____ activity. The chord can be presented melodically in the form of _____. Parts of the chord can be _____ among the voices. _____ tones can be added to create melodic links between parts of the chord. This can lead to the use of recurring _____ that add thematic content and interest to the accompaniment.
Solution 5 pedal tonic dominant tonal (tonic) are not reiterating motives (figures) ostinato focal (central) ornamental (embellished)	**Problem 5** Drone tones, also called _____ tones, can be used. Typically, the _____ and _____ pitches are used where strong _____ focus is desired. These tones (are) (are not) restricted to use in the bass voice. As with block chords, _____ rhythms and _____ can be used to embellish a drone. The closely related repeating pitch pattern is called an _____. Since this pattern can be reduced to a repeating _____ pitch, it can be seen as an _____ drone.
Solution 6 obbligato counter need not middle bass	**Problem 6** In homophonic texture, a secondary melody, called an _____ or _____ melody can be used. Like the principal melody, these secondary melodies (must) (need not) be placed in the soprano. Sometimes, it is refreshing to hear the melody in the _____ range of the texture or in the _____.

Instruction

Use this chord progression as the basis for illustrating the accompaniment patterns requested in the following problems.

Each solution includes several sample patterns. In a real composition, patterns would not change so frequently. Any pattern included in the solution frames could be used as a repeating figure.

Instruction

basic progression

Solution 7

The solution in this problem is only a sample. Variation in correct response is expected.

Problem 7

simple reiteration

Solution 8

The solution in this problem is only a sample. Variation in correct response is expected.

Problem 8

reiterating rhythmic motive

Solution 9

The solution in this problem is only a sample. Variation in correct response is expected.

Problem 9

alternating parts (emphasize root and fifth in bass)

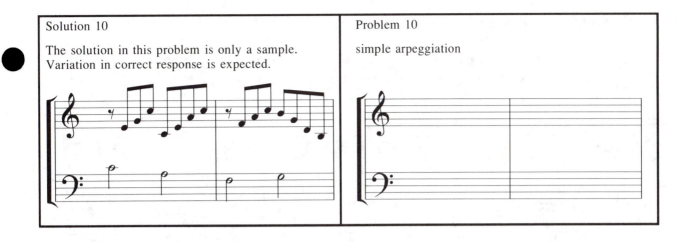

Solution 10

The solution in this problem is only a sample. Variation in correct response is expected.

Problem 10

simple arpeggiation

APPLICATIONS

1. Reduce Prelude 1 in C major (from the Well-Tempered Clavier, Book 1, J. S. Bach) to a harmonic core of thirty-five five-voice chords and write this reduction in the staff provided. How can this reduction help you read, play, memorize, and interpret this composition? Pay special attention to voice-leading. The progression contains some measure-long nonchord tones. Locate and label these ''slow motion'' nonchord tones.

Prelude No. 1 in C Ma (from the Well Tempered Clavier)   J. S. Bach

C:

2. Find a copy of Robert Schumann's Papillons, Op. 2 for piano. Listen to a recording of this composition while looking at the score. Briefly explain what textural variables and constants Schumann used to create unity and contrast in the first five short compositions of this character composition cycle. What texture patterns are displayed in each composition? How could you use this knowledge to rehearse each composition? What would you try to bring to the listener's attention in each case?

No. 1

No. 2

No. 3

No. 4

No. 5

3. Specifications for a Year-end Project

Presentation Length The presentation should take no more than 15 minutes not counting set-up time (overlap set-ups and strikes; the first presentation is set before class begins, last set-up struck after class ends).

Presentation Media Choice of media is variable (can include combinations of narrative, live performance, recording, handouts, transparencies). You are responsible for acquiring your own resources (recordings, sound equipment, performers, handouts, etc.)

Format of Work Submit a <u>typewritten</u> (done with typewriter or word processor), well organized paper with supporting material such as scores, transparencies, diagrams, and charts attached. The documentation can be organized as a portfolio.

Subject of the Project Choice of a topic is variable. It can be an original composition or an analysis of a composition in a style presented in this volume, especially accompanied melody. Consider selecting a theme and variations or a suite since these types of compositions often include the rich use of varied texture patterns. Use literature studied this semester for models. The analysis should have specific objectives. For example, you can use an analysis to develop an interpretation or plan for a rehearsal. You can use an analysis to closely examine and demonstrate certain composing techniques. Strive for an application of knowledge gained in this course.

Organization You will be graded on your ability to (a) organize and express your thoughts and (b) organize and coordinate the resources used in your presentation. Work from a well conceived thesis statement. The body of your presentation should support this thesis. End with a conclusion or summary that is consistent with the thesis and body of the presentation.

Guidelines (1) Strive for a coherent narrative. Do not assume that the music you present will speak for itself. Over-reliance on recordings will result in a loss of points.
(2) Rehearse the presentation so you can coordinate your resources smoothly while giving the presentation. This rehearsal will give you a solid sense of timing.
(3) Think about the true value of sharing your own discoveries and experiences with others in the class—what you can give to your classmates and what they can give to you. This time of individual presentation tends to be illuminating, stimulating, and expanding for everyone. Important ideas hitherto not covered in the class invariably come out at this time.

Evaluation <u>100 points distributed as follows</u>:

Presentation (45 pts):	efficiency, smoothness	[	]
	quality of resources	[	]
	content	[	]
Document (45 pts):	technical writing quality	[	]
	organization	[	]
	quality of layout/typing/graphics	[	]
Composite effect (10 pts)		[	]
	TOTAL	[	]

4. Option 1: Write an original composition in homophonic texture or use a melody you harmonized earlier in the semester. Experiment with various accompaniment patterns and arrangements of textural components. If you plan to write an original composition, try setting words to music. The mood and structure of the poetry will stimulate your thinking about your choice and manipulation of textural factors. Your thinking can also be stimulated by thinking about mood or character pieces. Write to support movement in dance, theatre, or video. Write for a medium that interests you (solo instrument, solo with accompaniment, ensemble, synthesizer, and so on).

5. Option 2: Write a series of examples or an arrangement that illustrates all the major points about homophonic texture included in this chapter. Arrange a folk song for instrument(s), voices, or a mixture of the two. Base these illustrations on phrases or periods written in previous chapters. Harmonize the melody and add accompaniment pattern, pedal, ostinato, or obbligato. Suggestions in the previous option will work here.

6. Option 3: Select a composition from your solo or ensemble repertoire that seems rich in patterns of homophonic accompaniment. Select a composition that you have not yet performed or wish to add to your repertoire. Attempt to create a "map" of the changing texture patterns. Discuss how this "map," the flow of components in the composition, melody pattern, and harmonic background all interrelate. Explain and illustrate how your awareness of these factors helped you learn, rehearse, interpret, and/or memorize the composition. A performance of the composition to show the result of your work would be a nice finishing touch.

INDEX